D1611459

Number Nine:
The Centennial Series of the Association of Former Students, Texas A&M University

Gone from Texas

Public Square, Waco. *Texas Collection, Baylor University, Waco.*

GONE FROM TEXAS

Our Lost Architectural Heritage

BY

WILLARD B. ROBINSON

TEXAS A&M UNIVERSITY PRESS

COLLEGE STATION

Library of Congress Cataloging in Publication Data

Robinson, Willard Bethurem, 1935–
    Gone from Texas.

    (The centennial series of the Association of Former Stu-
dents, Texas A&M University; no. 9)
        Bibliography: p.
        Includes index.
        1. Architecture—Texas—Mutilation, defacement, etc.—
Pictorial works. I. Title. II. Series: Texas A&M University, College Station. Association of Former Students. Centennial series
of the Association of Former Students, Texas A & M University; no. 9.
NA730.T5R59   720'.9764   80-5518
ISBN 0-89096-106-9

Manufactured in the United States of America
Second Printing

To our Texas ancestors, who knew and loved these buildings, now gone

Contents

List of Figures

Acknowledgments

During the several years that research and work on the manuscript for this publication were in progress, many individuals and organizations generously aided the development of the project. In the early stages of the work, Margaret Ann Robinson provided assistance in compiling data on buildings that no longer stand. Numerous librarians, archivists, curators, and historians provided information and illustrations.

Among these, I thank L. Tuffly Ellis, director, Texas State Historical Association; Marjorie Morey, Ginger Garrison, and Nancy Wynne, Amon Carter Museum of Western Art; Kent Keeth, Texas Collection, Baylor University; William McDonald, formerly of the Dallas Historical Society; Jane Kenamore, archivist, Rosenberg Library; Audrey Kariel, Marshall; Dorothy Glasser, Texas and Local History Department, Houston Public Library; Mrs. W. D. Cooper, Austin–Travis County Collection, Austin Public Library; Jan Czenkush, Barker Texas History Center, University of Texas at Austin; Mrs. Joe Welch, chairman, Fannin County Historical Commission, Bonham; Betty Cue, La Retama Library, Corpus Christi; Mary Cook, Laredo Public Library; Kathleen Upham, director, Swenson Memorial Museum of Stephens County, Breckenridge; Margaret Waring, librarian, Comanche Public Library; Susan L. Danforth, assistant curator of maps, Brown University; Arthur J. Willrodt, Columbus; Maria Watson, Daughters of the Republic of Texas Library, San Antonio; Henri Elizabeth Pepper, manager, City-County Museum, Sweetwater; Mary A. Sarber, head, Art and Southwest, El Paso Public Library; Patricia Chadwell, head, Genealogy and Local History, Fort Worth Public Library; John Davis, Institute of Texan Cultures, San Antonio; Linda Pringle, librarian, Bryan Public Library; Sue Kethley, librarian, Special Collections, Waco–McLennan County Library; Linda Frederickson, Photo Library, Texas Highway Department, Austin; Carolyn Ann Robinson, Lubbock.

The staffs of several agencies also were very helpful. I appreciate the assistance of the Archives Division, Texas State Library; Barker Texas History Center, University of Texas at Austin; Texas Historical Commission; Department of History and Genealogy, Dallas Public Library; Library of Congress; National Archives, Washington, D.C.; and Museum of National History, Smithsonian Institution.

In Galveston, Peter Brink, executive director of the Galveston Historical Foundation, and Evangeline Wharton, vice-president for programs, were very helpful in supplying data. In Houston, Peter Rippe, executive director, and Frances Lawrence, curator of photographic collections, Harris County Heritage Society, assisted me in obtaining information and photographs in their city.

Information on certain aspects of Spanish colonial architecture was compiled with support from a grant from the National Endowment for the Humanities.

During the concluding phase of the preparation of the manuscript, two other women provided invaluable assistance. I am grateful for the excellent typing done by Dorothy Washington, secretary, Museum of Texas Tech, in the preparation of several drafts. Finally, I thank my wife, Jeannie, for her suggestions on the manuscript, countless errands to locate information, and investigations of sites of buildings that have been razed.

Introduction

Over a century ago the legendary inscription *G.T.T.* appearing on the doors of vacant dwellings of the southern states attested to the fact that their former occupants had *Gone to Texas*. These Anglo-Americans, like other ethnic groups who had immigrated previously, brought with them to Texas their ideas and beliefs about beauty and cultural refinement, along with the will to express them in orderly communities and dignified building styles. Although the hardships imposed by the land, the natives, and rivals were formidable, the colonists stoically remained and produced a material culture that reflected the conditions of their times as well as their life-styles.

The generations of Texans succeeding the early immigrants enjoyed improving conditions. Success in their worldly endeavors produced affluence and the means to benefit from the happiness provided by architecture and other arts, including opera, music, and drama. These generations expressed their values in religion and education and their customs through the concepts of beauty they incorporated into many fine private and public buildings.

Throughout historic times, Texans developed considerable pride in their architectural achievements. By the end of the nineteenth century, buildings represented both material and cultural progress. They fulfilled basic needs for shelter, provided psychological security, and satisfied innate desires for beauty.

Unfortunately, however, many twentieth-century Texans, perhaps due to their own need for accomplishment or their lack of roots in Texas heritage, have had little appreciation for the achievements of the pioneers. As a result of the desire to rebuild in the name of progress, countless examples of fine historic buildings are now *Gone from Texas* in the wake of the bulldozer and the wrecking crane. Gone are the antebellum- and Reconstruction-period courthouses; gone are the late-nineteenth-century resort hotels and natatoriums; virtually extinct are the chautauquas and market houses. Gone are innumerable opulent public buildings and elegant homes, which at one time expressed pride in cultural attainment but which in recent times occupied sites needed for automobile parking or new aluminum-and-glass-faced office buildings. Gone, too, are countless outstanding examples of particular styles and craftsmanship and works by prominent architects and builders. Endangered are numerous late-nineteenth- and early-twentieth-century courthouses, jails, commercial buildings, and churches.

Our bent for destruction has been well documented by surveys, both formal and informal. Several years ago in Dallas an unofficial survey by Terry Searcy revealed that only 11 churches remained of 110 that were standing in 1910. In Galveston, according to Evangeline Wharton, vice-president for programs for the Galveston Historical Foundation, only about

35 of nearly 300 fine buildings designed by Nicholas J. Clayton remain. About one-fourth of the nearly 400 buildings recorded in the state by the Historic American Buildings Survey are gone. These historic structures are irreplaceable cultural resources; once gone, of course, lost skills and scarcity of materials, not to mention expense, prohibit their replacement. Any history of Texas architecture based solely upon a survey of extant buildings must be incomplete.

Actually, Texans began neglecting and destroying important buildings even during the nineteenth century. Many important structures—for example the Spanish missions—received little or no maintenance during that time. Other buildings were destroyed to make room for new structures. Community development made impossible the retention of certain buildings that have now disappeared—for instance, the antebellum courthouses. With the prevailing emphasis on growth and progress, there was little express concern or interest in preserving buildings with historic or architectural merit. Furthermore, tastes that reject the values of the fathers, while accepting those of the grandfathers, have further contributed to our lost heritage.

In addition to the intentional actions of man, time and catastrophe have taken a heavy toll. Natural deterioration has returned countless early indigenous shelters to the ground from whence they came; hurricanes and tornadoes have left in their wake vast blocks of twisted masses of lumber and broken masonry where buildings once stood. Fires have reduced innumerable structures to ashes—even while this book was in press the historic structure in which the Texas A&M University Press offices were located was virtually destroyed by flames (and subsequently demolished). Given, then, the accidental attrition caused by nature, it is even more important to save significant work from planned destruction by the machine.

With the structures that have been destroyed has gone a sense of time and place.

Buildings evoke the history of a city or community. Tangible evidence of the past found in extant architecture enhances the present by providing a time perspective and by creating through contrast and harmony a feeling of location or situation. Furthermore, a sense of continuity and permanence conveyed by surviving material culture provides psychological security. There is no way for future generations to replace the qualities and experiences lost with the destruction of the historic built environment. Moreover, designed and built when the life-style was slower, historic structures possess visual interest that is today difficult to develop in mass-produced buildings designed to facilitate quick assembly and to accommodate rapid activity.

Although the cultural value of historic buildings was denied by International-style architects during the twentieth century, today the Post-Modernism movement is again recognizing the importance of history. Fundamental needs for symbols and decoration are again being considered. Post-Modernists are searching for lessons to be learned from the past, and these can best be discovered by experiencing extant buildings, rather than viewing their vestiges.

Constructed before the development of mechanical environmental control systems, some historic buildings are more energy efficient than today's structures, with their large areas of glass. Breezeways created a cooling effect, and high ceilings allowed warm air to rise. Thick walls provided good insulation, operable windows gave efficient cross ventilation, and large attics afforded insulation between the roof and habitable spaces. These features were all intended to ameliorate life under natural conditions. Moreover, consideration for natural ventilation often influenced architectural form—an aspect that now is often not appreciated. Then too, many buildings were situated on sites where natural features shielded them against the cold winds in the winter and where windows caught the cool prevailing breezes in summer. These considerations certainly should attract study and re-use rather than more destruction.

It is the purpose of this study, then, through illustration of the architecture that has been lost, to survey the significant forces that gave buildings their form during their time. This may stimulate interest in endangered structures and create a better appreciation of the qualities they embody. At the same time, the examples illustrated and described have been selected to provide an accurate cross section of architectural history in the state from the Spanish colonial period to the turn of the twentieth century. In addition to the buildings now gone from Texas, this study includes structures that have been so denatured that their original character has been lost. Certain industrial buildings are included, regardless of aesthetics, in an effort to provide representations of functional types. Other private and public buildings were selected to exemplify exceptional concepts of aesthetics—beauty, symbolism, etc. This survey is not intended merely to lament the destruction of historic structures; it is intended to give a history of the types and qualities of works that once were in Texas, to explain how they came about, and to show what has been destroyed.

The history of architecture is much more than an account of the works of anonymous builders and talented designers or a discussion of styles. Rather, it should be a survey of conditions, both objective and subjective, influencing those works: environment, society, art, technology, and individuals. To appreciate the essence of the architecture of any given time it is essential to understand the conditions under which it was produced in terms of values current then, rather than through values of the times in which it is interpreted. Attitudes are subject to rapid change, often resulting in disregard for principles that later may be once again esteemed. Thus, interpretation is one of the objectives of this survey.

During the nineteenth century, the appreciation of architecture as art as well as an expression of progress prompted the publication of several artworks books, featuring photographs of architectural accomplishments in particular cities. It stimulated the publication of drawings and descriptions of buildings in newspapers, and it motivated railroads and boards of trade to extoll the virtues of handsome and durable buildings to nonresidents. Numerous illustrations from these sources are included in this volume. Contemporaneous writings are cited with the hope that the spirit of the historic times in which the buildings were created will be better appreciated in our own times. With the stress created by today's demands for speed and efficiency, individuals often look without seeing and sometimes see without understanding.

Several points should be noted: first, there has been an attempt to include illustrations representing a broad geographical distribution of architecture across the state. However, when West Texas communities were embryo settlements, such cities as Houston, Dallas, and Fort Worth were bustling centers of commerce, full of interesting buildings. Then too, extant photographic records are limited; textual references and descriptions exist for many important buildings for which no photographic documentation has been located. Finally, limitation in volume has naturally restricted the number of examples included.

Although it is understood that not all old buildings can or should be retained forever, an attempt has been made to illustrate works that were significant and should have been saved; for the most part they were among the best constructed in the state. The importance of the buildings that are contained in *Gone from Texas* is indicated by the fact that each probably would have been eligible for nomination to the National Register of Historic Places. It is hoped that illustration of works that have been lost and interpretation of their intended role may, in some measure, encourage preservation of remaining significant historic structures. Present and future generations should handle what is left of our cultural heritage with care. Tangible evidences of our roots are precious.

Gone from Texas

1

The Lost Prehistoric and Hispanic Heritage

ARCHITECTURE reflects the cultural history of mankind. In Texas, as elsewhere, buildings express the sociological and environmental conditions of the people who produced them. Even during prehistoric and early-historic times, indigenous shelters reflected the natural environments and traditions of the builders. During any era the types of structures erected reflect the nature of activities that are important in a community. As societies develop, cultural refinements and affluence are suggested not only by architectural function but also by style and technology.

The character of a community—rural or urban—is expressed in the forms and details of its dwellings and public buildings. Pride in cultural attainment is reflected in building beautification—configurations of masses and spaces, excellence and expressiveness of construction, basic principles of scale and proportion, and opulent ornamentation. Further, the iconographical content of architectural components often expresses the values of a particular individual or group. Symbols evoke sympathies and understandings or express purposes. For example, ecclesiastical architecture often displays a complex panoply of features relating to Christian concepts; governmental buildings frequently show features intended to communicate their official and patriotic functions.

In addition, environmental situations are revealed by the materials used and through spatial relationships, forms, and configurations of details. The manner in which structures are oriented to maximize nature's potential to heat and cool buildings reveals the builder's sensitivity to his environment. Then too, the manner in which various forms utilize wind and water is informative.

Historically, for those who would settle in the Texas country, diverse natural environments offered almost unlimited potential. In the contrasting meteorological zones, a variety of climates nourished the development of agriculture; in the differing terrains were innumerable sites favoring the establishment of communities; and a great range of building materials lay within the complex geological formations. In addition, the disparate flora and fauna supported by the land provided sustenance for colonists and their livestock.

During early historic times, members of various expeditions recorded observations of Indian architecture that reflected its setting. As early as 1582–1583, in the upper Rio Grande region, Antonio de Espejo and Diego Pérez Luxán on a journey to New Mexico found Patarabueye and Jumano villages in the vicinity of La Junta de los Ríos, near the confluence of the Río Conchos and the Rio Grande. These villages consisted of clusters of low, flat-roofed, rectangular buildings with walls of palings and adobe. The local Indians' utilization of the natural potential of the land was epitomized by a *ranchería* of freestanding houses—which the Spaniards named Santiago—located in an area where damp islands and bays of the river facilitated farming. Although they normally lived in pueblos, the Indians resided in flat-roofed houses set up in their fields while harvesting crops of beans and squash.[1]

Above and below the junction of the rivers were other pueblos, also consisting of houses with walls formed with mud-plastered pickets and roofs of adobe, probably placed over saplings, grass, and bark.[2] However, by the time the Spaniards visited these people, their population was diminishing, and by the latter part of the eighteenth century they had disappeared.

In the Panhandle, hundreds of miles to the north, architecture also revealed a close kinship between the Indians and their land. Sometime between A.D. 1200 and 1500 a pueblo culture—similar to the Arizona and New Mexico cultures—developed near the Canadian River. In this region Indians often selected promontories as sites for their villages, perhaps for defense. Using materials at hand, at the Antelope Creek site, about forty miles northeast of Amarillo, and at the Alibates site in Potter County, they constructed one-story pueblos with walls of horizontal masonry and double rows of stone slabs set on edge, oriented to the cardinal points. The walls tapered from three feet in width at the base to one foot at the top, and the spaces between the slab walls were filled with mud and rubble. Plastered on the inside with adobe, these walls enclosed chambers that were flanked by two semicircular spaces, which were perhaps used

for storage. Under the floors and outside the walls appeared cylindrical cists, which may have been used for burial and storage. On the interior of one of the Antelope Creek units, under a roof supported by four posts, were a firepit and a raised platform that possibly was an altar.[3]

The Panhandle pueblos evidently had been abandoned by the time Francisco Vásquez de Coronado and his *conquistadores* passed through the region in 1540 on their disappointing search for the mythical *Gran Quivira*. However, other explorers journeying through the different regions recorded the character of other Indian architecture. In 1601 the expedition of Juan de Oñate discovered in Kansas a settlement of Wichita Indians living in circular huts, fifteen to thirty feet in diameter.[4] In the seventeenth and eighteenth centuries, the Wichitas migrated south to the Red River region of Texas and Oklahoma where they continued to dwell in shelters of this type (fig. 1). During the mid-nineteenth century, on a reconnaissance of the Red River, Captain Randolph B. Marcy visited near Rush Creek a village occupied by the Wichitas and found the entire nation to be housed in forty-two lodges, each containing two families of about ten people (fig. 2).[5]

Like many of these other primitive Indians, the Caddo (Kadohadacho) tribes in northeast Texas ingeniously employed indigenous mate-

[1] Diego Pérez de Luxán, *Expedition into New Mexico Made by Antonio de Espejo, 1582–1583, As Revealed in the Journal of Diego Pérez de Luxán, a Member of the Party*, ed. and trans. G. P. Hammond and A. Rey, p. 62.

[2] Herbert Eugene Bolton, *Spanish Exploration in the Southwest, 1542–1706*, pp. 171–173; France V. Scholes and H. P. Mera, *Some Aspects of the Jumano Problem*, p. 271.

[3] Alex D. Krieger, *Culture Complexes and Chronology in Northern Texas with Extension of Puebloan Datings to the Mississippi Valley*, pp. 31–35, 42–43.

[4] Bolton, *Spanish Exploration in the Southwest*, p. 260; W. W. Newcomb, Jr., *The Indians of Texas: From Prehistoric to Modern Times*, p. 255. Newcomb goes on to say that the Wichita village consisted of houses structured with forked posts supporting horizontal logs. Against these frameworks were leaned poles with one end on the ground, the other against the frame. Other thin poles were tied to the frameworks horizontally, and the whole was covered with grass. Near the apex, four poles, symbolizing gods, were oriented to the cardinal points. Two low openings, closed with doors of grass tied to a willow framework, afforded entrance to the interiors of the huts, which contained beds of poles and grass and an upper platform reached by a ladder.

[5] U.S. Congress, Senate, *Exploration of the Red River of Louisiana, in the Year 1852*, 32d Cong., 2d sess., 1853, Senate Exec. Doc. No. 54, p. 77.

FIGURE 1. Wichita Village, North Fork of Red River. From a drawing by George Catlin (1834). *Smithsonian Institution Photo No. 1352-a, National Anthropological Archives, Bureau of American Ethnology Collection, Washington, D.C.*

During historic times, the Wichita Indians apparently continued to build shelters utilizing techniques that had been in use for centuries, but European (specifically, French) influence was at one time apparent in the works set up for defense. This drawing of an unfortified village in peaceful times shows a typical layout, fronting on water.

FIGURE 2. Wichita Village, Rush Creek. Lithograph. *Smithsonian Institution Photo No. 1386-g, National Anthropological Archives, Bureau of American Ethnology Collection, Washington, D.C.*

The Wichita Indians were skillful in using materials at hand to build shelters adapted to the climate. Like dwellings dated from previous centuries, these huts were on a circular plan with frameworks of poles, thatched with grass.

rials to create shelter and order within their environment. Living on hunted game and on harvests that included beans, pumpkins, and sunflowers, these peaceful natives set up circular houses up to fifty feet in diameter with walls of poles planted into the ground, arranged according to a plan similar to that of the Wichitas. The shelters had conical roofs made of frameworks of rafters and purlins tied together and thatched with bundles of grass—autochthonous shelters, expressing a civilized life in harmony with nature.[6]

The social order of the Caddo confederacies was reflected in the form and spatial arrangement of their shelters. The authority of the tribal leaders in the Hasinai confederacy was shown by their occupying the largest dwellings. During meetings, Hasinai captains occupied houses located across an open space from the governor's house. Nearby was a small shelter for the captains' pages. The other huts were situated around these.[7]

For their religion, which focused upon fire, the Caddo groups constructed large, round, thatched shelters. Typical of these was a large fire temple located between the Neches and Hainai tribes. Such temples contained an altar made of reed mats and a fire fed by large logs, which were always placed pointing to the cardinal points. Burning perpetually, these sacred temple fires furnished the coals to light the fires of the dwellings, which also were burned continuously and in the center of the home. It was feared that death would occur if the flames went out.[8]

However, while these East Texas Indians were civilized and relatively peaceful, other Indian tribes were nomadic and hostile. Alvar Núñez Cabeza de Vaca found the Karankawas—enemies of both France and Spain—to be a barbarous group, who lived in shelters of willow poles covered with skins or woven mats. The Coahuiltecans built huts of saplings and hides and were warlike, primitive hunters, although they eventually accepted mission life. Many settlers and travelers found the Kiowas and Comanches to be among the fiercest and most warlike. In addition, throughout many decades, other colonizers suffered from the hostilities of the nomadic Lipan-Apaches, who stole, burned, and murdered. Dependent upon the hunt and depredations, they relied upon easily moved conical tipis for shelters. As is well known, these tipis, set up by the women, consisted of thin poles covered with tanned buffalo hides (fig. 3).[9]

Naturally, the sedentary Indians already collected in communities, rather than these nomadic tribes, attracted the efforts of Spanish missionaries when they began work in Texas. Settled in the East Texas forests, the Hasinai Indians were suitably located to form a barrier against the feared French encroachment from Louisiana, if they could be Christianized and made loyal Spanish subjects—goals of the mission system, a joint venture between the Church and the Crown.

The earliest explorers and settlers, like the Indians before them, erected shelters that were responses to their environment. In 1685 the expedition of the intrepid French explorer, René Robert Cavalier, Sieur de La Salle, after missing its intended destination, the mouth of the Mississippi, hastily assembled near Garcitas Creek shelters that included buildings with walls of clay-plastered posts and roofs thatched with grass or reeds.[10]

[6] George L. Crocket, *Two Centuries in East Texas: A History of San Augustine County and Surrounding Territory*, p. 6. See also Fray Isidro Félis de Espinosa on the Asinai and their allies, quoted in "Descriptions of the Tejas or Asinai Indians," ed. and trans. Mattie Austin Hatcher, *Southwestern Historical Quarterly* 31 (1927):154–155.

[7] Newcomb, *Indians of Texas*, p. 297; Massanet, "Letter of Fray Damián Massanet to Don Carlos de Sigüemza, 1690," in Bolton, *Spanish Exploration in the Southwest*, pp. 377–378.

[8] Fray Francisco Hidalgo to the Viceroy, p. 52, and Espinosa on Asinai, p. 160, both in Hatcher, "Descriptions of the Tejas or Asinai Indians."

[9] Newcomb, *Indians of Texas*, pp. 43, 64, 68, 107, 116, 164, 198.

[10] Carlos E. Castañeda, *Our Catholic Heritage in Texas: 1519–1936*, 1:333; "Letters of Massanet to de Sigüemza," p. 362, and Alonso de León, "Itinerary of the de León Expedition of 1689," p. 398, both in Bolton, *Spanish Exploration of the Southwest*; Espinosa on Asinai, in Hatcher, "Descriptions of the Tejas or Asinai Indians," p. 155. Massanet records six shelters; de León, five.

FIGURE 3. Comanche Camp (ca. 1850). *From Edouard Charton, ed.,* Le Tour de Monde *vol. 1 (Paris, 1860),* p. 349.

These mobile shelters were typical of those used by the warlike nomadic tribes. Although most tipis were unadorned, some Comanche tents were painted with geometrical figures representing animals and humans, similar to those drawn by the women on the warriors' rawhide battle shields.

Intent upon negating this French threat to the Texas country, Alonso de León, Fray Damián Massanet, and three other Franciscan missionaries, with an expedition of 110 men, set out the following year for East Texas to establish a settlement. Arriving near a Hasinai village, they established, in the name of God and His Majesty the King, the first Spanish mission in East Texas: San Francisco de los Tejas. Using materials at hand, they felled pine trees, dug trenches, and planted posts into the ground vertically, side by side and tied together at the top. The enclosed spaces were then roofed with a framework of poles and bundles of thatch, using methods imported from Mexico rather than the techniques that had been used by the Indians.[11]

Other missions were subsequently constructed using similar techniques, although some may have had shake roofs rather than thatched. The primitive shelters thus produced were indigenous to their environment; however, they were susceptible to both fire and natural deterioration, and nothing remains of them.

While the construction techniques for these missions were indigenous, the siting appar-

[11]Ernest Allen Connally, "The Ecclesiastical and Military Architecture of the Spanish Province of Texas" (Ph.D. diss., Harvard University, 1955), pp. 49–62.

ently satisfied tradition. Perhaps Mission San Miguel de Linares de los Adaes, established in 1716 near the present Robeline, Louisiana, represented the typical exterior spatial arrangements. The church faced west, the traditional orientation employed by the Franciscans, who established the missions. Perpendicular to it at the east was the friary. The whole was then enclosed within a stockade, providing security from attack as well as creating a sense of containment.[12]

Just as the East Texas missions reflected the forests in which they were situated, establishments elsewhere suggested the character of their regions. Located on an island in the Rio Grande near El Paso del Norte, Mission Corpus Christi de la Isleta del Sur—the first mission in Texas—was established in 1682 to serve the Tiguex Indians, refugees from the Pueblo Revolt around Santa Fe. Lacking timber, the builders of the mission buildings and surrounding pueblo employed for the walls adobes (mud blocks formed from a mixture of mud and straw baked in the hot sun). Mud, of course, was plentiful and durable in the dry climate, and it provided good insulation against the hot sun. Moreover, building with adobe was a technique familiar to the Spanish colonists who were in charge of construction.[13]

The presidios established to protect these missions also combined indigenous construction with traditional principles for organizing space. Among these outposts was the presidio Nuestra Señora de Pilar de los Adaes, a fort established by Marquis de Aguayo. A wealthy resident of Coahuila, Aguayo was charged with the responsibility of re-establishing the East Texas missions in 1721, after they had been abandoned for several

years.[14] The knowledgeable Spanish engineer adopted principles of the bastioned system of fortification, a form that had evolved in Renaissance Europe, to design a wood-enclosed structure that a small number of men could defend from within. This geometrical arrangement of architectural components allowed defenders to flank all parts of an enclosure from within, so there would be no place where an enemy might conceal himself close to the stronghold. Similar to other early structures in East Texas, Los Adaes was geometrically laid out (fig. 4), but the buildings were primitive and decayed rapidly. Although stone defenses had been planned, as late as 1767 the buildings and the stockade were all still of wood, but the enclosure was rotten and in ruins. The presidio was abandoned in 1773, after Spain acquired Louisiana.

While principles of the art of fortification prescribed the configurations of the architectural components of the presidios, the geometry and location of the layout was influenced by the sizes of the garrisons and the terrain. The hexagonal enclosure of Los Adaes was designed to accommodate one hundred men. The larger Presidio Nuestra Señora de Loreto was formally laid out on an octagonal trace and also was provided with bastions on every other salient (fig. 5). The curtains and *baluartes* were carefully situated to control a nearby river.[15]

In theory, geometrical as well as hierarchical order was a requirement for town planning during Spanish colonial days. To encourage the development of communities that would be both functional and beautiful, planning was to conform to the "Ordinances concerning Discoveries, Settlements, and Pacifications." According to these ordinances, sites for towns were to be located near abundant farm-

[12] Henderson King Yoakum, *History of Texas from Its First Settlement in 1685 to Its Annexation to the United States in 1846*, 1:51; Connally, "Ecclesiastical and Military Architecture," p. 183.

[13] Paul Goeldner, *Texas Catalog: Historic American Buildings Survey*, p. 229; Works Progress Administration, *Texas: A Guide to the Lone Star State*, p. 564.

[14] Eleanor Claire Buckley, "The Aguayo Expedition into Texas and Louisiana, 1719–1722," *Quarterly of the Texas State Historical Association* 15 (1911):54.

[15] Juan Antonio de la Peña. *Derrotero de la Expedición en la Provincia de los Texas*, pp. 20, 23. See also Max L. Moorhead, *The Presidio: Bastion of the Spanish Borderlands*, pp. 30–31.

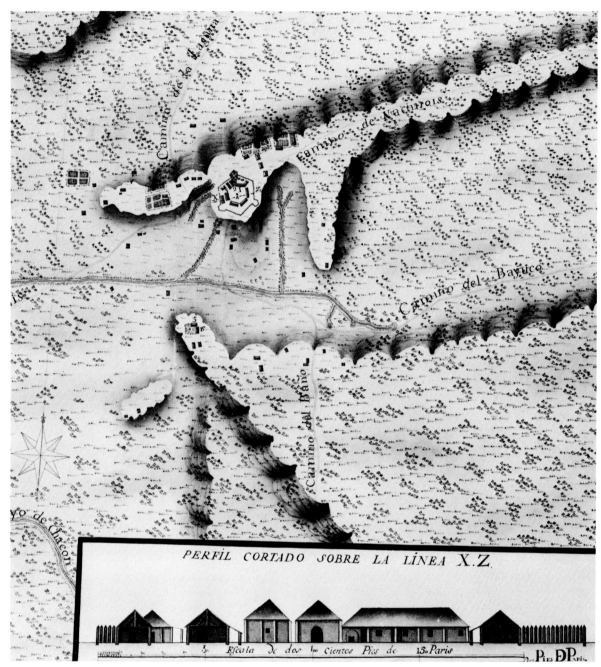

FIGURE 4. Presidio Nuestra Señora de Pilar de los Adaes, near the present Robeline, Louisiana (1721). Drawing by Joseph de Urrutia. Marquis de Aguayo, architect. *British Museum, London.*

1. Governor's house. *2.* Church. *3.* Guard house. *4.* Small gunpowder storeroom. *5.* Mission church. *6.* Missionaries' house.

Following the principles of the bastioned system, the defenses at Los Adaes were traced upon a regular hexagon of fortification, with *baluartes* ("bastions") on alternating corners. From the flanks of the three *baluartes* it was possible to enfilade all the spaces in front of the curtains (walls between the bastions). Within, the position of the buildings, with their picket walls and thatched roofs, suggested a hierarchy of order; a religious focus of the planner is revealed by the axial emphasis and the projection of the front of the chapel.

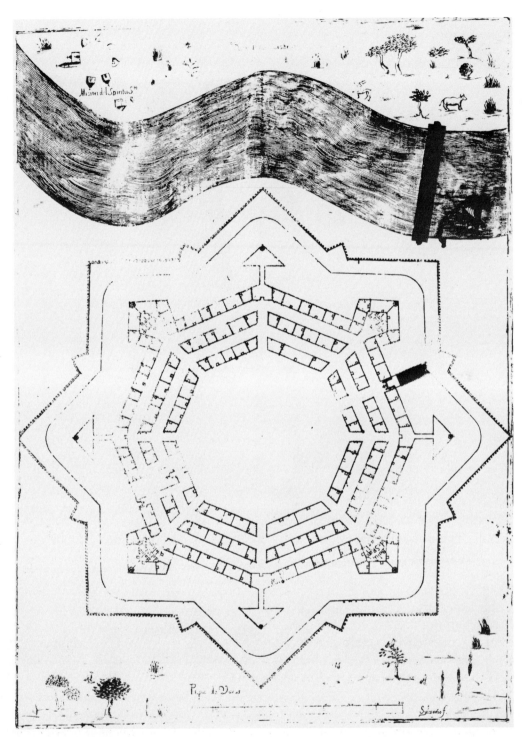

FIGURE 5. Presidio Nuestra Señora de Loreto, vicinity of Matagorda Bay (1722). Marquis de Aguayo, architect. *Archivo General de Indias, Sevilla.*

Established in the vicinity of La Salle's fort to discourage other French landings at Matagorda Bay, this stronghold revealed the importance attributed to it by the strength of its fortifications. The usual bastions at alternate salients were supplemented by redans (works with two faces forming salient angles, open at the back). All this was strengthened by a ditch surrounding the work.

In 1726 the fortifications were abandoned when the presidio was moved to the Guadalupe River.

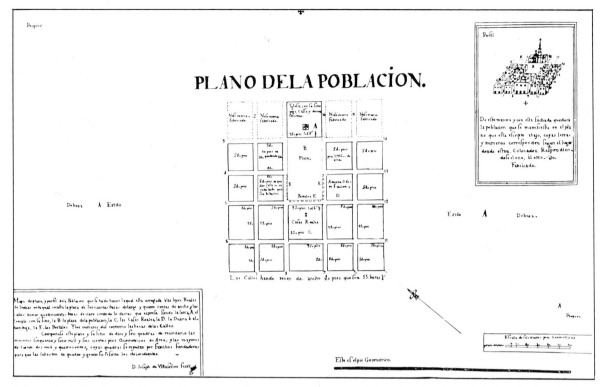

FIGURE 6. Villa de San Fernando de Béjar (San Antonio) (1731). Plan drawing (1730) by D. José de Villaseñor. *From Bolton,* Texas in the Middle Eighteenth Century, *facing p. 6.*

Shown on the plan of the *población*, which was oriented askew to the cardinal points, were such characteristic features as the *portales* surrounding the plaza. Although not isolated, the block for the *Yglesia* ("church") was situated on the northeast side of the plaza, allowing an approximate traditional orientation, with the narthex doors facing to the westerly direction.

lands, pastures, fuel, fresh water, and building materials. The nucleus of the community was to be a plaza, oblong and proportioned in size to the number of inhabitants. *Portales* ("porches") for the use of the merchants were to surround this plaza, relating it spatially to the enclosing buildings. Then, extending from this central space were to be several streets. To protect the community space, it was specified that the corners of the plaza point into the winds.[16]

Building sites within the towns were to be officially assigned according to the hierarchical order of Spanish communal organization. Close to the plaza, or community nucleus, were to be the *casas royales* ("royal houses") and the buildings for the *cabildo* ("council").

To avoid visual intrusion and distraction, the religious buildings were to be spatially isolated. To assert the authority of the church—as well as to provide for a transitional experience between exterior and interior space—it was required that, if possible, the church be elevated and that steps lead to the entrance. Then, to encourage the development of an esthetically unified community, it was specified that all buildings should be consistent in style.[17]

In 1731 the fifteen families who arrived from the Canary Islands to establish the Villa de San Fernando de Béjar (San Antonio) brought with them a neat plan, drawn by D. José de Villaseñor, which embodied these requirements (fig. 6). However, the selected location near the river and near the Presidio of San Antonio, which had been established in 1718, evi-

[16] Zelia Nuttal, "Royal Ordinances Concerning the Laying Out of New Towns," *Hispanic-American Historical Review* 4 (1921):743, 750.

[17] Ibid., p. 751.

dently forced modifications of the plan. In the final development, while the spirit of the law may have been fulfilled partially, some of the detailed requirements went unrealized. For example, the oblong space was divided into a military plaza and a public area by the placement of the parish church in the center (fig. 7). Today the military plaza is occupied by a city hall; the public plaza is a park.[18]

While the civil and military architecture in the early Spanish settlements was generally impermanent and without ornamental beauty, the missions along the San Antonio River (fig. 8) were developed into lasting and refined works. Although the first shelters were primitive, as early as possible the religious, while living in Spartan simplicity, determined to erect durable buildings, memorializing the eternal spirit of their labors. In the beauty of architecture and sculpture appeared lasting manifestations of spiritual zeal and inspiration.

Although components remain at each of the five San Antonio missions, none has survived intact from its peak of development. At the mission of San Antonio de Valero, planted in 1718, the church (1744) with its Spanish Baroque *retablo* ("reredos") front survives; gone are the convent, most of the shops, and the fortified enclosure (fig. 9).

The plan of San Antonio de Valero reflected the planning of the sixteenth- and seventeenth-century monastic colleges of Mexico, which in turn had been patterned after the Early Christian and Medieval monasteries of Spain.[19] A nearly rectangular compound, fifty *varas* wide (about 140 feet), enclosed by service units and convent, provided a space for everyday activities. A convent court, reminiscent of a Medieval cloister, spatially related the church to the convent, and the walls of this court and compound in front of the church formed an *atrio* ("atrium"), a common element in Early Christian churches. However, the vault spanning the nave of the church and a corner tower collapsed prior to 1762.

Over years of neglect, the buildings in the other missions also deteriorated. Established in 1720, San José y San Miguel de Aguayo—known as the "queen of the missions"—with its church in Ultra-Baroque (Mexican Churrigueresque) style fell into a sad state of disrepair during the decades following secularization in 1794. However, the San Antonio Conservation Society purchased its granary in 1933 and restored it. The following year other restoration work was accomplished under the Civil Works Administration, and most of the mission had been restored by the mid-twentieth century. Now it is maintained by Texas' parks department, and the church building, retained by the Roman Catholic Church after secularization, is still used. Nonetheless, the convent's walls, with their pointed-arch openings, remain as shells only.[20]

While significant portions exist, much of the historical work is also gone from the other three Spanish colonial religious institutions in the San Antonio vicinity. The mission church of Nuestra Señora de la Purísima Concepción de Acuña survives in fine original condition, but the enclosure and several other buildings are missing. At mission San Juan Capistrano, established in 1731, a church was begun but apparently never completed. However, a narrow chapel with a pierced *campanario* ("bell tower") faced east onto the quadrangle.[21] Capitalizing upon the favorable climate, this fine chapel served an exterior space where large numbers of Indians could be assembled. Most other structures are gone. The mission San Francisco de la Espada, established in 1731,

[18] Marion A. Habig, *The Alamo Chain of Missions: A History of San Antonio's Five Old Missions*, pp. 258–259; John W. Reps, *Town Planning in Frontier America*, p. 54.

[19] For comparisons see Trent Elwood Stanford, *The Story of Architecture in Mexico*, pp. 141–143; George Kubler, *Mexican Architecture of the Sixteenth Century*, pp. 314–320, 345–352.

[20] Works Progress Administration, *Texas*, p. 350; Habig, *Alamo Chain of Missions*, pp. 113–114.

[21] Miguel Celoria, "Spanish-Colonial Architecture: An Archaeological Approach," *Journal of the Society of Architectural Historians* 34 (December, 1975):295.

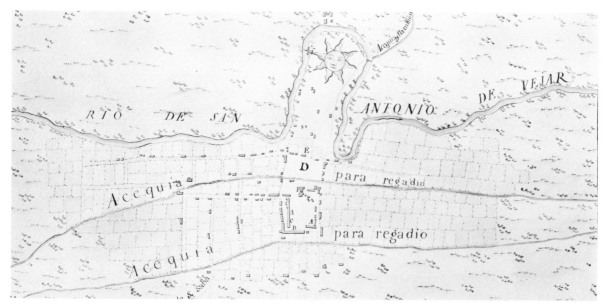

FIGURE 7. Town and Presidio of San Antonio de Béjar (1767). *British Museum, London.*
A. House of the Presidio. B. Captain's House. C. Guard House. D. Town Plaza. E. Royal Houses. F. Church.

    Apparently in response to terrain as well as to the requirements imposed by both the military and the civil settlement, the town of San Antonio had developed in an irregular pattern by the time this map was made. Also shown are the locations of the roads and the irrigation canals.

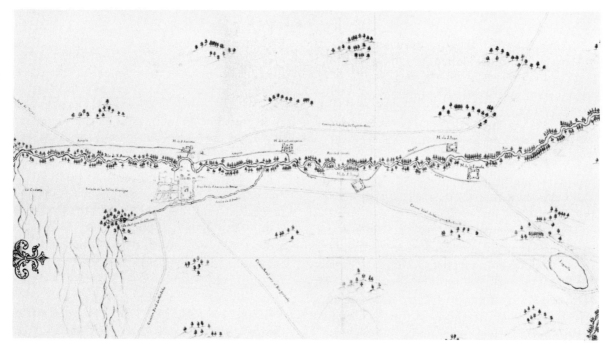

FIGURE 8. San Antonio Missions. *John Carter Brown Library, Brown University, Providence, Rhode Island.*
    Left to right: San Antonio de Valero, Nuestra Señora de la Purísima Concepción de la Acuña, San José y San Miguel de Aguayo, San Juan Capistrano, and San Francisco de la Espada.
    Situated relatively close together and all founded between 1718 and 1731, the San Antonio missions were the most successful of those established within the state. The sites chosen capitalized upon fertile farmlands, lush grasslands, and availability of water for irrigation.

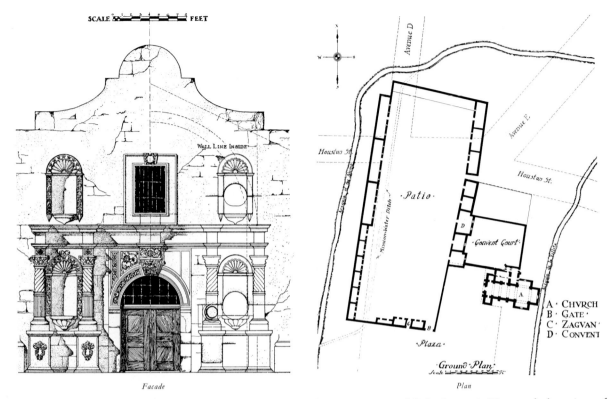

SCALE FEET

WALL LINE INSIDE

Facade

Patio

Avenue D

Avenue E

Houston St.

Houston St.

Convent Court

Plaza

A · CHVRCH
B · GATE ·
C · ZAGVAN ·
D · CONVENT

·Ground·Plan·

Plan

FIGURE 9. Mission San Antonio de Valero (Alamo), San Antonio (established 1718). Plan and elevation of church facade. *From Newcomb*, Spanish-Colonial Architecture in the United States.

Famous as the "Alamo," this mission was planted by Father Antonio de San Buenaventura Olivares adjacent to the San Antonio River. At the Alamo, as at other missions which were to follow, the first constructions were impermant huts or *jacales*. During the decades after its original functions were ceased, the mission underwent many changes. When the Alamo was defended by Texans during their war for independence, the church was a roofless ruin. At mid-nineteenth century the church served as a commissary store for the U.S. Army; the military restored the vaults. In 1883 the church building was officially purchased by the state from the Catholic church. The mission is now under the care of the Daughters of the Republic of Texas.

still includes a chapel and some fortifications (fig. 10).

The relative economic and cultural success of the missions was revealed by their architecture. While the handsome stone churches in the San Antonio vicinity indicated progress in civilizing the frontier, in other regions primitive log works, like those in the San Xavier (San Gabriel) River group (1748–1749), suggested a barbaric state, which persisted for over a century.

For the protection of the missions established during the mid-eighteenth century, several new military posts were set up by the Spanish. The presidio of San Luis de las Ama-

rillas de San Sabá was established in 1757 to defend several missions from the Apache Indians. San Sabá originally was a log construction; however, four years after its founding, work was commenced under the direction of Captain Felipe Rábago y Terán to replace these temporary structures with walls and buildings of rubble (fig. 11). Designed for occupation by one hundred soldiers and their families, San Sabá had fortifications that included two *torreóns* ("turrets"), one of which was positioned to allow enfilade fire along the fortified gate. However, all fell to ruins following the abandonment of the presidio in 1772.[22]

[22] Moorhead, *The Presidio*, p. 53.

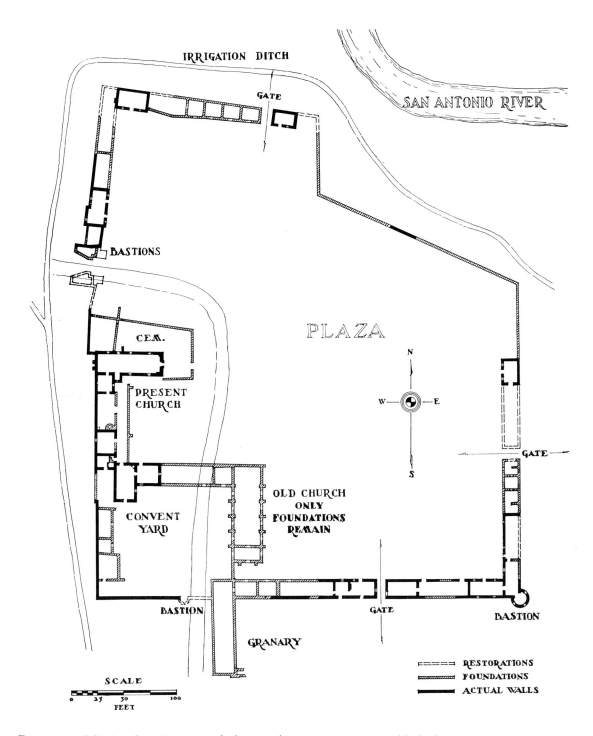

FIGURE 10. Mission San Francisco de la Espada, San Antonio (established 1731). Plan. *From Newcomb, Spanish-Colonial Architecture in the United States.*

While some parts of Espada survive in original form, others were either taken down or collapsed. Since it was feared that a church erected during the eighteenth century might fail structurally, it was razed stone by stone. Although some of the fortifications have been rebuilt, the *torreón* with its vaulted roof no longer stands. While only foundations of some structures remain, others have been reconstructed.

The charming chapel at Espada is still in use today. It is distinguished by a *campanario* and Moorish-style doorway.

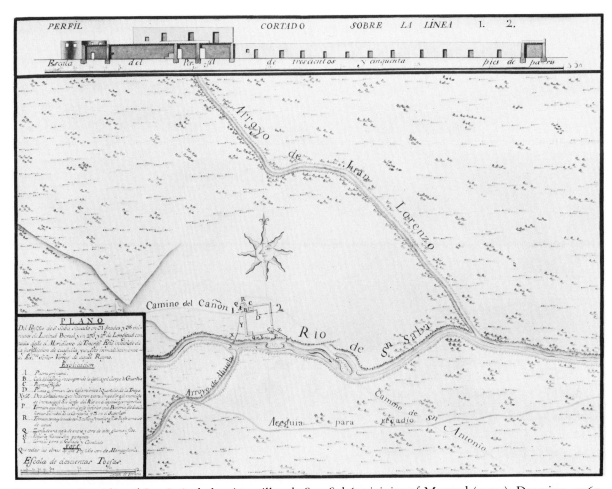

FIGURE 11. Presidio of San Luis de las Amarillas de San Sabá, vicinity of Menard (1757). Drawing, 1767. *British Museum, London.*

A. Main entrance. B. Captain's house. C. Private entrance. D. Plaza. O. Small Flank. P. Turret, with two cannons. Q. Ditch. R. Turret, with three cannons. Y. Corrals. X. and Z. Parapets.

Although the wood stockade that originally had been built proved to be strong enough to resist an Indian attack, authorities determined to erect substantial masonry fortifications. With *torreóns* and high masonry walls, the new works were Medieval in form. Appropriate for warfare in which primitive weapons, rather than cannons, were used, these contrasted with the Renaissance forms of earlier presidios.

While men in the service of the Church and the Crown significantly aided the pacification of central and east Texas, Spanish colonial ranchers also played an important role in civilizing the Texas frontier. Texas ranching had originated with the earliest missionary work. To provide food for the first missions, stock from the Mexican ranches, which had developed after Hernando Cortez introduced Spanish cattle into the newly conquered land, were trailed north by the Terán expedition of 1691–1692.[23]

However, while the East Texas missions maintained herds, the most successful ecclesiastical ranching operations developed along the San Antonio River. In addition to their farmlands, the San Antonio chain of missions maintained herds of cattle, sheep, and goats to supply food and to provide income. Located at appreciable distances from their missions, the ranches were operated by permanent residents stationed in headquarters dwellings, none of which remain today.[24]

Rancho de las Cabras ("Ranch of the Goats"), which may have belonged to Mission

[23] Sandra L. Myres, *The Ranch in Spanish Texas, 1691–1800*, p. 11; idem, "The Spanish Cattle Kingdom of the Province of Texas," *Texana* 4 (1966):235.

[24] Juan Agustín Morfi, *History of Texas, 1673–1779*, trans. Carlos Eduardo Castañeda, p. 102.

Espada, was perhaps representative of the *ranchos* ("ranch headquarters"). Reflecting frontier conditions, Las Cabras, like the missions, apparently was fortified against constant harassment by unfriendly Indians. Located near the present town of Floresville, it was surrounded by an enclosure and apparently had several bastions. Although only traces of the foundations remain today, it appears that a plaza, living quarters, and a chapel were contained within. From the security of these fortifications, the ranch Indians bravely ventured into the pastures to tend their livestock, which at one time included some fifteen hundred head of cattle and five hundred goats.[25]

At the time the mission ranches were thriving, secular ranching was just developing along the Rio Grande. The first ranching colony in this hot, arid region was established by José Vásquez Borrego, a rancher from Coahuila. Agreeing to treat the Indians with kindness and to endeavor to convert them to Christianity, Borrego proposed a settlement of thirteen families—all employees. In 1750 José de Escandón, who had been named governor of the province of Nuevo Santander (Tamaulipas), in which the lower Rio Grande was located, accepted Borrego's proposal, and the community of Nuestra Señora de los Dolores ("Our Lady of Sorrows")—now known as Dolores Viejo—was established near a point where Arroyo Dolores meets the Rio Grande. This establishment developed into a *rancho*; by 1754 there were 123 inhabitants and by 1757 there were 23 families. However, early in the nineteenth century Indian attacks forced temporary abandonment of Dolores, and eventually it was permanently vacated. Subsequently Nuevo Dolores was established on a new location. Today only lonely ruins attest to the past existence of the buildings at this and other ranches built at isolated locations.[26]

The sites for the *ranchos* were carefully selected to capitalize upon the terrain. Locations on high ground were preferred; these were defensible against attack and secure from floods. In addition, sites near water, firewood, and shade trees were preferred, when available.

The site layouts for the ranch buildings generally conformed to consistent patterns. Often the buildings were positioned to define central spaces—a tradition evidently imported from Spain to Mexico, thence to Texas. However, there are instances—for example at Los Ojuelos, a ranch founded between 1790 and 1810 in Webb County—where buildings were sited in line, forming streets or alleys. Even then, large open spaces still were apparent.

According to one observer,

the Mexican rancho, from Laredo clear down to the Gulf, adheres strictly to the one model; to describe one is to describe all, the differences being principally those of size and population.

There is always a "plaza" or "placeta" in the centre; if the rancho be unusually large, there may be two or even three such little squares, which serve all purposes of business, recreation, or, when necessary, religious function. From these radiate the streets, unpaved and dusty, sometimes shaded by the overhanging branches of trees, but oftener left to the full glare of sun and force of the wind.[27]

In response to fear of Indian attack, many of these ranches were fortified. At Los Ojuelos, a *torreón* was built, but it proved inadequate to prevent the Indians from reclaiming the springs that had attracted the settlement. Likewise, a *torreón* was built at Dolores Viejo, but it is in ruins. Fortifications at other ranches reportedly included palisades and stone walls, most of which are now gone. However, the fortified San Ygnacio Ranch buildings yet remain as a representative type of these civil defenses.

[25] Elo J. Urbanovsky, "Mission de las Cabras, Wilson County, Texas: Feasibility Report," mimeographed (Lubbock: Texas Tech University Department of Parks Administration and Horticulture, 1972).

[26] Florence Johnson Scott, *Historical Heritage of the Lower Rio Grande*, p. 57; Virgil N. Lott and Mercurio Martinez, *The Kingdom of Zapata*, pp. 132, 135–136.

[27] John G. Bourke, "The American Congo," *Scribner's Magazine* 15 (1894):600.

The earliest structures, as well as the later shelters of the *peónes* ("laborers") and *vaqueros* ("cowboys"), were primitive dwellings, sometimes flanked by arbors, all of which deteriorated rapidly. Using materials that nature provided, Spanish ranchers employed a type of *jacal* construction that differed from the *palisado* construction found in some other parts of the province (fig. 12).[28] Walls were constructed with crooked mesquite trees and branches laid horizontally between pairs of posts; roofs were thatched. Outside, a *horno* ("oven") was built of grass and clay for cooking and furnishing coals to heat the shelter during cold weather.

However, as soon as time was available, substantial buildings were begun for the *patron*, or owner of the ranch. Characterized by severe forms and details, these *casas grandes* reflected the climate as well as the danger inherent in frontier life and, at the same time, were consistent in style with the dwellings the ranchers had known before immigrating to Texas (fig. 13). Built by *peónes* and members of the ranch owner's family, the main houses were simple, massive cubes with walls of caliche block or brown sandstone and mud mortar. For protection not only against attacks by Indians—including Lipan Apaches, Comanches, and Mescaleros—but also against the burning sun, there were no openings for windows, only heavy panelled doors swinging on pivots or iron rings. For defense, builders provided *troneras* ("loopholes"), with cheeks carefully angled to allow complete coverage of the surrounding area with muskets. Among the fine examples of the fortified ranch dwelling were the José Ramírez house (figs. 14, 15)

and the Yzaguirre house. The former is now submerged in the Falcón Reservoir; the latter, built in what is now Jim Hogg County, has nearly collapsed from neglect.[29]

The roofs of the *casas grandes* were generally similar in style. The walls terminated in parapets extending several feet above the roof surface. A series of mesquite or cypress *vigas* ("beams") supported the roof. Demonstrating pride of accomplishment, the center *viga*, which was generally larger than the others, often bore the name of the owner, date of construction, and sometimes a religious inscription. Water from the roof, which was slightly inclined, was drained into barrels or tubs through openings in the parapet by *canales* ("drain troughs") cut from either wood or sandstone.[30]

In addition to the cubical *casas grandes*, stone-walled dwellings with gables and pitched roofs appeared. On these, the gable extended above the roof, which was either thatched with bundles of carrizo, sacahuiste, or sacaton applied in rows or covered with shingles. When available, cypress shingles were apparently preferred instead of grass. This style of architecture may have been brought to the Rio Grande from Ireland and northern England by Irish immigrants, who evidently were numerous along the border by the nineteenth century.[31]

Typically, several of these types of construction were employed on the eighteenth- and nineteenth-century ranches. At the time they were recorded by the Historic American Buildings Survey, the buildings of the San Bartolo Ranch—now also submerged—consisted of rectangular dwellings with some nearly flat and some steeply pitched roofs, originally covered, respectively, with *tipichil* (mixture of

[28] The term *jacal* or *xacal* originated with the Aztec word *xacalli*. *Xa* indicates straw, reed, bamboo; *calli*, house. In Mexico it now identifies virtually any form of shelter with a thatched roof. See *Vocabulario Arquitectónico Ilustrado*, p. 268. According to Bourke, "To make a 'jacal' the owner inserts half a dozen stout poles of mesquite or ebony or huisache at the proposed corners, and then fills in with a wattle-work which may or may not be daubed with mud, according to the exigencies of climate, the depth of the builder's purse, or his sense of the aesthetic" ("American Congo," p. 601).

[29] Eugene George, *Historic Architecture in Texas: The Falcón Reservoir*, pp. 32, 48, 54.

[30] August Santleban, *A Texas Pioneer*, pp. 23–24; George, *Historic Architecture of Texas*, pp. 38–39; "Historic American Buildings Survey Data Report," HABS No. Tex-3113, Library of Congress, Washington, D.C.

[31] Ada L. K. Newton, "The Anglo-Irish House of the Rio Grande," *Pioneer America* 5 (1973):33–38.

FIGURE 12. Palisade-walled dwelling, San Antonio (nineteenth century). *Daughters of the Republic of Texas Library, San Antonio.*

Although certainly dating from the nineteenth century, the dwelling on the right represents the type of *palisado* construction that was used from the time of the earliest settlements until the twentieth century. Palisade walls were widely used by both Spanish and French colonists, and other groups also adopted the technique. Since the only required tools were axes and shovels and since little skill was required, it was an expedient and rapid form of construction. After the posts had been planted in trenches the walls often were chinked and finished with mud.

FIGURE 13. *Casa Grande*, Nuevo Dolores, Webb County (1860). *Photo by author.*

The patronal house at Nuevo Dolores, a ranch established in 1859 by Cosme Martinez, overlooking the Rio Grande a short distance upstream from Viejo Dolores, was characteristic of the Latin *casas grandes.* Located on a 350,000-acre ranch, this was a massive work of sandstone. This building still stands, in ruinous condition. However, due to vandalism and neglect, it is deteriorating rapidly.

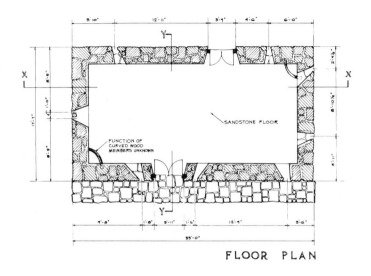

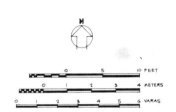

FLOOR PLAN

W. EUGENE GEORGE, JR., DEL.

FIGURE 14. José Ramírez House, Falcón (ca. 1810). *Historic American Buildings Survey, Library of Congress, Washington, D.C.*

The land on which this structure was originally located was part of a Spanish grant made in 1767 to José Clemente Ramírez. The cubical form is characteristic of the Spanish *casas grandes* that were built on the Hispanic ranches in Texas, as well as in Mexico to the south.

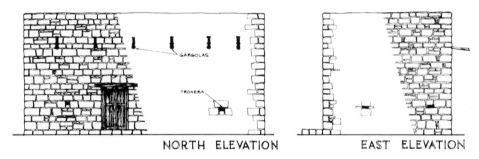

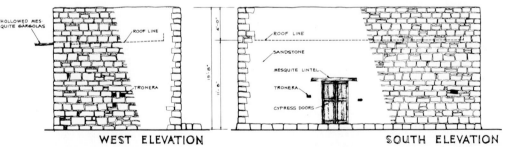

FIGURE 15. José Ramírez House. Elevations. *Historic American Buildings Survey, Library of Congress, Washington, D.C.*

The stones for the walls of the Spanish colonial ranch houses were generally quarried with an iron crowbar and dressed with a pick or small hand ax. Between two and three feet in thickness, the walls were made of masonry units laid in beds of mud mortar, with small stones filling the large voids. When completed, the walls were finished with a coat of plaster made from white sand and lime, which was produced in crude kilns from caliche, limestone, or marl found near the ranch headquarters.

FIGURE 16. San Bartolo Ranch, Zapata vicinity (1867–1876). *Historic American Buildings Survey, Library of Congress, Washington, D.C.*

The Hispanic colonial-style ranch headquarters structures usually included one or more cubical dwellings with several gable-roofed houses. Additions frequently were made to both types, often with gable-roofed rooms being added to the cubical forms.

Two houses in this group had rafter inscriptions. One read, *Se Edeifico Esta Casa el 1 De Eneio de 1867 Sirvo Ami Deueno Y la Honora* ("This building of this house the 1st of January 1867, Serving the honor of my master"); the other, *Ce Edifico esta Casa el Dia de 16to Junio en el año de 1876 sirvo ami deueno* ("This building of this house the 16th day of June in the Year 1876 serving my master"), Luis Gutierres [signature].

lime, sand, and gravel) and hand-split cypress shakes (fig. 16). Located across the Rio Grande from Guerro, which furnished many settlers to the Texas side of the river, the San Bartolo buildings exhibited details similar to those found in Mexico.[32]

These Spanish-Mexican dwellings included straightforward provisions for existence in the wilderness. They reflected their environment, and they expressed the austere life-style of their occupants. Located in the cool evening shade along the east exterior walls of the houses, which were oriented with the long axis in a north-south direction, was a *banqueta* ("masonry seat"), where the family could relax after working during the hot days. Without and within, the walls were plastered and whitewashed—evidently to protect the walls from erosion and to reflect light on the interiors. Expressing the role of Catholic dedication in everyday life, the focal point of most

interiors was a likeness of the Virgin set within a plastered or wood-lined niche, often decorated with flowers. Some of what little furniture there was may have been brought north from Mexico, but most was probably built on the *rancho* and was functional in design.

Although events during the first half of the nineteenth century changed the political allegiance of the owners and occupants of these ranches and towns, little cultural change occurred. Pride in traditions, inheritance, and race assured that eighteenth-century customs, traditions, and beliefs would continue to prevail during the nineteenth century along the Rio Grande. Moreover, the country between the Nueces River and the Rio Grande did not become a part of Texas until the mid-nineteenth century—in some regions ranch grants were made by Mexico as late as the 1830's. Throughout the century ranchers and town dwellers continued to build in the same form, although developing affluence was reflected in the finesse of details and materials of

[32] George, *Historic Architecture of Texas*, pp. 39–40.

FIGURE 17. Jesus Treviño House, San Ygnacio (1851–1871). *Historic American Buildings Survey, Library of Congress, Washington, D.C.*

Although the interior of the Treviño house still retains its original character, the exterior has been altered with the addition of a frame gable roof, thus changing the character of the building. This apparently was necessitated by the deterioration of the original roofing.

The roofs of these Spanish-Mexican ranches generally were similar in construction. *Vigas* hewn to a rectangular cross section, spaced about two feet apart, supported split or sawn *tablas* ("planks") or cypress *latias* ("billets"). Over these were placed the roofing, made of layers of mud and grass, gravel, and then a layer of *tipichil*.

The Treviño house, while retaining a simple form, shows some of the more refined details that became common. In this complex the corners are enhanced with cut stonework. In addition, the *canales* are noteworthy carved stone features.

construction (fig. 17). The decline of hostilities on the frontier resulted in the appearance of large openings in the walls.[33]

In the villas near these ranches, the architectural character also was similar to that of Mexico, but building forms and details reflected the primitive local conditions. An early traveler in San Antonio described some *jacales* there as "huts . . . erected of thin crooked muskeet [*sic*] logs, placed endwise in the ground, the crevices 'chinked and daubed' . . . without windows, and flooring and thatched with prairie grass. . . ." A few years later, another visitor noted that the basic types of shelters consisted of "windowless cabins of stakes, plastered with mud and roofed with rivergrass, or 'tule'; or low, windowless, but better thatched, houses of adobes. . . ." In El Paso,

with an arid climate where trees were scarce, numerous flat-roofed adobe dwellings, similar to those in San Antonio, were constructed by people of Spanish-Mexican descent (fig. 18). The dwellings of the *peónes* were one story with flat roofs and had few openings to the street. If windows appeared, they generally were without sashes and were protected by wooden or iron *rejas* ("grilles"). According to one San Antonio visitor who observed houses like these, "a man might think of himself in Palestine." Sometimes a courtyard was formed by the building and walls that were added (fig. 19). Within, the court may have been landscaped with plants, some of which may have been imported from Mexico.[34]

Like buildings in the Spanish-Mexican tra-

[33] Information on Mexican land grants was provided by Florence Shuetz, historian, Falfurrias, Texas. On the cultural development of this area, see Jovita Gonzales, "Social Life in Cameron, Starr, and Zavala Counties" (Master's thesis, University of Texas, Austin, 1930).

[34] William Bollaert, *William Bollaert's Texas*, ed. W. Eugene Hollon and Ruth Lapham Butler, p. 217 (the visit was made in 1843); Frederick Law Olmsted, *A Journey through Texas*, p. 149; Auguste Frétellière, "Adventures of a Castrovillian, 1843–1844," in Julia Nott Waugh, *Castroville and Henry Castro, Empresario*, p. 92.

FIGURE 18. El Paso. View (ca. 1900). *Texas State Historical Association, Austin.*

The use of Hispanic building traditions continued well into the twentieth century. A series of adobe cubes, plastered *jacales*, arbors, and crude fences formed an interesting juxtaposition against the Victorian-era El Paso County Courthouse (*upper right*) and the Federal Courthouse and Post Office building (*upper left*). Virtually every component of the built environment seen here is now gone.

FIGURE 19. Unidentified dwelling, El Paso (ca. 1900). *Texas State Historical Association, Austin.*

Apparently located on the outskirts of El Paso, this dwelling was typical of many adobe houses with flat roofs. Located to the left was the hemispherical *horno*. The courtyard was a family activity area.

Although the means were primitive, the residents attempted to ameliorate the natural environment. Protection from the burning sun was provided by a few trees and a flimsy arbor over the main door.

dition elsewhere, these expressed their situation and the values of their builders. With walls of stone or adobe two to three feet thick and with few openings, the cubical buildings appeared severe, but they were relatively well insulated and comfortable in the hot climate. When plastered and whitewashed, they looked neat, and the outside finish reflected the heat. On the exterior, visual relief from austere form was provided by ornamental *canales*, which often were cut from sandstone into a variety of interesting forms. As the owners achieved some degree of prosperity, simple brick or stone ornamentation appeared at the tops of parapet walls.

While most of the town dwellings were on a single level, occasional two-story houses appeared. As in the one-story cubes, a secluded courtyard often was formed by the multilevel building and its walls. A ground-story arcade open to this outdoor space provided a shady area. If the use of the building conformed to Mexican precedent, the upper story contained a family apartment, possibly a chapel, and a balcony, an arrangement providing for good ventilation by the breezes.

The form and details of these exteriors of the Hispanic houses, then, expressed structural strength and personal pride in architecture, while the spaces of the interior provided physical security and psychological warmth. Large, organic spaces attested to the unity of Latin families. By mid-nineteenth century San Antonio evolved into a picturesque city, with a juxtaposition of these Spanish-Mexican adobe and masonry cubes and *jacales*, along with the later additions of German- and American-styled shelters, most of which are gone. Numerous examples of the Latin development have disappeared from El Paso, too, in the wake of urban renewal; many others probably will go soon.

In the Latin communities, differing secular functions were rarely expressed through variation in form. The masonry or adobe box served public as well as residential uses. Often located side-by-side, the buildings bordered the streets, creating alleylike passages, in European fashion.

While the early Spanish colonial and Mexican provincial buildings were unadorned cubes, affluence often brought the addition of elaborate decorative details on the surfaces (fig. 20). Dignified Classical details, appropriate to the massiveness of the traditional cubical buildings, often attested to the wealth and cultural attainments of the owner and at the same time provided public enjoyment. Although ornamental details were occasionally cut from stone, in Laredo the early buildings had walls of plastered rubble, with parapets of brick laid to form a variety of decorative details. In Roma bricks were used for entire walls, wherein the openings were surmounted by Classical entablatures with moldings and dentils formed with molded bricks.

The parochial churches of Spanish colonial Texas likewise reflected the cultural heritage of the builders. In Laredo, a town founded in 1755, *Iglesia Antiqua* ("old church") was a charming edifice built in 1764, apparently with Spanish Baroque details; however, it was razed near the end of the nineteenth century. In San Antonio, aside from the missions, the most prominent building was the parochial church, Nuestra Señora de la Candelaria y Guadalupe (1734), built on a cruciform plan similar to an early adobe chapel at the mission of San Antonio de Valero (fig. 21). Barrel vaults spanned the nave and transepts—much as they did in the mission churches—and pendentives supported a drum, dome, and lantern high above the crossing. The dark interior was spacious and certainly provided the psychological mystery appropriate for the religious services.[35]

While these early adobe, stone, and log buildings were being hastily assembled by Spanish colonists during the early part of the nineteenth century, events were transpiring in Spain and Mexico that would have a profound impact on the political and economic development of Texas. In the wake of the corruption and archaism that had developed abroad, the

[35] Habig, *Alamo Chain of Missions*, p. 259.

FIGURE 20. Farias House, Laredo (late 1800's). *Laredo Public Library.*

In the design of this dwelling traditional refinements of details appear. The boxlike forms were similar to those that had appeared in ranch houses during the early years of settlement. However, large openings suggest that maintaining security was no longer a problem. Stone quoins and a decorative cornice treatment reveal the builder's concern for architectural refinement. Similar forms with a wide variety of details also appeared throughout El Paso.

This building was razed in 1972 to make space for a supermarket.

FIGURE 21. Church of Nuestra Señora de la Candelaria y Guadalupe, San Antonio (1734). *Daughters of the Republic of Texas Library, San Antonio.*

It was specified that the structure of this church be on a cruciform plan, thirty *varas* long (about eighty-three feet) and six *varas* wide (about seventeen feet), with a principal altar in the sanctuary and side altars in each of the two transept arms. However, Padre Juan Agustín Morfi, in his *History of Texas, 1673–1779,* opined that the work was "so poorly constructed that it promises but a short life." It did survive, though, and later it was incorporated into the San Fernando Cathedral. While parts of the building have been restored, the front is no longer visible.

Mexican revolution broke out. Finally, in 1821 Mexico won independence from Spain.

As is usual in times of turmoil, architecture languished during the period in which Mexicans were struggling for independence. Due to frequent changes in civil and military offices, garrisons and public buildings were much neglected. With little money and few available workmen, authorities ignored civil and ecclesiastical architecture alike. Typical of the communities where construction and maintenance were much retarded were Nacogdoches and San Antonio. In 1812 the former was entirely abandoned; during the struggle the buildings deteriorated, and by a decade later many evidently had not been rebuilt. To improve conditions and to secure the country following the winning of independence, immigration was needed—in 1820, there had been only three thousand people in Texas.[36]

In contrast to Spain, which discouraged settlement in Texas by foreigners, Mexico recognized that one of the most efficient means of developing the country was to encourage immigration from other lands. In 1825 the co-state of Coahuila and Texas passed a colonization law specifically inviting the immigration of foreigners and Mexicans alike. Land was offered to those of good moral character who would swear before an *ayuntamiento* ("municipal government") that they would support the federal and state constitutions, and that they would observe the Catholic faith. Subsequently numerous immigrants arrived from the United States and other foreign countries.

The colonization law also authorized the establishment of new towns upon vacant lands. As in Spanish times, laws were passed to control town planning. However, in response to the recognition of conditions that differed between Mexico and Spain—where the Laws of the Indies had originated—the requirements developed at home differed from those that had been instituted abroad. In the Texas region, planning was regulated by the *Laws and Decrees of the State of Coahuila and Texas*. According to laws governing town planning, the commissioner in charge should carefully select the site for his town. Typifying the desire to establish order in the wilderness, the principal lines of the town were to run north and south, east and west. The center space from which the main streets were to emanate was to be the principal or constitutional square. The streets were to be straight, and a ferry was to be provided at each river crossing where a highway to the town passed. To facilitate surveying, streets were to be parallel, if possible.[37]

Virtually all the towns founded within Mexican Texas essentially conformed to these requirements during their early years. Included among these new communities were Villa San Patricio de Hibernia (1830), on the left bank of the Nueces River where the *Camino Real* crossed, and Villa de la Santísima Trinidad de la Libertad (Liberty) (1831), located in the far eastern section of the state. Even in Nacogdoches, already laid out under Spanish law, consideration was given to resurveying the town according to the new requirements. However, since conformity to Mexican laws would have required the division of existing lots, the razing of business buildings, and the destruction of soldiers' barracks, officials decided to allow the streets to remain in their original patterns.[38]

The original plat of Liberty followed the Mexican plan specified by the *Laws*. Sixteen leagues of land were granted for the community itself, and forty-nine blocks comprised the

[36] Population figures for the period are estimates only. David M. Vigness, *The Revolutionary Decades*, states the population to have been 2,500 in 1820 (p. 24). A report by Juan M. Almonte, cited in Kathryn Stoner O'Connor, *The Presidio of La Bahía del Espíritu Santo de Zuniga 1721 to 1846*, lists the 1806 population of "Bexar" at 5,000 and Goliad at 1,400. In 1834 the combined population of Bexar, Goliad, Victoria, and San Patricio was 4,000 (p. 95).

[37] *Laws and Decrees of the State of Coahuila and Texas in Spanish and English*, pp. 15–21.
[38] Ernest Allen Connally, "The Ecclesiastical and Military Architecture of the Spanish Province of Texas" (Ph.D. diss., Harvard University, 1955), pp. 243–244; Winnie Allen, "The History of Nacogdoches, 1691–1830" (Master's thesis, University of Texas, Austin, 1925), p. 129; A[mos] [Andrew] Parker, *Trip to the West and Texas*, p. 151.

"inner town." The *plaza de mercado* ("market place") formed the central public space. The square on the east evidently was to be reserved for the church, and the block on the west was designated for public buildings. Other blocks adjacent to the square were set aside for other public functions. While the square on the west has served continuously as a site for municipal buildings, the other blocks became locations for commercial and public buildings.[39]

As was usual, the Anglo-American settlers, who formed the majority in these towns and the surrounding farms, built with techniques they had known before immigrating. Many had originated in the southern United States; hence, they constructed in thir new environment rough, frame structures and cabins with cribs of horizontal logs, similar to those in other regions in the South. Relatively little knowledge of building techniques appears to have been obtained from the Mexicans who were already in the state.

During this era, of course, it was difficult to obtain public buildings. Such shelters as were finally built for any purpose were crude works, generally of logs. For example, a courthouse raised for the municipality of Liberty in 1831 apparently was made of rough-hewn timbers, some twenty-two feet square, and was located in a grove of pines.[40] Throughout the forested regions this was typical.

While the *Laws of Coahuila and Texas* authorized the collection of property taxes to finance the construction of churches in the new towns, little ecclesiastical work of pretension resulted. As early as the 1820's Baptists, Methodists, and Cumberland Presbyterians were preaching in Texas. Most Anglo-American immigrants, coming from the southern United States, belonged to these denominations, and few converted to Catholicism as required by law.[41] These Protestants placed rela-

tively little emphasis on the need for elaborate architecture as a setting for the religious experience. All they required for assembly was a grove of trees, a porch, a private cabin, or the courtroom of a courthouse. In areas already populated by Latins, on the other hand, missions and other existing churches continued to serve the needs of the residents.

Other architecture of the Mexican period in the Texas region reflected other considerations, including economic status and political disunity. At the close of the Mexican revolution, the states had little money. In an effort to recover, the government placed high tariffs on goods imported from the United States. This encouraged smuggling, which, according to Mexican officials, required measures for control.

The success of the colonization program contributed to other governmental problems. Encouraged by the General Colonization Law, the stream of immigration rapidly increased the population. By 1830, Austin's colony alone contained more than 4,000 people; in 1836 one writer estimated the population of Texas to be about 25,000, of whom 7,000 were Mexicans.[42] With the Americans and their institutions threatening to take over the country completely, General Manuel Mier y Terán urged the Mexican government to initiate action to assure Mexican control. As a result of his recommendations, a decree was passed to curb immigration from the United States. This same law also authorized the establishment of forts and customs houses to control tariff and immigration.[43]

The locations for customs houses were scattered widely. Buildings and garrisons appeared in San Antonio, Goliad, Anahuac, Galveston, Victoria, and Tenoxtitlán. In addition, Fort Terán and a fort at Velasco were established on

[39] "Liberty," Historical Files, Texas Historical Commission; Charles W. Fisher, Jr., "A New Look at Liberty's Seven Courthouses, 1831–1972," mimeographed, p. 2.

[40] Fisher, "Liberty's Seven Courthouses," p. 4.

[41] According to the historian Yoakum, "nineteen twentieths of the colonists neither observed or believed in the religion prescribed in the Mexican constitution" (*History of Texas* 1:4).

[42] Orceneth Fisher, *Sketches of Texas in 1840*, pp. v, 34–35.

[43] Vigness, *The Revolutionary Decades*, pp. 107–110.

the east bank of Galveston Bay. However, the design of these posts apparently followed no typical plan.[44]

The law forbidding further immigration and establishing these military works had antagonized the independent Texans. Although in 1834 laws were passed allowing additional immigration and nullifying the religious requirements, other forms of oppression continued.[45] Finally, events transpired that would result in war for Texas' independence.

[44] *A Visit to Texas in 1831*, pp. 60–61.
[45] Vigness, *The Revolutionary Decades*, p. 148.

Most of the architectural heritage of the Hispanic era leading to Texas independence is gone. While some masonry works remain, most of the wood and adobe buildings deteriorated or were destroyed by storms. Others burned as a consequence of man's carelessness. Still others were ripped apart in subsequent years to make room for larger, more durably built structures. While it obviously was impossible to retain much of this heritage, it seems unfortunate that the legacy Texas took with her into independence is so little visible today.

2

A Potpourri of Culture and Architecture

DURING the first years following the revolution (1835–1836), the economic and political situations in Texas were not propitious for architecture, public or private. In addition to the devastation remaining in the wake of hostilities, the financial condition of the republic was poor. Although the towns and homes that had been neglected or burned during the war were rebuilt, the threat of Mexican invasion and Indian hostilities created insecurity. Poverty and strife, then as always, were certainly deterrents to cultural advancement.

Key to the development of the Texas country was settlement. Immigration from the United States was strong right after the revolution as a result of poor crops and a panic in America during the late 1830's. The flow of settlers was interrupted, though, by two Mexican invasions in 1842, the first of which entered Goliad, Refugio, and San Antonio and the second of which again entered San Antonio. But after fears of hostilities with Mexico ceased in 1844, immigration again got underway. Now prosperity along with the promise of annexation attracted settlers. Furthermore, as Mexico had done previously, the republic and then the state offered free land to entice immigrants. Educators, mechanics, and farmers all were needed if the sparsely populated country were to prosper and advance culturally.

Even before statehood and before American immigrant trains began crossing the Red River and the Sabine River, foreign immigration had already been underway. Seeking a new life, but at the same time the opportunity to continue their native languages and customs, immigrants from Europe collected in colonies within the new state. Among those who sailed across the Atlantic to form communities in the Republic and State of Texas were colonists from France.

Texas had appealed to some Frenchmen while it was still a province of Spain. In 1818 a group of Napoleonic exiles, ex-soldiers, and several other nationalistic types formed on the banks of the lower Trinity River an ephemeral settlement, which they named Champ d'Asile ("Field of Asylum").[1] However, this settlement survived for only a short time.

More successful were the efforts of empresario Henri Castro, an ambitious Frenchman who in 1827 had become a naturalized citizen of the United States. In 1842, Castro received a contract from the Republic of Texas to settle six hundred families on a tract of land in Indian country west of San Antonio. Two years later, with colonists from Germany and

[1]Frederic Gaillardet, *Sketches of Early Texas and Louisiana*, trans. James L. Shepherd III, pp. 121–131.

FIGURE 22. Laurent Quintle House and Store, Castroville (ca. 1850). Side view. *Historic American Buildings Survey, Library of Congress, Washington, D.C.*

Constructed by Laurent Quintle, this was a two-and-a-half-story building with storage cellar and attic. Entered through two pairs of French doors, the one large ground-story room was used for commercial purposes. A residence was contained in four rooms and a hall on the second level, accessible only by a stair and a porch located on the back side. A small interior stair provided access to the attic.

The building possessed warmth and charm, characteristic of French immigrant architecture. The limestone the walls were constructed of was of course indigenous to the region. Porches and the broken pitch in the roof contributed to the handsome character of the building.

France, principally Alsace, he founded the town of Castroville. To encourage settlement in this community, each family was assigned a lot, was furnished with building materials for a house, and was given 640 acres of farmland on the Medina River.

In addition to their language and social customs, Castro's settlers imported their own form of town planning and architectural styles (fig. 22). Named after Castro's friends and rel-

atives or for European capitals, streets were laid out on a simple grid pattern with a central space reserved for community activity. Conforming to centuries-old practice in New France, a site for the Catholic church, the community's focal point, was located adjacent to this town square (fig. 23). At first a temporary shelter was set up on this location to house worship. Then a substantial church building of stone was designed on a basilican plan by

FIGURE 23. Town Square and St. Louis Catholic Church buildings, Castroville. *Courtesy Robert Q. Johnson, Castroville, Texas, from files of the Institute of Texan Cultures, San Antonio.*

The styles of the churches near the square reflected the development of the community and surrounding area. The second church building, which replaced an 1846 temporary shelter, was completed in 1850. Both were in Gothic style.

A few years later, wanting a larger, more distinguished building, parishioners supported construction of a third edifice (*right*), which was some 50 feet wide and 150 feet long. It was completed about 1870. In this the character of the ecclesiastical architecture of the builders' homeland was apparent. Although the third church still stands, finials have been removed, the steeple changed, and the doorway modified.

The square is now landscaped and all the buildings except the church on the right are gone.

Emmanuel Domenech, a priest, and the cornerstone was laid in 1844. The third building, which still stands with some modification of original details and which was erected beside the previous structure, has a cornerstone that was blessed in 1868.[2]

The quaint ethnic character of the French settlements was noted in 1854 by Frederick Law Olmsted. Describing Castroville, with its houses of picket walls and steeply pitched thatched roofs and its Catholic churches— two of which were standing at the time—he wrote, "The cottages are scattered prettily . . .

[and the community] might sit for the portrait of one of the poorer villages of the upper Rhone Valley." Only Castro himself, apparently, lived in a stone house. Founded in 1847, following the establishment of other French settlements of Quihi (1845) and Vandenberg (1846), D'Hanis was "like one of the smallest and meanest of European peasant hamlets." The houses had walls "made of poles and logs placed together vertically and made tight with clay mortar . . . the windows without glass . . . the roofs covered with thatch of fine brown grass, laid in a peculiar manner, the ridge-line and apexes being ornamented with knots, tufts, crosses or weathercocks."[3] While

[2]This discussion of Castroville's founding and layout is drawn from Walter P. Webb and H. B. Carroll, eds., *The Handbook of Texas*, 1:309; *The Texians and the Texans: The French Texans*, pp. 20–21; Samuel Gideon, "The Quaint Old Town of Castroville," *Frontier Times* 2 (September, 1925):12–14.

[3]Frederick Law Olmsted, *A Journey through Texas*, pp. 276, 280.

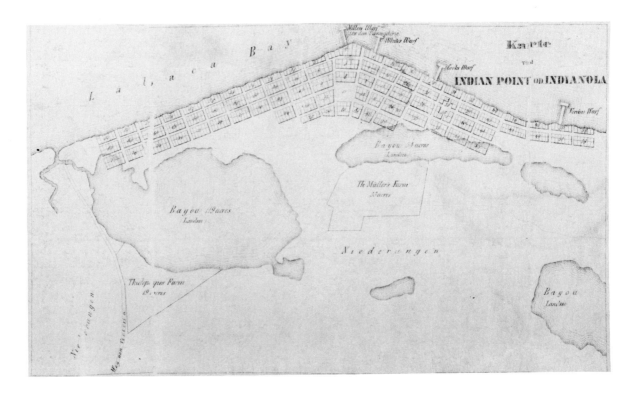

FIGURE 24. Indianola (founded 1844). Plan (1860). *General Land Office, Austin.*

Founded by Prince Carl Zu Solms-Braunfels on the west shore of Matagorda Bay, Indianola was a port of entry for many German immigrants. Prior to the Civil War it became a county seat and prospered economically. However, the town was destined for oblivion. After several hurricanes devastated the community, the town began to fail. The diversion of shipping to other coastal cities contributed to the decline of the once prosperous community. Finally the county seat was moved to Lavaca, and Indianola was abandoned. Today a 1936 granite slab marks the site.

the towns in which these were located did not grow large, some of their foreign character has survived, although many of the early buildings have disappeared.

In North Texas, environments unbenign to the skills of the immigrants made other French settlements less successful. New Icaria was established in 1848 in Denton County, but it survived only a few years. In 1855 under the leadership of Victor Considérant, a follower of the socialist Charles Fourier, another group of French immigrants formed the utopian settlement of La Réunion on the West Fork of the Trinity River in Dallas County.. Lack of agricultural know-how, poor farmland, and decreasing finances forced abandonment of La Réunion in 1857 or 1858. Some of the residents moved then to the town of Dallas, where they continued some of their customs.[4]

[4]Webb and Carroll, *Handbook of Texas*, 2:29; *The French Texans*, pp. 24–25.

By far the most extensive European immigration to Texas was conducted by the *Adelsverein* (Society for the Protection of German Immigrants), an organization formed for the benefit of immigrants seeking to escape unsatisfactory political, economic, and religious conditions in Germany. Although there had been some earlier immigration in the 1830's—for instance, in the founding of Industry (1838)—thousands came to Texas in the 1840's and 1850's to establish other new towns. In 1844, under Prince Carl of Solms-Braunfels, commissioner general of the society, tracts of land were purchased for communities. Chief among these towns were New Braunfels, founded in 1845 by Prince Carl, and Fredericksburg, founded in 1846 by John O. Meusebach. Other settlements included Sisterdale, Boerne, and Comfort. Bettina, a German communist community in which the people were to live in a common house and share all

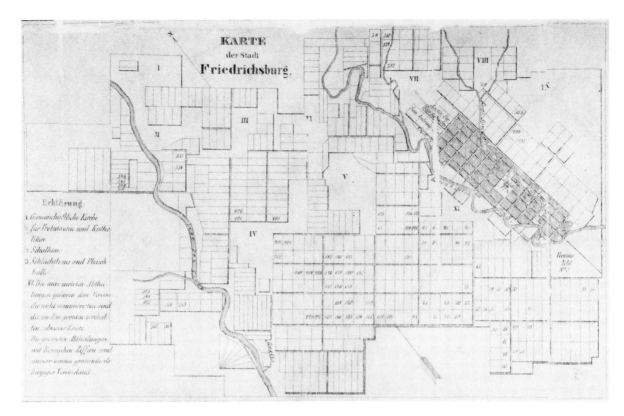

FIGURE 25. Fredericksburg (founded 1846). Plan. *General Land Office, Austin.*

Located in the Hill Country, Fredericksburg was founded by a group of German immigrants led by John O. Meusebach. In the vicinity, immigrants discovered large quantities of oak and limestone, which were extensively used in their architecture.

the work and profits equally, was founded in 1847 near the Llano River; however, it lasted less than a year.[5]

In the German communities, the main plaza was identified as a market place, although there were variations in its form and location. In the community of Indianola (1844), the *Marktplatz* occupied the center of an elongated grid (fig. 24). At New Braunfels the public space was centered on the intersection of the two main streets, making it quite prominent. Fredericksburg was planned with a large, oblong square, 600 feet by 920 feet (fig. 25). Forming the focal point in the center of this space and thereby emphasizing its community role was the *Vereins Kirche* ("society church") (fig. 26).

Where Olmsted was intrigued with the uniform style of the French settlements, Roemer was struck by the diverse architecture of the

German hamlets. In both Fredericksburg and New Braunfels, settlers lived in shelters that revealed the exigencies of the times. Those who could not afford to expend much labor lived in Mexican-type shelters, formed from unhewn picket walls, whose cracks were filled with grass and clay. The roofs of these dwellings were of thatch, canvas, or oxhide. Other Germans lived in Anglo-American-type log houses built of oak trees, which were abundant.[6]

Many settlers employed *fachwerk* ("half-timber") walls for their houses, as well as barns. A form of half-timber construction common in Europe in the Middle Ages, this technique was continued in later centuries as a tradition in the eastern provinces of Germany.[7] Immigrants brought it to Texas, as well as to other states. In Texas, *fachwerk* houses had

[5] Webb and Carroll, *Handbook of Texas*, 1:152, 181, 386, 643, 884, and 2:271, 616.

[6] Ferdinand Roemer, *Texas, with Particular Reference to German Immigration and the Physical Appearance of the Country,* trans. Ostwald Mueller, p. 229.

[7] Richard W. E. Perrin, *Wisconsin Architecture*, p. 16.

FIGURE 26. *Vereins Kirche*, Fredericksburg (1846–1847). *From* Seth Eastman Sketchbook.

As part of its obligations to settlers it brought to Texas, the Society for the Protection of German Immigrants agreed to erect a building for religious services. Built on an octagonal plan according to the design of Dr. Schubert, the church was open to all denominations. Although it was modeled after a European church, the resemblance to a coffee mill prompted some to label it the *Kaffeemuehle* ("coffee mill").

In 1897 the building was demolished. In 1930 a replica was built for a museum. Unfortunately, in the reconstruction the original *fachwerk* ("half-timber") walls, each of which was eighteen feet in height by eighteen in length, were eliminated, thereby ruining the character of the building.

FIGURE 27. J. L. Forke House, New Braunfels (1850's). *Historic American Buildings Survey, Library of Congress, Washington, D.C.*

This was a characteristic German *fachwerk* dwelling, with adobe and brick nogging. Stone also was often used in *fachwerk* dwellings.

In other German buildings there were other forms of half-timber work, wherein the panels were filled with sticks, mud, and grass. One variation was accomplished by boring holes, one and a half inches in diameter, into the sides of the wooden posts and inserting into these saplings or branches, which were covered with grass and mud, coated with lime plaster.

FIGURE 28. Ferdinand Kneip House, Round Top (ca. 1850). *Historic American Buildings Survey, Library of Congress, Washington, D.C.*

Built by Conrad Schuddenagem, a German immigrant, this two-story dwelling was a durable work of stone. The walls were finished with stucco and whitewashed. A two-story gallery across the front and a steeply pitched gable roof, an American feature, contributed to the handsome character of the building. German influence is also shown in the location of the building adjacent to the street.

timber frameworks of oak or cedar secured with mortise, and tenon joints secured with treenails (pegs). Limestone or brick nogging then ordinarily filled the panels of the framework. A fine example of *fachwerkbau*, now gone, appeared in the J. L. Forke House, New Braunfels (fig. 27). In response to the hot climate, the German Texans, like others, usually added porches to the traditional form.

With German immigration came excellent stone masons. Employing the abundant limestone and sandstone of the Hill Country, they skillfully built houses with walls of stones, often roughly hewn with a hatchet. The walls contained openings spanned either by wooden lintels or segmental arches. Among the fine stone constructions were the Heinrich Dietz House, Fredericksburg (1848), and the Ferdi-

nand Kneip House, Round Top (fig. 28), both of which have been destroyed.

Stone, delicate wooden punch work, and jigsaw ornamentation were also employed in the construction of many Sunday houses in Fredericksburg. Farm and ranch families who resided on lands located long distances from town constructed small one- and two-room stone dwellings with lofts. They stayed in these houses when they came to town on Saturday to socialize, to shop at the stores, and to attend church on the following day. To relieve the austerity of stone's massiveness and to satisfy the German love for detail, decorative figures such as the quatrefoil were incorporated into the ornamental features of the porches, where evenings were spent visiting.

With prosperity and cultural advancement

artistic sophistication appeared, reflecting the German homeland. Among the many German immigrants were talented artists, including Rudolph Melchior, who had done theatrical design and painted portraits and landscape designs before immigrating to Texas in 1853. To delight the eye, Melchior and other artists decorated the wooden walls and ceilings of homes with beautiful freehand paintings and stencil designs in bright colors. Many of the stencils were applied in linear patterns around door and window openings. Representative in New Braunfels was the Guadalupe Hotel, now gone, which, according to Olmsted's description, had pink walls, stenciled panels, and scroll ornaments in crimson—all by an unknown artist. In other buildings graining representing various handsome woods also enhanced interiors.[8]

While the colorful decoration appearing on many of the neatly kept dwellings showed a love for delicate beauty, other qualities of the German character were reflected in the functional types of buildings constructed. Although many did not appear until the latter part of the nineteenth century, community buildings attested to the fraternal nature of the German life-style. For example, Turner Hall, Galveston, was built in 1858 by a Turnverein Lodge; the building was expanded during the latter part of the century to accommodate increasing social activity (fig. 29). Also the product of German society was the Galveston Garten Verein—a social club formed in 1876—which constructed a pavilion with charming gingerbread trim. The pavilion, where members danced to the lively tunes, was extensively damaged by fire in 1979 but then restored.[9]

Further contributing to the ethnic diversity of early Texas settlements were groups from Bohemia and Moravia, from Poland, Ireland, and Norway. Primarily agrarians, the Bohemians and Moravians (Czechs) settled on lands that were favorable to farming and established, among others, the communities of Shiner and Praha. Like many other immigrant groups, they built straightforward dwellings. As the Germans did, they formed organizations, and near the turn of the century they built meeting halls, which also were used for dancing—an important aspect of their culture. Perhaps the most remarkable feature of the architecture produced by these Czechs is some of the interiors, where skilled artists recreated with paint the style of decoration they had known abroad.[10]

Polish farmers moved into Texas in substantial numbers during the 1850's. On Christmas Eve, 1854, on an open prairie, Panna Maria ("Virgin Mary") was established by Father Leopold Moczygemba and a small group that was joined by others in subsequent years. Later, several other communities, including Czestochowa (Cestohowa), were founded.

As is usual in new communities, the first Polish shelters were primitive, but these eventually were replaced by durable buildings. First, the immigrants in Panna Maria built huts of pickets with thatched roofs. Ultimately, they replaced these huts with fine houses with stone walls, similar to the houses they had known in Poland.[11] As was characteristic of these immigrant communities, the church, which formed a nucleus for the settlers' lives, became the dominant built landmark of the area. Situated upon an eminence, the Immaculate Conception Catholic Church (1877–1878), which replaced an 1856 building, closely resembled innumerable other rural religious edifices. It was distinguished by a simple form containing the nave and a centrally positioned rectangular tower, which promi-

[8] The Texians and The Texans: The German Texans; Rudolph Melchior Papers, Historical Files, Institute of Texan Cultures, San Antonio; Olmsted, A Journey through Texas, p. 144. For an illustration and discussion of graining techniques, see Lonn Taylor, "The McGregor-Grimm House at Winedale, Texas," Antiques 108 (1975):515–521.

[9] "Turner Hall," HABS No. Tex-21, Library of Congress, Washington, D.C.; Ellen Beasley, "History in Towns: Galveston, Texas," Antiques 108 (1975):482–483.

[10] The Texians and the Texans: The Czech Texans, pp. 5–13.

[11] See T. Lindsay Baker, The Early History of Panna Maria, Texas.

FIGURE 29. Turner Hall, Galveston (1858). *Historic American Buildings Survey, Library of Congress, Washington, D.C.*

The communal nature of the Texas-German society was indicated by the establishment of numerous community halls—many of which were in isolated rural locations. Those built by the end of the nineteenth century were often large, to accommodate dances and other social activities. Although they frequently were straightforward in design, occasionally they were enhanced with various decorative details.

Noteworthy features of Turner Hall include the large Doric columns. All the openings are flanked by woodwork representing Doric pilasters, which supported an entablature on both the first and second floors. Turner Hall was later purchased by J. T. Albert and was converted into a residence.

nently announced the entrance. Other Polish communities with buildings of similar character included New Waverly and Czestochowa. Fortunately, since they have not been threatened by urbanization, most of the early Polish public works still stand. However, in Bremond, two Polish Catholic churches, dating from the late nineteenth and early twentieth centuries both have been razed (fig. 30).

Like the Europeans, immigrants from the United States moved to Texas searching for new opportunities and a better life. From Kentucky and Tennessee and from the Gulf Coast states came the two main streams to occupy the lands and establish new communities.

While many immigrants settled in the ru-

ral areas, others, as occupants as well as entrepreneurs, helped found towns. During the days of the republic and early statehood, new community names appeared with remarkable frequency. As speculative ventures by proprietors—some of whom were prominent men—many towns existed only on paper as ideas; however, when conditions were favorable, many others developed into successful settlements.

Among the keys to successful community founding were healthful natural environments and abundant natural resources. Locations along rivers near the crossings of frequently traveled roads were favored, and sites surrounded by abundant timber for the manufac-

FIGURE 30. St. Mary's Catholic Church, Bremond (1879). *Courtesy St. Mary's Catholic Church, Bremond.*

During the 1870's, Polish people, many of whom were farmers, immigrated to Bremond and the surrounding region. After meeting in homes, the Polish Catholics of the area determined to build this church. In 1879 Father Mosiewicz conducted the first services in the frame house of worship.

In 1908 this was replaced by a large brick edifice in Gothic Revival style, after which the first building served as a Sunday school until 1936. In 1970 the masonry church was razed and the ground broken for the present contemporary church.

ture of lumber were considered advantageous. Stone that could be quarried conveniently likewise added to the attraction of a community, as did clay for the manufacture of bricks. Fertile soil for farming and grass-covered pasture land also increased the potential for economic advancement.[12]

As foreign immigrants did, so Anglo-Americans brought to Texas the customs and architectural traditions of their homes states. Town plans conformed to conventions that had spread across the southern states.[13] Regardless of terrain or location, they consisted of rectangular blocks and lots—arrangements that were easy to survey and that fulfilled a psychic need for organization in the unordered natural environment.

While the basic grid was universal, the dimensions of the blocks and streets varied across the republic and state. Near the Red River, in such towns as Clarksville and Paris, the streets were quite narrow and blocks were small—perhaps reflecting the Upper South origins of the early immigrants who settled

[12] Newspapers published during these times contained many advertisements for new towns and extolled the features of the chosen sites. See, for example, *Matagorda Bulletin*, August 2, 1838; *Telegraph and Texas Register* (Houston), December 25, 1839; *Telegraph and Texas Register* (Columbia), August 30, 1836.

[13] Edward T. Price, "The Central Courthouse Square in the American County Seat," *Geographical Review* 58 (1968): 49–51.

in northern Texas. In communities south of these, however, the components of the grid often were more spacious.

Generally, the town plan was developed with one side parallel to an adjacent stream, river, or bayou, producing orientations at angles to the north-south, east-west lines. However, in many other towns true north-south, east-west orientations were preferred, and additions often were laid out in the direction of the cardinal points. Within these grids, one or more blocks were reserved as public spaces to accommodate community activity and to provide sites for the main public buildings of the town or county—arrangements that evidently had been brought to Texas by settlers from the upper and lower South.

The public spaces provided sites for important social functions. The public square was the point of arrival in a community; it was the location of the community well or cistern, the gathering place for the "courthouse society," the site of political speeches. As the focal point of the town it attracted commercial intercourse (fig. 31). The significance of the community space was well expressed by one unknown reporter in Fort Worth when he wrote that it "is the grand popular exchange and commercial room for exhibition and sale of the entire products of the country."[14]

Deed restrictions were often placed upon the property that had been donated to the public. At the time he contributed the public square to Dallas County, newspaper accounts speculated that John Neely Bryan had specified that if the square were ever abandoned the land would revert to his heirs. Likewise, reporters suspected that the courthouse site in Fort Worth had been deeded for use only as a public square. At the turn of the century, because of such a deed restriction, Houston officials declined to change the site for a new courthouse.[15] However, in other county seats,

such as Clarksville and Sulphur Springs, original courthouse sites on the town square were abandoned late in the nineteenth century—the sites are now parking lots.

The commercial architecture appearing around the public squares developed through several stages. The first business buildings, of course, were simple wood-framed boxes, often with false fronts and decorative cornices. In time, these were replaced by stone- or brick-walled buildings with timber structural work. In the masonry fronts along the sidewalk there were generally three or four openings, spanned by Roman arches and filled with French doors surmounted by fanlight windows. When built of rubble, the fronts were often covered with stucco into which were tooled or onto which were painted lines to represent masonry coursing. When the buildings were of ashlar, textures and tool markings often contributed to the character of the front. On fronts built with bricks, a variety of patterns often added interest—near the end of the century the decorative potential of stone and brick was extensively exploited in rural communities. Fortunately, many of these buildings still stand.

A wide variety of merchandise was available in these antebellum commercial buildings. According to one visitor in Galveston, within were offered "curious assemblages of all manner of miscellaneous articles, in almost every department of human wants and occupations. Unlike the shops of Europe, in which one article, or, at most, perhaps some few of the same genus, constitute the staple commodity of the

---

[14] *Fort Worth Daily Gazette*, January 16, 1879.
[15] *Fort Worth Daily Gazette*, February 8, 10, and 20, 1890, and December 23, 1892; *Houston Daily Post*, July 3, 1895.

Concerning a question over the location of a new Harris County courthouse, the county judge observed, "The [original] site was deeded to the county upon the condition of its use for courthouse purpose. It is in an excellent location, convenient to different portions of the business district and a more suitable location could not be found. To use the site for a purpose other than that for which it was deeded would involve complications." In Jefferson, however, D. N. Alley attempted to repossess a public square and courthouse that had been vacated, but the district court ruled against him (see *Dallas Morning News*, January 11, 1891). In Sweetwater the Texas and Pacific Railroad, which laid out the town, retained—and still retains—ownership of the public square.

place, these stores much more nearly resemble a series of modern museums. . . ."[16]

While most of the Texas communities with commercial buildings of this kind around a public space were platted on simple grids of modest size, the state capital was laid out on an imposing plan, with the commercial sites platted along a broad avenue leading up to it. Among the matters pressing the administration of the new republic following the winning of independence was the site for the seat of government. After being briefly located at West Columbia, the government was moved to Houston. Then in 1839 a commission headed by Edwin Waller was appointed to select a permanent location and was provided with instructions to govern planning. This agency selected a site near the existing settlement of Waterloo, at the edge of the frontier. The scenic and healthy location in the hills along the Colorado River, it was hoped, would foster settlement of the uninhabited western region.

Official directives required that a number of spaces in the capital plan be reserved for public use. The act authorizing the permanent location of the seat of government specified: "the . . . agent, before the sale of lots, shall set apart a sufficient number of the most eligible for a Capitol, Arsenal, Magazine, University, Academy, Churches, common Schools, Hospital, Penitentiary, and for all other necessary public buildings and purposes."[17] Following these specifications, Waller surveyed the town of Austin (fig. 32).

Incorporating the required spaces, the new seat of government was laid out on a formal plan, which was considered appropriate for the capital of the republic and which reflected the cultural aspirations of its founders. Conscious of the need for sites that would complement monumental architecture, agent Waller developed a gridiron layout with a prominent public focal point that recalled Philadelphia, although the sensitive utilization of landforms recalled Washington, D.C. Four blocks in the grid, which were located on an eminence, were reserved as a pedestal for the future capitol. A depression extending south from this site to the river was transformed into Congress Avenue, the main traffic artery. Around the capitol square, lots were reserved for the government of the republic, including the Navy Department and War Department. Four public squares were reserved, along with a courthouse-jail space. In formal pattern, other lots were specified for churches and market, and on another height forty acres were reserved for a university—the concept for which also recalled the original plan for Washington, D.C.[18]

If the monumental plan of Austin fulfilled the noble aspirations of its designers, the early architecture, destroyed many decades ago, reflected the primitive and hostile conditions of the frontier. Francis Moore, Jr., described the capitol as a temporary log or frame structure. According to Moore, "The buildings occupied by the heads of the several departments, are generally log cabins, fitted up in a neat and commodious style." However, while Austin buildings may not have represented the height of luxury, at least one article in a local newspaper claimed that the houses of Austin were ". . . better buildings than were built the first year in Houston."[19]

Probably the two most sophisticated early buildings in the capital of the republic were the president's house and the French Legation. Located on a hill east of Congress Avenue, the president's house (1839) was described by a contemporary as "the best building in the place; it is two stories high, has a portico in front and rear; and although, if situated in any one of the larger towns of the United States,

[16] Charles Hooton, *St. Louis' Isle, or Texiana*, p. 12.

[17] "An Act for the Permanent Location of the Seat of Government," *Telegraph and Texas Register* (Houston), January 16, 1839.

[18] Roxanne Kuter Williamson, *Austin, Texas: An American Architectural History*, pp. 1–6; Katherine Hart, *Austin and Travis County: A Pictorial History, 1839–1939*, introduction; Webb and Carroll, *Handbook of Texas*, 1:85.

[19] Francis Moore, Jr., *Map and Description of Texas*, p. 130; *Telegraph and Texas Register* (Houston), July 31, 1839.

FIGURE 31. Public Square, Waco. *Texas Collection, Baylor University, Waco.*

During the nineteenth and early twentieth centuries, many public squares across the state presented scenes similar to this. Farmers crowded the public space with wagons laden with their products. However, the public square was not always pleasant to the casual visitor. On hot, dry days it was dusty; on cool, rainy days it was muddy. Nonetheless, these were accepted as routine conditions, and trade and social intercourse proceeded.

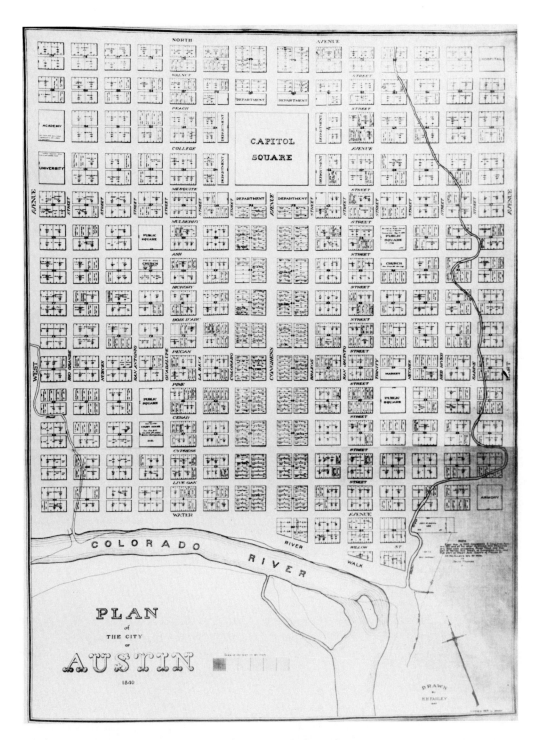

FIGURE 32. Austin (founded 1839). Map. *General Land Office, Austin.*

The officials who set forth the official requirements for the capital of the republic carefully specified that spaces be reserved for important public buildings. The space reserved for the capitol is still used as originally intended, but the political change from republic to state obviously eliminated the need for space for certain governmental functions. In addition, the public square at Trinity and Mulberry (now 10th) streets is occupied by a Baptist church; the public square at Trinity and Pine (now 5th) streets is the location of a fire station and the O. Henry House Museum; the other two public squares are parks. The space reserved for a courthouse and jail is now commercial.

would attract little or no attention, appears almost a palace contrasted with the houses of the frontier hunter."[20] However, in 1843, four years before the house burned, unsatisfactory building techniques became obvious: "The green wood necessary to use had become loose and it was . . . falling to pieces."[21] The French Legation, which still stands, is a one-story frame house with a formal plan and a roof with dormers, reflecting the origins of its intended occupants.

At the time these buildings appeared, it was stated, perhaps optimistically, that Austin had only about one hundred houses. Nonetheless, with splendid faith in the future, one writer anticipated times when "neat cottages and . . . great mansions [would] be scattered abroad over the country, combining to form a picture of beauty and loveliness unsurpassed. . . ."[22]

As in Austin, settlers in other rural areas of the republic and early state erected expedient shelters, which were indigenous to the land. Utilizing materials at hand, they tried familiar techniques, then sometimes modified them to suit the climate and the available materials. Roemer observed the concern for adaptation in the New Braunfels region when he wrote that "most people had no idea as to which particular type of construction was most suited to the climate."[23] In response to the new environment, roof forms and coverings were developed for the greater rainfall, openings were modeled to suit the temperature; and orientation was selected with respect to the prevailing breezes.

Early adventurers journeying into the wilds of Texas certainly transported only the most essential tools with which to construct their shelters and probably brought few or no building components. In 1849, Edward Smith

wrote, "The emigrant should carry with him all requisite carpenter's tools (except axes) of the best quality. . . ." He also recommended that the settler carry a few sash frames, disassembled, but then noted that windows were not universally found in Texas homes. The tools of most early immigrants probably included axes for felling trees and cutting joints, an adz for hewing, and perhaps a froe for riving shingles. Other recommended tools included hammers, whipsaws, and augers, one and a quarter or one and a half inches in diameter. These implements were all that were required to build a log cabin in the wilderness; nails facilitated construction but were not essential.[24] Log houses displayed more refined craftsmanship than the primitive log cabins.

Following selection of a cabin site, which should be elevated, well drained, and near water, the orientation of the building ordinarily was established carefully with respect to the prevailing breezes. In 1848, Viktor Bracht's instruction to settlers specified: "It is best to have the entrance to the house face south or southeast, and put windows in the north side of the house, in this way cool south breezes can be passed through the house during the warm months."[25]

In Texas, although other variations appeared, two basic plans were followed: the single crib and the double crib, also known as a dogtrot cabin, in which the rooms were separated by a breezeway (fig. 33). While one-story cabins were common, a number of log dwellings appeared with an attic, to which ladders or stairs provided access (figs. 34, 35). The upper spaces of these story-and-a-half cabins were used for sleeping and for storage. Many single-room dwellings apparently became double cabins when second cribs and covered breezeways were added some years later. Then too, lean-to rooms of wood frame

[20] *Austin Telegraph*, December 11, 1839. See also Williamson, *Austin, Texas*, p. 11.

[21] William Bollaert, *William Bollaert's Texas*, ed. W. Eugene Hollon and Ruth Lapham Butler, p. 198.

[22] *Austin Telegraph*, December 11, 1839.

[23] Roemer, *Texas, with Particular Reference to German Immigration*, p. 93.

[24] Edward Smith, *Journey through Northeastern Texas*, p. 90; Viktor Bracht, *Texas in 1848*, trans. Charles Frank Schmidt, pp. 133–135.

[25] Bracht, *Texas in 1848*, pp. 133–134.

FIGURE 33. Sanders-McIntyre House, Stoneham vicinity (1826). *Historic American Buildings Survey, Library of Congress, Washington, D.C.*

Built while Texas was with Coahuila, a co-state of Mexico, this was a representative double-crib cabin of the era. It was built by K. P. Sanders, an immigrant from Florida, for Margaret McIntyre and her two sons, who had immigrated from Ireland. The charming gable-roof form with a plastered stone fireplace at one end was typical in regions where both stone and timber were available.

FIGURE 34. Tom Ireland Cabin, Webberville vicinity (ca. 1845). *Historic American Buildings Survey, Library of Congress, Washington, D.C.*

This indigenous cabin is similar to many cabins built in the timbered regions of the state. The form, made up of two cribs of cedar logs separated by a dogtrot, all under a common gable roof, was employed innumerable times. In this cabin the usual fireplace of mud and sticks had apparently been replaced by one of bricks. At one time the cabin probably had a porch.

Maintenance of chinking was a common problem. In this cabin, much of the material between the logs had deteriorated.

FIGURE 35. Louis Jones Cabin, Center vicinity (1830–1836). *Historic American Buildings Survey, Library of Congress, Washington, D.C.*

Built by Logan Smith, this was a story-and-a-half cabin with a lean-to porch, a form essential in the South for providing a shaded area for routine family activities during the hot months. Many cabins were eventually covered with boards and battens or weatherboards to present a more sophisticated appearance than logs provided and to reduce the problem of maintaining the chinking.

The breezeway on this cabin had been closed when the picture was taken. At one time the chimneys were apparently located entirely within the end rooms.

or stone were sometimes attached on the north side, and porches were usually attached to the south side.

In the hot regions of Texas, the life-style revolved around outdoor living during much of the year. In the breezeway, according to one observer, "the farmer sits, eats, washes, and frequently sleeps, fanned by the lovely southwest wind."[26] Porches, placed to be swept by the prevailing breezes, were also indispensible for protection from the sun and rain. According to Bracht, "Porches . . . form a part of nearly every cabin. . . . Strictly speaking, in Texas during ten months of the year, one lives either out-of-doors, or at least in rooms that permit a free circulation of air. . . . During nine months of the year the porch is the most pleasant place of abode both by day and by night." F. L. Olmsted also noted the active living function of the veranda when he described a Texas cabin with a gallery that extended across the whole front and served "for a pleasant sitting-room in summer, and for a toilet-room at all seasons."[27]

Log-cabin fabric, of course, reflected the environment of the site; yet log construction, although simple in concept, accommodated considerable varieties of material and shape of the individual components. In East Texas logs

[26] Smith, *Journey through Northeastern Texas,* p. 101. According to the author, a double log cabin, exclusive of shingles, could be built by three men for $75.00.

[27] Bracht, *Texas in 1848,* pp. 133–134; Olmsted, *A Journey through Texas,* p. 60.

were commonly pine; in the south-central regions they were cedar, pecan, or elm; in the Hill Country they were generally post oak or cedar. In form, the logs were sometimes round or unhewn, occasionally split in halves with one face hewn, sometimes hewn flat on two sides like planks, occasionally hewn to rectangular cross section, but often only roughly trimmed on two sides—all depending upon the available time, skill, and inclinations of the builders. Among the commonly used corner interlocks were the simple V joint and the complex dovetail, the former of which was easy to cut, the latter of which required considerable skill with an ax.[28] In the southern part of the state, the chinking between logs was frequently Spanish moss and mud. In other instances, the interstices were filled with wooden wedges, which were forced tighty between the logs and plastered with mud. In the Hill Country, Germans used rocks and mortar. Clay mixed with grass binder was commonly used for filling spaces between logs in other regions. In the early years the roof coverings in damp climates were of riven shakes or clapboards running parallel with the ridge. If shingles were employed, they were usually of pine, oak, cedar, or pecan, applied to laths laid across hewn or unhewn rafters.

Openings were not cut into the walls until the roof was completed, and therefore they could appear many years after the cabin had been occupied. After the openings were made, the logs were supported by uprights either pegged or nailed into ends of the sawn logs. Although sashes sometimes may have filled window openings, most early descriptions indicate that glass was rare in early cabins; ordinarily cloth or rawhide was placed over the openings to allow light to enter when the door was closed.[29]

The door opening was naturally the first cut made in the walls. In the wilderness, this opening was closed with a shutter made of thin puncheons, pegged or nailed together. However, as conditions on the frontier improved, eventually doors were made of lumber. The most primitive door hinges were leather or wood, but hand-wrought metal pivots and strap hinges were also used.

Like the main sections of Texas log cabins, the chimneys reflected the conditions of the wilderness in which the dwelling was built. In areas where stone was easily quarried, masonry fireplaces and chimneys were usual. However, in East Texas, where stone was not so readily available, they were made with wood and mud. Such fireplaces were fabricated by setting up four vertical poles, to which small wooden staves were attached on the inside. Over these were then placed long "cats," comprised of grass, Spanish moss, or pine needles, rolled together with clay from a slough. Finally the whole was often plastered with a layer of mud, producing a wall thickness of nearly six inches. Although not as durable as stone, these nonetheless served well.[30]

Although relatively few remain today, in the southerly rural, forested regions log dwellings predominated on the architectural scenes. One observer was fascinated to note that Ashbel Smith—one-time surgeon general of the Texas army—lived in a common two-room log cabin, built with partially hewn logs and simply furnished. In the town of Houston, Sam Houston, president of the republic, also had lived in a cabin with a dogtrot. In other forested regions, too, cabins were basic shelters. During the era of the republic, in order to receive clear title to free land in the Peters Colony in northcentral Texas, grantees were obligated to build a good cabin.[31]

On the frontier, log construction also played an important role in civilian defense works,

[28] See Terry G. Jordan, *Texas Log Buildings: A Folk Architecture,* for an excellent survey of log construction in Texas.

[29] Bracht, *Texas in 1848,* pp. 133–134; Olmsted, *A Journey through Texas,* p. 184; A[mos] [Andrew] Parker, *Trip to the West and Texas,* pp. 119, 126.

[30] For additional information on log cabins, see the files on cabin construction at the Institute of Texan Cultures, San Antonio, and Jordan, *Texas Log Buildings,* pp. 95–99.

[31] *A Visit to Texas in 1831,* p. 31; Seymour V. Connor, *The Peters Colony of Texas,* p. 39.

none of which remain today. In 1834 pioneers under the leadership of Silas M. and James W. Parker erected a series of log cabins and surrounded them with a stockade, which they named Fort Parker. For this they employed arrangements of fortifications that had been used earlier by settlers in Kentucky and Tennessee for such forts as Harrod (1774) and Nashborough (1789).[32] As was usual, the cabins of the eight or nine families comprising the settlement formed a part of the enclosure. Although the original works are gone, a replica constructed in 1936 in Limestone County provides an impression of the early private forts.

In the isolated timberless, semiarid frontier regions, adobe was the material most often used by settlers to fortify their habitations. On the north bank of the Rio Grande, in the vicinity of the town of Presidio, Ben Leaton built adobe fortifications upon the ruins of the Spanish mission El Apostol Santiago, a Spanish outpost established in 1684. Begun in 1848, and designed by its builder to defend against the incursions of both Mexicans and Indians, Fort Leaton (El Fortin) consisted of a forty-room house arranged around a courtyard and fortified with thick walls, a crenellated parapet, and towers with loopholes at the corners, all of which deteriorated after the work was abandoned, but which is now being restored by the Texas Department of Parks and Wildlife.[33]

South of Leaton in the 1850's, another settler, Milton Faver, built fortified baronial houses named Cibolo and Cienega, with perimeter walls three to four feet thick and turrets on diagonal corners. Utilizing techniques similar to those employed in the previous century by the Spaniards, the builders of Cibolo constructed a roof supported by cottonwood logs, over which was placed a layer of sotol covered with mud.[34] Cienega apparently was similar.

Indigenous techniques also were employed by the military of the Texas republic and the United States when they established frontier-defense posts. With little money in the treasury, the republic faced the formidable task of defending the frontiers against Indian depredations and Mexican encroachment. Lacking a strong military force during the 1836–1845 era, the republic relied upon the Texas Rangers. In order to civilize the area along a planned road from Austin north to the Red River, posts were to be constructed at intervals. However, except for the Texas Ranger posts—Fort Fisher (1837), Bird's Fort (1841), and Fort Colorado (1836), a stockaded work incorporating two-story blockhouses on diagonal corners—little military architecture of consequence was realized during this era.

After Texas was annexed to the United States, organized programs for frontier defense were vastly expanded. Along the Rio Grande a program of border defense was developed by the U.S. Army, according to the stipulations of the Treaty of Guadalupe Hidalgo, and along the inland frontiers—which were constantly moving—military posts for Indian control were essential. Near the Rio Grande, in the early years, since the government was unable to obtain clear title to some sites, the military architecture was temporary and expedient. To provide the promised protection of Mexicans from Indians residing in Texas, the United States established several posts, including Ringgold Barracks (1848), later renamed Fort Ringgold. Although this post, along with such others as Fort McIntosh (1849) near Laredo and Fort Bliss (1848) near El Paso, were called forts, usually there were no fortifications—only open complexes of buildings grouped in orderly patterns.[35] While buildings at Fort Bliss were adobe, those at Fort McIntosh were flimsy wooden shelters;

[32] Webb and Carroll, *Handbook of Texas*, 1:630.
[33] Leavitt Corning, Jr., *Baronial Forts of the Big Bend: Ben Leaton, Milton Faver and Their Private Forts in Presidio County*, p. 20.
[34] Ibid., p. 60.
[35] However, prior to the Civil War, earth fortifications were constructed at Fort McIntosh and at another post farther down the Rio Grande, Fort Brown (established 1848). These consisted of fronts with ramparts designed to withstand attacks supported by cannons.

however, at the latter these eventually were replaced by handsome masonry buildings.

In the inland areas, too, chains of posts were established to control the Indians. This approach resembled the national defense strategy for the midwestern United States, which consisted of a line of forts extending north from Fort Smith, Arkansas. For Texas, the military developed a chain of five posts, extending north-south through the center of the state in regions with climates ranging from hot and humid to semiarid. In the selection of sites for these military posts, officers considered ecological advantages.

On an unstable frontier, the military adopted indigenous building methods similar to those already employed by civilians. At Forth Worth (1849) officers dwelt in Anglo-American types of double log cabins with breezeways separating the log cribs; some of the enlisted men occupied shelters with picket walls, although several buildings were frame. Many of the buildings at Fort Graham (1849) were set up with walls of logs hewn to rectangular cross sections and roofs of either shingles or clapboards. Double log cabins also were built for officers at Fort Croghan (1849), and *jacal*-type shelters with shingle or thatched roofs were thrown up at Fort Inge (1849), the southernmost post in this chain.[36]

In 1851 due to scepticism about whether the posts were in the best locations for the defense of the frontier, the secretary of war ordered the revision of the entire Texas system.[37] To the west a group of new posts was established,

after which lands between the old and new chains were settled. Forts in this second chain included Fort Belknap, Fort McKavett, Fort Mason, Post on the Clear Fork of the Brazos (Fort Phantom Hill), and Fort Davis, all established during the 1850's. With buildings of stone and adobe, the architecture of these posts was more permanent than that of the earlier forts. At Fort McKavett and Fort Mason a number of buildings were constructed with native stone by German masons who lived in the vicinity.

When the Civil War began, most of these posts were abandoned, after which the buildings rapidly deteriorated. However, following the cessation of hostilities, many were reoccupied, and several new forts were established. These included Fort Concho (1867), a post largely comprised of masonry buildings, and Fort Richardson (1867), a post with palisade-walled structures as well as frame and stone buildings—although soldiers occupied temporary shelters of canvas while the more permanent quarters were under construction.[38]

At Fort Davis, under the direction of Lieutenant Colonel Wesley Merritt officers' quarters of cut limestone quarried locally replaced the original picket-walled shelters. However, orders were eventually issued forbidding the use of masonry. Subsequently, adobe was the material employed at this lonely post in the hot southwest, with stone being used occasionally where strength was important, such as for foundations and for the corners of buildings. Much of the adobe work of Davis is gone, although the National Park Service has done some restoration.[39]

While the main objective of these forts was the protection of settlers, expeditions, and travelers, the military also contributed to the welfare and culture of the frontier settlements. Concerned about the influence of location and

[36] Details on these early forts may be found in U.S. Congress, House, *Report of the Secretary of War*, 32nd Cong., 1st sess., 1851, House Exec. Doc. No. 2; various field reports edited by M. L. Crimmins in the *Southwestern Historical Quarterly* 42 (1938–1939):122–148, 215–257, 351–387, and 53 (1949): 76; and Olmsted, *A Journey through Texas*, pp. 285–286.

[37] See "General Order No. 1" in House, *Report of the Secretary of War*, 32d Cong., 1st sess., 1851, House Exec. Doc. No. 2. In the selection of sites for posts it was ordered that consideration be given to the protection of the inhabitants of Texas, the defense of the Mexican territory, and the economy and facility of support troops with respect to forage, fuel, and adaptation of the surrounding country to cultivation.

[38] War Department, *Circular No. 4: A Report*, pp. 185–186, 198.

[39] Forts in the new chain are described in "Special Order No. 3" in U.S. Congress, Senate, *Report of the Secretary of War*, 36th Cong., 1st sess., 1859, Senate Exec. Doc. No. 2, p. 357; M. L.

architecture on health, post surgeons maintained records of observations on the effects of environment on the soldiers in barracks and hospitals. According to a published report, which included statistics on sickness and mortality, the records were intended for use not only by the military but also by civilian physicians.[40]

The military also brought other architectural and cultural refinements to the frontier. At Fort Davis there was a school; at such other posts as Fort Richardson, there were reading rooms. In some instances post chapels provided settings for religious services and weddings. Then too, these posts provided locations for settlers to establish commercial enterprises, bringing goods to the frontier for both civilians and troops. Finally, military bands provided some cultural entertainment.

Thus, defense needs were joined with the public and residential needs of European and American immigrants in the development of the early architecture of Texas. Each group provided for its needs for shelter in a manner that reflected the land and the group's cultural origins. Although significant examples of buildings from this era remain, many of the best are gone.

Significant progress, then, was made in the civilizing of the Texas frontier by the various ethnic groups. Still further advances were to occur with the development of other aspects of Anglo-American culture.

Crimmins, ed., "Colonel J. K. F. Mansfield's Report of the Inspection of the Department of Texas in 1856," *Southwestern Historical Quarterly* 62 (1938):312, 360–362; idem, "Fort McKavett, Texas," *Southwestern Historical Quarterly* 38 (1934):28–32; U.S. War Department, Surgeon General's Office, *Circular No. 4: A Report on Barracks and Hospitals with Descriptions of Military Posts*, pp. 228–229; Robert M. Utley, *Fort Davis National Historic Site, Texas*, pp. 7–8, 20.

[40] Ibid.

3

Reflections of Anglo-American Cultural Advancement

WHILE the military was helping to civilize the frontier, intellectual and cultural advancement began to appear in other sections of the republic and state. As is well known, it was the intellectual inclinations of some immigrants that led to the establishment of the utopian communities of La Réunion and the Bettina Colony (1847), although neither settlement possessed the economic substance to endure.[1] Anglo-Americans from the South and East brought with them, too, cultural awareness and patterns for institutions, as well as a nostalgic receptiveness to trends in art and architecture from the established regions of America. The development of appreciation for decoration, illustration, and music seemed to go hand in hand with an admiration for architectural beauty. As the mid-nineteenth century approached, those who could afford them and who enjoyed the other fine arts generally added to their buildings the refinements of formal planning and sophisticated decoration.

Eastern trends in the fine arts were communicated to other Texans by those who had recently immigrated. In addition, printed advertisements conveyed outside cultural influences. At mid-century, Eastern art unions, advertising in local newspapers, provided Texans with opportunities to obtain not only art work but also subscriptions to periodicals publishing articles on taste. In 1849 the American Metropolitan Union, through an advertisement in the *Northern Standard*, offered literature "composed of contributions from the most Eminent Writers of the Country; together with SPLENDID ENGRAVINGS. . . ."[2]

Later, the American Artists' Union announced the purpose of "cultivating taste for the fine arts throughout the country . . . with a view of enabling every family to become possessed of a gallery of Engravings, BY THE FIRST ARTISTS OF THE AGE. . . ." An engraving could be purchased for one dollar. In 1856 the Cosmopolitan Art Association offered for three dollars a lottery ticket for either "the annual distribution of works of art" and a "splendid" engraving titled *Saturday Night* or a subscription to one of a group of magazines, including *Harper's Magazine*, *Godey's Lady's Book*, and *United States Magazine*, all of which were tastemakers of the period.[3] Although it is impossible to ascertain the amount of influence these publications had on architectural taste in Texas, the announcement of lottery prizes won by persons in Texas indicates that there were a significant number of subscribers.

---

[1] The Bettina Colony was a German group made up of professional men, musicians, and artists.

[2] *Northern Standard* (Clarksville), May 5, 1849.

[3] *Standard* (Clarksville), December 9, 1854; *Texas Republican* (Marshall), December 27, 1856.

People with affluence and refinement, who are likely to have been familiar with the magazines mentioned, built formally to express cultural and economic advancement, rather than with the spontaneity appropriate to the land and primitive frontier conditions. Although straightforward log and adobe structures are admired today, in their time they were not much appreciated for their rustic beauty. While an occasional traveler may have commented on neatness of construction, beauty was perceived only when decoration and refined finishes were incorporated into buildings. Many log cabins were eventually covered with weatherboards or stucco, giving a more sophisticated appearance—partially because they produced more maintenance-free and tight walls, but also because of the lack of admiration for rustic types of construction. Early Texans desired more architectural refinement than these indigenous works provided. The development of sawmills powered by steam, water, and oxen, the establishment of brick kilns, and the opening of stone quarries all provided the potential to build formally.

As the affluence of the republic and state developed, nostalgia and the demand for culture, as well as the desire to publicize the station of the owners, created a need for buildings with architectural distinction. Moreover, in a mood consistent with concepts expressed by eastern writers, Texans believed that sophisticated architecture would have a positive influence on the attitudes of people. One writer, commenting on the impact of art on both taste and morals, contended that when objects of taste are placed "before the public . . . the sure consequence will be a refinement of taste, an elevation of mental character. . . ."[4]

During the 1840's and 1850's, eager to avoid provincialism in building and to express cultural finesse, Anglo-American immigrants made use of the Greek Revival style, which had been popular in the states they had come from.

The formality and repose inherent in this mode provided for farms and fledgling communities not only the order and beauty so much admired but also an appropriate setting for the formal Southern life-style of east and southeast Texas. Moreover, the uncomplicated beauty and the rectilinear quality of the Greek proved appropriate for the available material resources and skills.

Like most nineteenth-century styles, the Greek Revival had been imported from England to the East Coast of the United States. Interest in the style was stimulated originally by the publication of measured drawings of ancient Greek architecture by Stuart and Revett in the *Antiquities of Athens*, a book intended to improve taste by providing knowledge of work that had been previously unknown.[5]

Individuals who pondered about an appropriate character for American architecture rationalized that the Greek inspiration was appropriate from other points of view. Some believed the relative simplicity and economy of style to be satisfactory for the United States, still a young developing country. Some also believed that only degenerate taste preferred the ostentatious decoration required by picturesque styles; hence the simplicity of the Greek recommended it for those with refined taste. Then too, there seemed to be hopes that the uniformity of the style might contribute to both the visual and the patriotic unity of a country where there was much individuality and diversity of attitudes. Finally, still others seem to have believed that the style symbolized democracy.

As a result of these ideas, the popularity of the Greek spread across the country. In the East the style became popular around 1820 and remained fashionable for more than two decades; in Texas, the style was prominent during the 1840's and 1850's.

[4] "Architecture in the United States," *American Journal of Science and Arts* 17 (1829):109.

[5] James Stuart and Nicholas Revett, *Antiquities of Athens, Measured and Delineated*. The four-volume new edition was published in 1825–1830. The original edition had been published in 1762–1816.

FIGURE 36. Jasper Collins House, Carthage (1850). *Historic American Buildings Survey, Library of Congress, Washington, D.C.*

A wood-framed, clapboard dwelling, this building exhibited fine Greek Revival details. Identical tetrastyle porticoes were placed on three sides; on the fourth—the least important—a distyle portico was used. This multiplication of porticoes was unusual in Texas. The entablature of the one-story house exhibited characteristic moldings and proportions. All the columns were rectangular, with a slight entasis near the capitals.

This house, built by Jasper Collins, was later sold to the Baptist church for use as a parsonage, but is now gone.

The Greek Revival was a style based upon precedent and intellectual order. Basically, beauty was derived from details inspired by ancient Classical Greek architecture and from symmetry, proportion, and harmony of parts. On the exterior, the natural beauty of materials only occasionally played a role in the success of the style in Texas. Builders could simplify details and fashion them from lumber and moldings, rather than copy the stone models of antiquity, and still retain the essential character of the mode.

The facades of Greek Revival houses usually had five bays (each door and window opening formed a bay), but on large houses or inns there were seven bays, and occasionally on a small dwelling a three-bay front appeared. Following the precedent in other southern states, the window sashes were often double hung, but, to provide better ventilation in the hot, humid climate of South and East Texas, they were frequently triple hung, thereby providing more open wall area for ventilation. When triple hung, the window openings extended down to the level of the floor. To provide security and privacy, shutters, usually painted deep green, were provided.

On wooden Greek Revival buildings with clapboard-covered walls, the corners and entablatures were also noteworthy details. The exterior corners were finished with a vertical feature, often simply a narrow board terminating at the architrave with an embryonic capital or occasionally with a fully developed pilaster fashioned from boards and moldings. On frame as well as masonry buildings, the parts of the entablatures were formed with boards and standard moldings (fig. 36).

The Greek Revival cottages, like the larger dwellings, generally conformed to one of three

FIGURE 37. Nathaniel Raymond House, Austin (1857). *Historic American Buildings Survey, Library of Congress, Washington, D.C.*

    With walls of stuccoed brick on limestone foundations, this house was built on a typical Greek Revival plan with a central hallway. This central space was flanked on either side by two symmetrical rooms. A graceful stair at one time enhanced the hallway. In 1893 the building was remodeled, and later it was used by the University of Texas for storing playground equipment and for housing white rats, which were used by the biology department. In the 1950's it was razed.

basic plans: a central hall with a single room on either side, a full-length central hall with two rooms on either side (fig. 37)—the typical plan of earlier Georgian houses in the East—and a six-room type wherein a central hall extended through half the width of the house and opened into a back room through a wide doorway ordinarily closed by sliding doors.[6] Generally in the central-hall, four-room type plan, as in many Georgian houses, the fireplaces were built back to back and centered along the walls between the rooms, but in the central-hall, two-room plan fireplaces were centered on the exterior end walls (fig. 38). However, additions frequently were made to the back side of any of these plans, thus resulting in a departure from its basic simplicity.

    Porticos (called galleries in the nineteenth

century) formally announced the entrances to the Greek Revival houses. On two-story Greek Revival dwellings—which conformed to the same plans as the one-story cottages—several types of porticos appeared. Although a one-story porch occasionally was employed, most porticos extended the full height of the house and were surmounted by either a simple entablature or an entablature with a pediment (figs. 39, 40). The plan of the second floor was usually identical to that of the first, with a central hall and exterior doors at each end similar to the entrances on the ground level. The balcony necessitated by the second-story doors was designed either as an integral element of a two-story portico or as a form cantilevered from the wall and flanked by two-story columns. On the Brown-Denison-Moore House, Galveston (ca. 1858), the portico was storied with a hipped roof covering the balcony. Another fine example of the storied portico appeared on the W. W. Brown-

[6] There were, however, exceptions to these three patterns. In Washington County, the Red House, a mid-nineteenth-century dwelling, had plans resembling an English Colonial house type with central back-to-back fireplaces.

FIGURE 38. George Pessony House, Palestine (1854). *Historic American Buildings Survey, Library of Congress, Washington, D.C.*

Into this wooden-framed building were incorporated characteristic Greek Revival details. As was typical, fireplaces were located at the gable ends. A wide classical frieze and a distyle portico with triangular pediment created monumental character. Wide corner and portico pilasters, noteworthy features that were somewhat unusual in Texas, repeated the proportions of the columns.

FIGURE 39. Douglas House, Bullard (1854). *Historic American Buildings Survey, Library of Congress, Washington, D.C.*

Dignity and repose characterized this fine two-story Greek Revival building. Surmounted by a pediment, the porch was a two-story arrangement with square columns. A cornice decorated with modillions added distinction to the design. The details of the doorways and windows were typical.

FIGURE 40. Peter Walton House, Plantersville vicinity (1854). *Historic American Buildings Survey, Library of Congress, Washington, D.C.*

Built during a period of prosperity created by cotton trade, this was another fine example of the Greek Revival style. The typical five-bay front was enhanced by the fine pedimented entrance portico. The delicate railing juxtaposed against heavy columns of colossal order created interesting contrast. The shafts of these columns apparently were built up from straight boards. Also noteworthy were the superimposed pilasters that were used in place of corner boards.

ing House, Chappell Hill (1856), which is collapsing (fig. 41). On the Collins-Camp House near Navasota (1860's), the porch was supported by square, two-story columns, while the balcony was independently supported by one-story columns (fig. 42).

Within Texas several regional variations of the Greek Revival forms appeared, among which was the raised cottage—a dwelling with the main floor elevated well above the ground on brick piers or walls. Utilized in the Mississippi Valley, evidently to protect floors from damp ground and floods, this type of dwelling appeared in East as well as South Texas— even where groundwater was not a problem.

Among the fine examples of the raised cottage, now gone, were the William Madison Sledge House, near Chappell Hill (fig. 43), and the Alexander House near Marshall (fig. 44).

Immigrants also brought into the Lone Star State knowledge of other regional residential work with antecedents in the Mississippi Valley, where French colonial work combined architectural forms that had evolved in France with those from the hot West Indies (fig. 45).[7] Hipped roofs with the steep pitches of France were extended to create the dominant shelter-

[7] Charles E. Peterson, "The Houses of French St. Louis," in *The French in the Mississippi Valley*, ed. John Francis McDermott, p. 20.

FIGURE 41. William Westcott Browning House, Chappell Hill (1856). *Historic American Buildings Survey, Library of Congress, Washington, D.C.*

Located on a once-prosperous plantation, this was one of the finest Greek Revival houses in its region. The hipped roof, terminated at a captain's walk, and a two-story portico located on the north side both contributed to the formal monumental atmosphere of the dwelling. The house was structured with a heavy cedar frame secured with mortise and tenon joints.

The openings were finely detailed. At the formal entrance wide, paneled doors were flanked by side-lights; above this entrance were three transoms. This main entrance was framed by a lintel with crossets and a flared casing. Other doors and large six-over-six-light windows provided light and ventilation through the rooms and hall.

FIGURE 42. Collins-Camp House, Navasota vicinity (1860's). *Historic American Buildings Survey, Library of Congress, Washington, D.C.*

Although the plan, five-bay front, and gabled roof were typical of many Greek Revival houses throughout the state, the configuration of the porch and balcony were not common. The porch was supported by square columns with moldings and trim representing capitals and neckings, while the balcony was independently supported by similar columns on a smaller scale. These entrance features, along with the double doors flanked by rectangular sidelights and surmounted by a rectangular transom comprised the most significant features of the building; elsewhere the details were much attenuated.

FIGURE 43. William Madison Sledge House, Chappell Hill vicinity (1850's). *Historic American Buildings Survey, Library of Congress, Washington, D.C.*

Also known as the John Smith House, this was a good example of the raised cottage form, which produced a *piano nobile*. The entrance was approached up a wide flight of steps terminating at wide porches. On this dwelling a hexastyle porch roof supported by square columns extended across the back while a formal tetrastyle portico enhanced the front. Both porches provided access to a twelve-foot-wide central hall. Although at the time it was recorded by the Historic American Buildings Survey this dwelling had a brick-walled ground story, the spaces under the first floor were usually entirely open, with only a lattice filling the perimeter spaces between pedestal supports. Unfortunately the stately character of this house was obliterated when the second floor was removed—according to rumor, because the family who had purchased it feared the wind in the second story.

FIGURE 44. Alexander House, Marshall vicinity (ca. 1860). *Historic American Buildings Survey, Library of Congress, Washington, D.C.*

This was a fine Greek Revival raised cottage with exterior walls finished with both clapboards and boards and battens. A basement entered from the side was situated under part of the structure. The veranda extended from three sides, thus providing cooling shade for the walls. Unfortunately this handsome home, like so many built during the antebellum era, has been lost.

FIGURE 45. Des Mazieres Store and Residence, San Antonio (1853–1854). *Historic American Buildings Survey, Library of Congress, Washington, D.C.*

Built by Francis Louis Des Mazieres, this was a fine example of design that reflected the experience of the builder and the conditions of the environment. The wide porch, originally supported by iron braces, and the broad, overhanging roof were features that recalled the French colonial work of Louisiana. The walls of lime-and-gravel concrete, finished with lime-whitewashed stucco, provided satisfactory insulation in the hot climate.

As was common on most buildings of the time, the openings were fitted with wooden shutters to provide security and ventilation. However, by the time this photograph was taken, the shutters obviously had been removed. Simple refinements, including columns with rudimentary capitals, modestly enhanced the work.

ing forms of the West Indies over continuous balconies. The porches thus formed were eight or nine feet wide and supported by thin columns. They effectively protected the walls from the sun's hot rays, keeping the interiors cooler, as well as providing shady areas for sitting, eating, and sleeping during the hot months. In addition, the overhangs protected plastered walls from erosion caused by rainfall. The entire residence story was raised well above the damp ground.

Other regional features of antebellum houses appeared in the interiors. In East Texas generally either the walls of the frame houses were sheathed with rough-sawn boards over which wallpaper was stretched or they were finished with lath and plaster, covered with wallpaper. In south-central Texas the interiors were often finished with center-matched planed boards, painted, stenciled, and decorated with representational configurations, German fashion.

In the mid-nineteenth century, throughout the civilized regions of the state, techniques of painting pine to simulate other materials were finely developed. In south-central Texas fine examples of interior paneling and exterior doors appeared, all grained to represent walnut or cherry wood—pine was workable, and the graining provided beauty and weatherproofing. In other instances fireplace trim, often built up with boards and moldings to form Classical design features, was marbleized with paint to represent stone.

While these attractive Greek Revival houses were ordinarily built of either wood or masonry, near the Gulf coast concrete made from lime or cement, with seashells as aggregate, was used. The technique of building with this material, which had been used as early as the seventeenth century along the South Atlantic coast, was published in Texas newspapers, hence was commonly known along the Gulf coast. In early Houston numerous dwellings

FIGURE 46. Conrad Meuly House and Store, Corpus Christi (1852–1854). *Historic American Buildings Survey, Library of Congress, Washington, D.C.*

This structure was built by Conrad Meuly, a Swiss immigrant-merchant, utilizing the local material of oyster-shell concrete. Plain walls provided the background for elaborate decoration. Delicate ironwork—probably from New Orleans—enhanced the porch, and the acanthus motif decorated the architrave.

The front part of the ground floor was used for a store while the remainder of the spaces served residential functions.

appeared with walls of "shellcrete." Elsewhere near the coast, oyster shells were included as an aggregate in the material, as in the Conrad Meuly House, Corpus Christi (1852–1854) (fig. 46).

Lime concrete also was used frequently in Seguin. When visiting the community in 1854, Frederick Law Olmsted observed this technique of wall construction: "A number of buildings in Seguin are made of concrete—thick walls of gravel and lime, raised a foot at a time, between boards, which hold the mass into place until it is solidified. As the materials are dug from the cellar, it is a very cheap mode of construction . . . and is said to be as durable . . . as stone or brick." By mid-century lime with gravel was also known in Houston.[8] In

some cases cement may have been substituted for lime, since in 1848 it had been reported that hydraulic cement was being manufactured on the banks of the Guadalupe River, near Seguin.[9]

Regardless of structural technique, these handsome frame and masonry antebellum houses were ordinarily built by masterbuilders without drawings but according to written descriptions forming an official agreement between the owner and builder. Specifications were usually brief on workmanship but sometimes quite detailed in describing plans, wall construction, and building materials.[10]

Usually the agreement did not specify archi-

[8] Frederick Law Olmsted, *A Journey through Texas*, p. 231; *Telegraph and Texas Register* (Houston), January 10, 1851. The mixture was made of twelve parts gravel and one part lime; forms were 1½×17″ pine boards.

[9] *Northern Standard* (Clarksville), December 23, 1848.

[10] Examples of such contractual specifications may be found in Washington County, Deed Records, Office of the County Clerk, Vol. N, p. 551 (a copy of these specifications for this house was provided by Mrs. Charles Bybee, Houston); and San Augustine County, Deed Records, Office of the County Clerk, Vol. E.

FIGURE 47. James H. Raymond House, Austin (1850's). *Austin–Travis County Collection, Austin Public Library*.

Similar to Woodlawn, another house by Abner Cook, which is still standing in Austin, the Raymond House was distinguished by a two-story colonnade in the Ionic order and by a second-story balcony. The house was located on the corner of a street intersection, and the main portico fronted on one of the streets, while a smaller secondary portico was provided on the east side. As was typical of Greek Revival structures, the house had a central-hall-type plan.

tectural style or configurations of decorative features. These evidently were provided by the masterbuilder, according to his own inclinations, probably with the approval of the owner, and perhaps with published sources serving as guides. Available pattern books that could have been used as references included Asher Benjamin, *The Practice of Architecture* (1836), and Minard Lefever, *The Beauties of Modern Architecture* (1835), both of which published illustrations of Greek details. Some pattern books illustrated procedures for laying out some features.

In addition to the design, the masterbuilders provided the materials for construction. They often sawed and planed their own lumber, sometimes made their bricks and quarried their stone, manufactured their doors and sashes, then provided all the necessary labor for assembly, thus providing complete services. However, finished building components also were available from catalogs of manufacturers located in the eastern states.

Representative of the experience the masterbuilders brought to Texas were the backgrounds of Charles G. Bryant (1803–1850)

and Abner Cook (1814–1884), who were among the most talented of the antebellum builders. Although little is known about his education, Bryant, who may have been the first professional architect in the state of Maine before immigrating, was trained as a housewright and designed and built some fine Greek Revival houses in Bangor. In 1839 he moved to Texas, where he designed several buildings, including the Galveston County Prison and Court Room (1847–1848), which, ironically, is in Gothic Revival style.[11]

Abner Cook also immigrated from the East Coast region and evidently learned his occupation through first-hand experience. Following departure from his home in North Carolina at the age of twenty-one, he began his career in Macon, Georgia, then worked for a brief period in Nashville, Tennessee, before moving to Texas in 1839 at the age of twenty-five. Although he stayed in Huntsville for a brief period, he lived in Austin most of his career and

[11]See James H. Mundy and Earle G. Shettleworth, Jr., *The Flight of the Grand Eagle: Charles G. Bryant, Maine Architect and Adventurer*.

erected a good number of public buildings as well as many fine houses. Among the structures built by Cook, now gone, was the James H. Raymond House, an 1850's Greek Revival mansion (fig. 47).[12]

Other large houses similar to those constructed by Abner Cook appeared in other thriving communities. In the commercial centers of antebellum Texas, wealthy businessmen and bankers built noble Greek houses that they felt appropriately expressed their attainment in taste and wealth. San Antonio, for example, was the location of the James Vance House, an excellent work that is now gone (fig. 48). Among the most remarkable Greek Revival houses were those with galleries extending down the sides as well as across the front. Built in 1850, the B. L. Holcombe House, a large two-story work, was distinguished by broad front and side galleries (fig. 49).

One of the largest and most unusual Greek Revival buildings to appear in Texas was the Tacitus Clay House (ca. 1836) in Washington County. The dwelling was nearly eighty feet square, with a central hall on both the first and second floors; the entire third floor was used as a ballroom. As occasionally happened in hilly country, the house was built on the edge of an incline, providing a basement that could be entered from ground level at the back. On the exterior a three-story portico with porches extending from each floor created an imposing appearance. Unfortunately, the house was destroyed in 1915, and apparently no good photos clearly illustrating its original quality exist.

The Clay House was razed after a storm caused damage that was considered at the time to be irreparable. Countless other handsome Greek Revival houses have also been lost to hurricanes and tornadoes; many others have burned. During the antebellum era builders viewed buildings as permanent creations to be retained by successive generations; they were expendable only to acts of God. At mid-century the general view on the importance of preserving buildings was expressed by the English critic, John Ruskin, when he wrote: "*We have no right to touch them. They are not ours. They belong partly to those who built them, and partly to all the generations of mankind who are to follow us.*"[13] However, as is well known, attitudes change, and many of these fine Greek Revival buildings have been lost to the planned actions of man.

Shortly after mid-century the Greek Revival began losing its popularity in the Texas communities with the closest ties to eastern tastemakers. In Galveston, the Italianate style, which had become fashionable in eastern cities during the 1840's, appeared in several fine houses. The James Moreau Brown House (Ashton Villa), which was built in 1858–1859 and still stands, now as a museum house, is a remarkable expression of this mode. Gone, however, is the W. L. Moody House (1859–1860), also in Galveston, a fine building distinguished by its consoles and window openings spanned with segmental arches—characteristic features of the Italianate (fig. 50).

Meanwhile, though, the Greek Revival had also appeared in some of the commercial buildings of Texas. Perhaps stemming from a tradition of the early years, when rural cabins and houses served as inns, many Greek hotels and stagecoach inns were built to resemble large houses, recalling the eighteenth-century hostelries in other parts of America. Included among these Classical public buildings was the Capitol Hotel, which served as the state legislative hall from 1837 until 1839, when the seat of state government was transferred to Austin (fig. 51). Taverns with similar forms and Classical detailing included the Old Stagecoach Inn at Chappell Hill (1852), a building that had lost most of its decorative features by the 1970's but that did retain a noteworthy Greek-fret frieze.

Other antebellum hotels were masonry-

[12] George L. Landolt, *Search for the Summit: Austin College through Twelve Decades, 1849–1970*, p. 86.

[13] John Ruskin, *The Seven Lamps of Architecture*, p. 201.

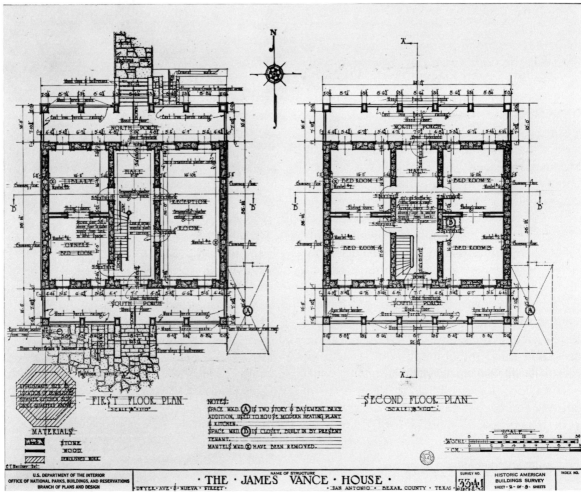

FIGURE 48. James Vance House, San Antonio (1859). John Fries, architect. *Photo, Daughters of the Republic of Texas Library, San Antonio; plan, Historic American Buildings Survey, Library of Congress, Washington, D.C.*

Attributed to architect John Fries, the Vance House was distinguished by fine details. The entablature was decorated with a dentil course, and plain limestone walls were relieved by quoins. The front porch was distinguished by an ornamental iron railing, while the back porch displayed wood railings. Before the building was razed to provide a site for a branch bank building, it had served several nonresidential purposes, including a cafe and an art school. Already gone at the time this photograph was taken were the fences and landscaping.

FIGURE 49. B. L. Holcombe House (Wyalucing), Marshall (1850). *Historic American Buildings Survey, Library of Congress, Washington, D.C.*

Built by Beverly Lafayette Holcombe, this house, with its six-bay front, was a large dwelling with monumental character. The colossal colonnade contributed to the visual impact of the design.

Also known as *Wyalucing,* an Indian term meaning "home of the friendless," the house served as a residence for a relatively short time. From 1880 until 1961 it was used as a classroom and music building for Bishop College, a Negro institution. Finally in 1962 the building was razed.

FIGURE 50. W. L. Moody House, Galveston (1859–1860). *Historic American Buildings Survey, Library of Congress, Washington, D.C.*

Originally built for Thomas M. League, this was a fine, three-story dwelling with balconies on the back. The plan was in the form of an L. On the front was a two-story portico.

The building served several owners. Following the Civil War it was converted into a boarding house; then it became the home of W. L. Moody. During the twentieth century it was used as a Catholic high school.

FIGURE 51. Capitol Hotel, Houston (1837). Thomas William Ward, builder. *Harris County Heritage Society, Houston.*

This frame building served as the capitol of the Republic of Texas from 1837 until 1839. After the seat of government was moved to Austin, the structure was remodeled into a hotel.

This seven-bay structure was representative of many antebellum Texas hostelries. As was common, these early hotels were residential in style and scale. The broad porches and the dormers, which were provided to ameliorate the heat, reflect the response to his environment by the builder, who was an Irish immigrant hired in New Orleans. In 1882 this frame building was razed to make room for a Renaissance Revival hotel.

walled buildings fitting into the business sections of towns. Among the early durably built structures with Classical details was the Menger Hotel in San Antonio, which was one of the first hostelries in the state with commercial character.

In Texas, as in other states of America, the Greek Revival style also appeared in the buildings for educational institutions. During the years of the republic and the antebellum state, numerous academies, colleges, and universities were established, providing Texans with opportunities to receive education at home rather than traveling to other states, as had been necessary in previous years.

While the Greek mode was considered by most educated individuals to be a satisfactory form for any building associated with noble cultural purpose, for colleges and universities

it was considered further to have an impact on students' minds. On a national level this point of view was expressed by Joseph R. Chandler at the dedication of Girard College (1833–1847), a monumental Greek-styled building in Philadelphia: "The adoption of the grandeur and beauty of an ancient architecture . . . must be considered with regard to their influences on the mind and character of the pupils. . . ."[14] Builders may have had similar hopes for the architecture of other college buildings in the United States, on a scale smaller than Girard.

As in the older sections of the United States, the first institutions of learning were estab-

[14] Joseph R. Chandler, quoted in Albert Bush-Brown, "College Architecture: An Expression of Educational Philosophy," *Architectural Record* 122 (1957):154.

lished by benevolent and religious groups. In 1837 the Independence Female Academy—the first authorized by the Republic of Texas—was opened, and thereafter schools appeared in all areas of settled Texas. Throughout the republic and state, the Masonic lodges sponsored many academies; for example, by 1856 the Milam Masonic Lodge, with individual assistance, erected a building for the education of girls.[15] At the same time other agencies operated, for profit, academies for both males and females. After graduating from these, many students entered colleges, which, during the antebellum period, were privately financed.

During the antebellum period, several charters for the establishment of colleges and universities were issued to churches. In 1837, the Congress of the Republic authorized the University of San Augustine, although its doors were not opened to students until 1842. In 1840 a charter was issued for Rutersville College, a Methodist school originally located in Fayette County but moved first to Chappell Hill and then to Georgetown, where it became Southwestern University. The Baptist church opened Baylor College in 1846 in Independence, and the Presbyterian church opened Austin College in 1849 in Huntsville. Saint Mary's Institute, San Antonio, began work on its first building in 1853.[16]

Patterned after those of institutions in the East, the curricula of the colleges at the lower levels included basic courses in reading, writing, and arithmetic, but the upper levels were filled with studies of the classics, including "History of Rome, History of Greece . . . Virgil, Cicero's orations, Livy, Horace . . . Herodotus and Thucydides. . . ." Interestingly, architectural drawing was also listed among the courses at the University of San Augustine.[17]

Buildings providing the setting for these studies of the classics were designed, appropriately, it was felt, in the Greek Revival style. In Huntsville, specifications drawn up for Andrew Female College, a Methodist institution chartered in 1853, called for Classical details similar to the original main building at Austin College (1851–1852), which still stands on the campus of Sam Houston State University. According to the requirements, the simple rectangular building was to have a portico, "supported by four fluted wooden columns . . . of size of those at Austin College with Ionic carved capitals. . . ." (However, the capitals on the Austin College building were Tuscan.) The doors also were characteristically Greek with "two doors from outside into passage—*Double* with upper and side transoms, made and finished as the front door in Austin College. . . ." This building served Andrew College until near the end of the century, when it closed; today nothing is known of the temple.[18]

Other colleges and universities also initiated academic programs in Greek Revival edifices. Baylor Female College at Independence once was housed in a fine Greek Revival building (fig. 52), and Waco University, with which Baylor later merged, in the 1860's erected a pair of buildings in restrained Greek style (fig. 53). Soule University, chartered 1856, in 1858 built a three-story masonry edifice with a rusticated base and walls articulated by pilasters; it was razed in 1911.[19]

Although these college buildings—by virtue of style and location—were certainly prominent in their communities, the most dominant structures in most antebellum towns were the temples of justice and the churches. Located on the blocks set aside for public use, the

[15] *Standard* (Clarksville), May 31, 1856.
[16] *Telegraph and Texas Register* (Houston), July 29, 1837; William Ransom Hogan, *The Texas Republic: A Social and Economic History*, pp. 149–150; Walter P. Webb and H. B. Carroll, eds., *The Handbook of Texas*, 1:125 and 2:521, 647; Joseph William Schmitz, *Mission Concepción*, p. 29.
[17] *Red Lander* (San Augustine), March 12, 1846.

[18] David Hoffman, "A Building Specification for Andrew Female College," *Newsletter of the Society of Architectural Historians, Texas Chapter* 6 (December, 1977):11. For an illustration of the Austin College building, see Willard B. Robinson, "Temples of Knowledge," *Southwestern Historical Quarterly* 77 (1974):450.
[19] Webb and Carroll, *Handbook of Texas*, 1:125, 2:638.

FIGURE 52. Main Building, Women's Campus, Baylor University, Independence (ca. 1857). *Texas Collection, Baylor University, Waco.*

Baylor University was chartered by the Republic of Texas early in 1845 and was opened the following year at Independence. The institution originally had both male and female departments, but disagreements among trustees, the administrators, and faculty led to the creation of Baylor Female College with this monumental building with Classical form and details on its campus. Thereafter, Baylor University remained a men's institution until 1886.

Baylor Female College remained in Independence from 1865 until 1886, when it was moved to Belton where it finally became known as Mary Hardin–Baylor College. Today only the columns of this building still stand; they have been restored as monuments to the campus at Independence.

FIGURE 53. Classroom Buildings, Waco University (1860's). *Texas Collection, Baylor University, Waco.*

In 1861 Waco University was opened under the direction of the Waco Baptist Association. During the decade these beautifully proportioned buildings were erected. Simple Greek Revival details—including five-bay fronts, Classical cornices, and entrances with double doors, rectangular sidelights, and transoms—contributed to stately appearances.

In 1886 Baylor was moved from Independence to Waco and combined with Waco University. Afterward these buildings were remodeled and additions were made to convert them into dormitories—Maggie Houston and Ertha Lee Cowden halls—which were used by Baylor after the schools merged.

courthouses were the focal points of the counties and county seats. Activities within and without the courthouse walls provided the basis for social intercourse. Although the nineteenth-century subjective importance of these buildings and their value to society has been somewhat obscured by time, one writer on American architecture provided some perspective when he wrote: "Place in a village a handsome public monument, or pillar, or church, and . . . villagers will be bound more to one another, and their village, than those of another."[20] Limited means prohibited the construction of large, pretentious buildings that would express this attitude. Nonetheless, in the Republic of Texas there was considerable pride in public buildings, and this was expressed through formal design.

When the republic was formed, the existing twenty-three Mexican municipalities became counties, and the *casas consistatoriales*

("houses of government") became courthouses.[21] While organization and government were at first patterned after the Mexican municipalities, even the earliest courthouses were patterned after Anglo-American paradigms. Although a one- or two-room cabin, about sixteen feet square, with either picket or horizontal log walls, was commonly the first shelter for the activities of any county, within several years work generally was underway on a frame or masonry structure with more sophistication than these indigenous works possessed. Similar to Virginia courthouses, the typical Texas county seat during the republic and early state was a building with a courtroom on the ground floor and offices on the second floor. Representative of these edifices—none of which remain—was the Harris County Courthouse. Late in 1837 the county invited bids on a courthouse

[20] "Architecture in the United States," p. 108.

[21] Charles W. Fisher, Jr., "A New Look at Liberty's Seven Courthouses, 1831–1972."

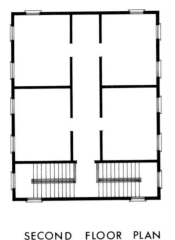

SECOND FLOOR PLAN

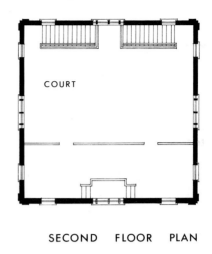

SECOND FLOOR PLAN

0   4   16 FEET

0   4   16 FEET

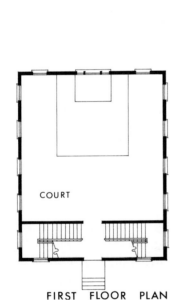

COURT

FIRST FLOOR PLAN

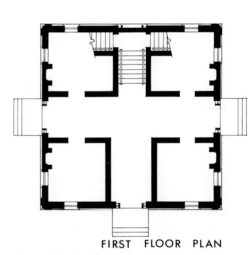

FIRST FLOOR PLAN

FIGURE 54. Liberty County Courthouse, Liberty (ca. 1845). *Drawings by the author.*

The plans of the Liberty County Courthouse are similar to those used for several courthouses built during the time when Texas was a republic. Apparently the tradition of placing offices on the first level and the courtroom on the second was brought west by settlers who migrated from the Southeast.

FIGURE 55. Van Zandt County Courthouse, Canton (1857). *Drawings by the author.*

The plans are typical of the antebellum Texas courthouses erected during the 1850's. Centrally positioned corridors intersecting in the center divided the ground floor into offices, an arrangement that also provided for good natural ventilation by the breezes. The courtroom then occupied the entire second floor. Although the dimensions varied, many counties utilized this basic scheme in either square or rectangular configurations.

36 feet in length by 24 feet in breadth . . . two stories high, the lower story 12 feet in the clear, the upper 11 feet between floor and joist; a frame building of good materials weatherboarded . . . the lower part to be finished off with the judge's seat, jury box, bar, clerk's box and table, with nine windows to the lower story, of 24 lights 8 by 10 inches each, and three doors 8 feet high by 4 wide . . . in the upper story a passage six feet in width shall run crosswise the house so as to construct two rooms on each side. . . .[22]

The third Liberty County Courthouse, a building thirty-two by forty feet, commenced circa 1845, was similar, but access was through a hallway, which contained a stair (fig. 54).

Most of these early courthouses were replaced in the mid-1850's. New brick or frame buildings were made possible by the prosperity created by trade and good cotton crops. In contrast with the courthouses of the republic, the late antebellum temples were built according to a new scheme, which, like the plan they replaced, was imported from the Southeast, probably Virginia. These temples of justice were either rectangular or square. (Symbolically, in some ancient times four-square forms represented stability and permanence.) In contrast to the earlier types, ground-floor corridors, usually extending through the building in both directions, divided the area into four offices. On the second floor rather than the first, the courtroom occupied the entire space (fig. 55). Whether square or rectangular, virtually all plans conformed to this interior arrangement. Among the earliest county buildings to be built in this form, the Harrison County Courthouse, Marshall (1849–1851), was in a cubical form with a cupola. However, there were examples that did not conform to this pattern, for instance, the Gillespie County Courthouse (1860) in Fredericksburg (fig. 56).

Constructed by masterbuilders according to written specifications—although plans appar-

ently were used occasionally—the square antebellum courthouses were designed with four fronts that were either similar or identical, in contrast with county governmental buildings in the northern states, which commonly emphasized one main facade.

In Bonham, specifications for the Fannin County Courthouse (1859), which was to be "built of good brick or Sulphur rock," called for a sixty-foot-square building "with four fronts alike. . . ." Demonstrating the importance of this requirement even in cases where doors were not actually installed in all sides was the Van Zandt County Courthouse. Although a stairway to the second floor blocked the installation of an operable door, specifications called for four identical fronts, thus requiring the installation of "a false or imitation door. . . ." The Dallas County Courthouse (1855) was similar but with dimensions of fifty feet on a side. David P. Fearis was contracted to build for Ellis County, to replace a fifty-nine-dollar log house, a courthouse on a smaller scale than Dallas', only twenty-four feet by thirty-six, with two stories.[23] Yet other fine examples were the Fayette County Courthouse in La Grange (1855–1856) and the Gonzales County Courthouse (1849) in Gonzales (fig. 57).

Numerous fine antebellum courthouses were constructed. However, today they are all gone, largely due to the importance placed upon the retention of the original public square as the site for the courthouse to be built, thus necessitating razing of the old buildings before the new were built after the Civil War.

To complete the governmental units of the typical county seat, jails were required for the enforcement of law. Calabooses were ever-present reminders of retribution in the name of law and order. Structures that were free-stand-

[22] *Telegraph and Texas Register* (Houston), October 21, 1837.

[23] Fannin County, Commissioners Court Minutes, vol. B, June 8, 1859, p. 17; Van Zandt County, Commissioners Court Minutes, vol. A, p. 242; *A Memorial and Biographical History of Dallas County*, p. 200; *A Memorial and Biographical History of Ellis County*, p. 80.

FIGURE 56. Gillespie County Courthouse, Fredericksburg (1860). *Historic American Buildings Survey, Library of Congress, Washington, D.C.*

This building with plastered masonry walls served county functions in the German community of Fredericksburg until the 1880's, when a new edifice was erected, using the plans of San Antonio architect Alfred Giles. This early building was somewhat smaller than most antebellum courthouses. County officers were housed in the bottom story, and the courtroom was contained on the second floor, which was reached by exterior stairs.

After the 1880's courthouse was completed, this structure served as a post office until 1939, when it was razed to make room for the present federal building.

FIGURE 57. Gonzales County Courthouse, Gonzales (1849). *From the collections of the Dallas Historical Society.*

Contributing to the stateliness of this edifice were five-bay fronts framed by corner pilasters supporting a fine entablature. As was common, a cupola surmounted the hipped roof.

Unlike most courthouses, this building was located adjacent to the town square, rather than on it. Laid out during the Mexican period, the square of Gonzales was originally an open space.

ing rather than attached to the courthouse reinforced this symbolism to some extent.

While the antebellum courthouses were generally situated symmetrically, in the middle of the public square, the locations of the lockups followed no standard pattern. Often appearing somewhat as afterthoughts rather than integral parts of the county government, they sometimes were placed at a corner of the public square, but frequently appeared on a lot located a block or more away—a less convenient situation but perhaps more desirable, since it isolated criminals from the center of social activity.

These antebellum works for detention required strong walls, floors, and ceilings, yet the types of materials that were available were limited. The soft bricks and lime mortar that could be had often were not satisfactory, unless reinforced with iron, since they could be easily chipped or broken apart. Consequently the typical antebellum jail—few models of which remain—was a work of wood, sometimes reinforced with iron.

Near mid-century masonry was employed in some jails, though. After considering several different plans, a committee appointed by the county commissioners of Fayette County selected the proposal of William Lewis for a two-story brick jail. The plans—for which Lewis received twenty dollars—called for eighteen-inch-thick walls to enclose two rooms on the lower story and two rooms separated by a corridor on the second story, with "at least one of the cells to be made secure by lining it with boiler iron, or by bay iron crossed and riveted."[24] Although these early buildings ordinarily displayed few conventional stylistic details, the Galveston County Prison and Courtroom (1847) was decorated with Gothic Revival features (fig. 58).

Stylistically the most pretentious and durable buildings were those for state and federal governments. Crowning the eminence reserved for it in the original plan of Austin, the state capitol was the largest Greek Revival edifice to be built in Texas (fig. 59). Built with funds awarded to the state as compensation for lands ceded the United States at annexation, this was the first permanent capitol in the state and was contemporary with such other Greek Revival American state houses of legislature as those in Indiana and Michigan. The rectangular form, with a portico centered on the long side and a central tower, recalled the Iowa capitol (1840) and the Alabama capitol (1851), both also in Greek Revival style.

Complementing the Classical theme of the well-established antebellum Texas town were the churches, which increasingly appeared in Greek style, providing unity between dwellings and other public buildings in the same mode. While churches from the Spanish and Mexican periods continued to be used—for example, an early mission church in San Patricio was used by the Irish—many frame and masonry works were set up by Anglo-Americans according to the architectural traditions and religion they brought with them.

At first Protestant church groups met in houses of the settlers or in small chapels. While the shortage of churches was frequently noted by observers,[25] during the 1830's and 1840's many new buildings began appearing in Texas communities as well as in rural regions. By 1850 one writer reported that there were 341 houses of worship in Texas.[26] With the development of affluence in the congregations and with the increase in numbers of buildings came the stylistic distinction of the Greek Revival.

The Texas Greek Revival church displayed Classical details similar to those found in other

[24] Fayette County, Commissioners Court Minutes, vol. A, p. 247.

[25] Edward Stiff, *The Texan Emigrant* (p. 16), observed, "throughout the whole extent of Texas, at the present time, there is but one protestant house that is exclusively appropriated to the worship of God, and few there are who enter that." In an 1839 article (September 18) in the *Telegraph and Texas Register* (Houston), the importance of churches as expressions of religious sentiment was noted, but then the concerned reporter exclaimed, "Alas, how few there are in the city!"

[26] Homer S. Thrall, *The People's Illustrated Almanac, Texas Handbook and Immigrant's Guide, for 1880*, p. 744.

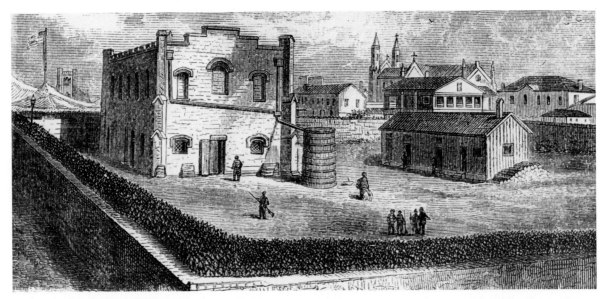

FIGURE 58. Galveston County Prison and Courtroom, Galveston (1847–1848). Charles G. Bryant, architect. *From Edward King,* The Great South, *courtesy Bowdoin College Library, Brunswick, Maine.*

Unlike many early Texas jails, this building was decorated with Gothic Revival buttresses, which may have been functional but which were probably only ornamental. Other decorative details included window hoods and a parapet. Wall construction was molded brick.

FIGURE 59. Texas State Capitol, Austin (1852–1854). John Brandon, architect. *Archives Division, Texas State Library, Austin.*

With walls of cream-colored limestone (oolite), the structure was an imposing antebellum monument. The base was composed of pitched-faced ashlar with horizontal rustication; above this, the exterior walls of the middle section were finished with cut stone, with quoins in strong relief. The composition was terminated with a wide entablature. A portico supported by fluted columns with Ionic capitals formally announced the entrance. Above the roof a tower rose to a height of about a hundred feet. The present capitol now stands on this site.

sections of the country. The roof usually had a Classical slope—appropriate for the typical temple form. A wooden entablature with proportions similar to those found on houses and public buildings terminated the walls. Originally, openings, which have now often been modified with the installation of stained glass, were usually simple rectangles with double-hung sashes. To communicate the spiritual purpose, which might not have been otherwise apparent, a tower or belfry, decorated with wooden pilasters and an entablature, often was placed upon the apex of the roof at the front—apparently in some cases several years after the building was completed.

The plans of these churches were naturally as simple as the forms. Although the First Baptist Church, Austin, used a square plan, most plans were simple rectangles. At one end of the nave or auditorium was located the chancel of the Episcopal and Lutheran churches and the rostrum of the Baptist, Methodist, and Presbyterian churches. Often this was flanked on either side by small rooms containing storage or sacristies. At the entrance of the edifice was often a balcony (which in antebellum times was used by slaves). In Catholic, Lutheran, and Episcopal churches a communion rail separated the clergy from the congregation, and Classical details decorated the chancel.

While these Greek Revival churches were certainly admired for their designs, which expressed repose and dignity, the purity of the mode began declining as the Civil War approached. First, the popularity of the Greek had diminished, and other styles were becoming fashionable in other sections of the United States. Then, even while the Classical mode was popular, other styles were preferred for some types of buildings. As a result of the decline of the Greek Revival in Texas, transitional details appear in works dating from the early 1860's through the 1870's.

In the typical transitional designs, the Classical form was retained for the mass of the church, along with Greek Revival entablatures. However, the entrance vestibule was sometimes brought forward and transformed into a tower, as in Saint Joseph's Catholic Church (1860) in Galveston, designed by Joseph Bleicke, a wood-framed structure, which fortunately still stands. Universal in these transitional designs was the use of Gothic pointed arches, which created a mixture of styles. At the same time these transitional works were being built, the "pure" Gothic Revival style appeared in some churches, particularly those of the Catholic, Lutheran, and Episcopal denominations, all of which had a strong attachment to formal liturgy. In the early examples of this style the plans were similar to Greek Revival buildings, but the roofs were steeply pitched, and buttresses—often decorative rather than structural—were stressed vertically on the exterior walls. In both masonry and wood-frame buildings, openings were spanned by pointed arches. A fine example of antebellum Gothic Revival, now gone, appeared in Christ Episcopal Church, Houston (fig. 60).

The designers and builders who most favored the Gothic Revival before the Civil War were certainly those with the strongest ties to Catholicism. The association of the revival mode with the era of the great Gothic cathedrals of Europe—manifestations of intense dedication to God—motivated designers to use Medieval stylistic features, even though economy of means may have restricted their use to simple forms. Typical of these architects was Father Pierre Yveres Keralum, an intrepid missionary who designed several churches in South Texas in Gothic Revival style. Among these was the Church of Our Lady of Refuge of Sinners, Roma (1854) (fig. 61). Interestingly, although the Gothic was used extensively for ecclesiastical buildings, it never became fashionable for residential buildings in Texas.

While Texans—particularly those who were concerned about moral improvement—were justly proud of their religious buildings and other public structures, they also expressed concern for state public works designed to benefit society—including a peniten-

FIGURE 60. Christ Episcopal Church, Houston (1859). Edwin Fairfax Gray, architect. *From an 1869 map by W. E. Wood, courtesy Harris County Heritage Society, Houston.*

This was a fine example of antebellum Gothic Revival style. The high, centrally located tower, pointed arches, and buttresses extending above the roof eaves all contributed to the distinctive ecclesiastical image of the edifice.

The building served Houston Episcopalians for about four decades. In 1876 it was expanded, according to the plans of Henry Congdon. After deterioration of the fabric became a problem, it was razed.

tiary, a lunatic asylum, and an institute for the blind. The dire need for a penitentiary was noted in 1840 by one reporter, who certainly expressed public sentiment when he opined: "Every principle both of humanity and public economy have [*sic*] been outraged in the enactments relating to crime." Later, in 1842, a bill authorizing establishment of a national penitentiary for the republic was passed by the legislature, marking, according to one reporter,

"a new impulse to moral improvement."[27] However, funds were insufficient, and no buildings were realized at that time. Still faced with the need for a state facility, authors of the 1845 constitution provided for construction, and in 1848 three commissioners were appointed by the governor to select a site and

[27] *Telegraph and Texas Register* (Houston), December 9, 1840, and January 5, 1842.

FIGURE 61. Church of Our Lady of Refuge of Sinners, Roma (1854). Father Pierre Yveres Keralum, architect. *Historic American Buildings Survey, Library of Congress, Washington, D.C.*

The designer of this building, Father Keralum, was born in Quimper, Brittany. He became a cabinet-maker and then studied architecture in Paris, France. After practicing architecture in France, he became a missionary of the Oblates of Mary Immaculate. In 1848, he and several other priests arrived in Galveston. Several years later he designed this fine church in Roma.

Only the tower of the 1854 building remains. The nave was razed to make way for a larger space in the mid-1960's.

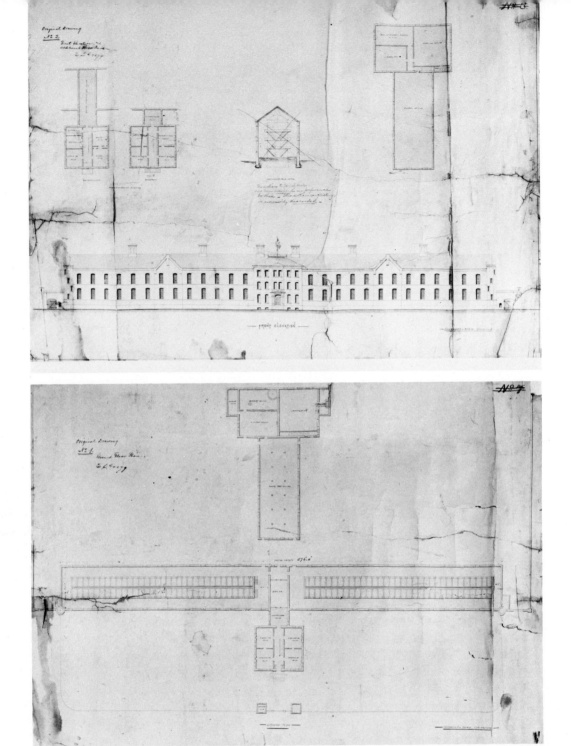

FIGURE 62. Texas State Penitentiary, Huntsville (1849). *Archives Division, Texas State Library, Austin.*

Throughout the early part of the nineteenth century, many prisons were constructed in the United States. Much reform had developed in the treatment of prisoners, and the Texas State Penitentiary was designed to fulfill the requirements of the new reform. Included among the new facilities were a chapel, dining hall, and freestanding cells.

Basically, the building was straightforward in style. However the main access was decorated with pilasters and a pediment. Although strictly functional, the corner towers, with their castellations, added interest to the composition. The extent to which this plan was realized and is extant is difficult to ascertain. Changes in procedures, installation of new facilities, and rises in prison population have necessitated changes throughout the years.

FIGURE 63. Asylum for the Deaf (Institute for the Deaf), Austin (1856). *Austin–Travis County Collection, Austin Public Library.*

Formerly located on South Congress, this institution was established in 1856 and was opened the following year. The goals of the school were to educate and train deaf children.

In 1886, a third story was added, and the building was expanded laterally, but eventually the structure was completely razed.

oversee construction. Finally in 1849 work got underway on the state penitentiary in Huntsville, under the supervision of masterbuilder Abner Cook (fig. 62).[28]

The State Lunatic Asylum, the Institute for the Blind, and the Institute for the Deaf all were located in Austin and erected in 1856–1857 in Italianate style. Providing distinction to the insane asylum (Austin State Hospital), which still stands, were substantial

[28] *Democratic Telegraph and Texas Register*, March 1, 1849.

walls of masonry, corner quoins, balconies, and a bracketted cornice, all characteristic of the Italianate. In the building for the Institute for the Blind (1856), which is on the Little Campus of the University of Texas, a similar character was achieved, although the design was somewhat more straightforward, with contrast provided by polychromy. The Institute for the Deaf, which has been destroyed, however, was a frame structure (fig. 63).

Thus architecture during the periods of the republic and antebellum statehood, all too much of which is now gone from Texas, was characterized by contrast. The early work was indigenous to the land and often revealed responses to the environment; on the other hand, it often reflected the origins of the builders. In later work, when times were more prosperous, historical styles following eastern trends provided manifestations of order and cultural advancement. However, the Civil War terminated all these developments. Thereafter, developments in technology and changes in taste would have a strong impact on the evolution of communities and their architecture.

Fortunately many fine Greek Revival buildings and a few examples of other historical styles dating before the Civil War remain in East and South Texas. However, indigenous cabins from the antebellum era are mostly gone (although some, which have been protected by weatherboarding or other materials, remain). Some of these Classical and indigenous buildings are preserved in museums, while others still serve active functions. None of the Greek Revival courthouses remain, and only a few jails survive. Progress required that many buildings in towns be replaced. Countless structures located in rural areas simply rotted away as they were abandoned.

4

Evolution in Technology and Taste

As is typical of conflicts among states or nations, the American Civil War had a lasting detrimental impact on the states' economies and public attitudes. In the South the spirit of optimism and the prosperous times of the 1850's, which had made possible the construction of a number of fine public and private buildings, was transformed into a condition of depression and poverty. The aura of sadness emanating from a heavy loss of life and from the destruction of property created melancholy psychological scars—attitudes that were reflected in the early material culture of the postbellum period through somber character of form and color.

The Civil War had even retarded the development of the West Texas country. After the withdrawal of Federal troops from the frontier forts, the Indians were no longer inhibited from raiding settlements. Living in fear, many civilians were forced to "fort up" in log cabins surrounded by stockades, and new immigration was halted. Further settlement of the western wilderness was not feasible until after the war, when the Indians could be confined to reservations.

However, the war had stimulated developments in transportation and industry that were to be instrumental in rapid recovery. Among the benefits to postbellum society was the stimulation of railroad construction, which finally tied the country together, culturally as well as physically. With the driving of the silver spike near Promontory, Utah, in 1869, the East and the West were connected by the Union Pacific Railroad. Later other transcontinental routes would cross other sections of the country, and, during the years following, the communication of ideas and the transportation of materials to areas that had formerly been remote contributed to both economic and cultural development.

Also during the war, industrial development had been encouraged by government subsidies. Although originally the stimulus was to increase the production of items necessary to wage battle, during postwar years manufacturers easily shifted from the making of munitions to the production of goods that would improve the quality of life. In Austin, for example, a foundry that had been established by a military board to produce cannons and munitions was converted to produce plows and spinning jennies. Other foundries and industries followed suit, and a number of new factories also sprang up. Notable among these in San Antonio was a steam factory owned by Major Kampmann, "a splendid store edifice . . ." designed to manufacture moldings, sashes, and blinds as well as to cut stone.[1]

Through sharecropping, through the development of the timber industry, and through increasing commercial activity in the coastal

---

[1] *San Antonio Express*, June 25, 1868. Information on the era may be found in Ernest Wallace, *Texas in Turmoil: The Saga of Texas, 1849–1875*, p. 127.

cities, the economic condition of Texas began improving during Reconstruction. In the west, the economic situation improved with the growth of the cattle and sheep industries. During the years following the Civil War, ranching was stimulated by increasing demands for beef in eastern cities, in western gold camps, and in military establishments. Consequently large, profitable ranches were developed on the grasslands of West and South Texas, and functional rural buildings sparsely dotted the outlying regions.

On the semiarid Lower Plains, where timber suitable for building was scarce, and on the High Plains, which were devoid of trees, shelters built before the arrival of the railroads were of adobe or stone, only occasionally of logs. The first dwellings were dugouts placed wholly underground or half-dugouts placed partially underground into the sides of inclines. Both provided living places that were cool in summer, warm in winter and required minimal amounts of timber. Roofs were covered with poles and dirt, and the walls were earth, sometimes lined with stone; few remain.

In areas where stone was on or near the surface, masonry structures were set up. Heinrich C. Schmitt (Hank Smith), a German immigrant who had worked in various parts of the United States before settling permanently in Texas, built with limestone. While temporarily living in a dugout in the late 1870's, Smith built his Hacienda Glorieta on a site near a spring in Blanco Canyon. This was a two-story house with stone walls, laid up using lime manufactured on the ranch (fig. 64). Subsequently, outbuildings and corrals also were built with rocks. Unfortunately, after a fire in 1952, the house is now a ruin.[2]

After the railroads reached the westerly regions, sawn lumber became economical, and large wood houses, barns, and stables appeared at the ranch headquarters, which were strategically located to operate large spreads.

Box construction was widely used for ranch buildings. To provide maximum economy of materials, the houses were built like boxes, with walls of one-by-twelve boards nailed to a floor platform of widely spaced two-by-sixes. Thin strips covered the joints between the boards, and a light frame roof covered with shingles completed the shell—there was no wall framing. This technique was used extensively on the plains, where all material had to be imported, and it was even employed for a courthouse in Leakey and a jail in Floydada.

As the open-range era came to a close at the turn of the century, the ranch headquarters grew larger; buildings were sited in accordance with both convenience and the terrain. Bunkhouses, usually located near the service structures, were provided for the cowboys when they were not on the range. Stables, built of stone or sawn lumber, provided shelters for their horses, and blacksmith shops were built to house the implements essential to the farrier's art and other required metal working, such as wagon-wheel repair. Carriage houses provided protection for buggies and tack, and on the large ranches office buildings were provided. Windmills and storage tanks, which were often landmarks of the open range, were also often a part of the building complexes. Representative of these large headquarters was Las Escarbadas, now mostly gone, which was located in Deaf Smith County near the New Mexico boundary (fig. 65).

Many fortunes were accumulated during the latter part of the century by entrepreneurs investing in these ranches, in industrial enterprises, and in other ventures. The concentration of wealth produced a class of affluent individuals with the means to foster art and architecture on a large scale. Although the Panic of 1873 temporarily retarded progress, the demand for architects, masons, stonecutters, carpenters, plasterers, and painters increased fairly steadily.

The conditions creating the new wealthy class also brought about the development of a

[2]Flukey Smith interview, Crosby County, Texas, July 20, 1975.

FIGURE 64. Hank Smith Ranch, Crosby County (1877). *Crosby County Pioneer Memorial, Crosbyton.*

A native of Rossbrunn, Germany, Heinrich Schmitt (Hank Smith) established this ranch in 1877 in Blanco Canyon. After working at various occupations and serving in the Confederate army during the Civil War, he was commissioned to develop the ranch by an individual in Philadelphia. However, his sponsor went bankrupt, and Smith took over the property.

This stone house was on a simple, central-hall-type plan. It also served as a post office for many years. In 1952 the dwelling burned, and today only a lonely, three-sided shell of stone remains.

FIGURE 65. Las Escarbadas Ranch Headquarters, Deaf Smith County (1880's). *Library of Congress, Washington, D.C.*

Ranchers demonstrated sensitivity to their environment in the placement and construction of buildings. Most of this complex was situated on a south slope, below the brow of a tableland, which protected it from the cold winter northers; buildings were oriented with their broadsides to the south, providing for good cross ventilation from the prevailing breezes during the hot months. The headquarters house was built with caliche rock walls about two feet thick, thus providing good insulation; it was only one room deep, making it efficiently ventilated. A porch shaded the south facade.

Virtually all is gone. After the ranch was abandoned in the twentieth century, the structures were vandalized and deteriorated rapidly.

new leisure class. The labor saved by mass production and mechanization provided the middle classes time for recreation and cultural refinement. Now they could enjoy pleasurable activities and some of the arts. At the same time, the development of public services improved the quality of life.

All this, of course, had a revolutionary impact on the type, magnitude, and opulence of the architecture that was required to fulfill the physical and emotional needs of society. The railroads created demands for large service structures and bridges with long spans, as well as depots designed to enhance the travel experience. The middle class provided the patronage necessary to finance such pleasure palaces as natatoriums and skating rinks and such cultural entertainments as opera houses and chautauquas. The improvement of public welfare required buildings for fire protection and health care. Then, to express worldly status and attainment, the affluent class demanded large mansions in European historical styles. At the same time, public buildings became larger and more elaborate in design.

Vital to the economic improvement and increased settlement that made all this feasible in Texas was the expansion of transportation systems during the last half of the nineteenth century. Railroad building had been commenced in the antebellum period, but fewer than five hundred miles of tracks had been completed when the war began. The extension of lines through remote sections of the state made possible the transportation of the people and goods essential to the development of the land and resources. To be sure, the railway companies carefully planned their routes to capitalize on the potential of the country.[3]

To stimulate railroad building, Texas, like other states in the nation, offered land as bounty. The policy of awarding sixteen sections of land for every mile of railroad laid, which had been initiated in 1854, was continued after the war, although the Texas and Pacific Railway Company received twenty sections per mile.[4]

On some of this land the railway companies developed new towns, which yielded profits from the sale of lots as well as from fares and freight. Among the early railroad towns, Calvert was laid out in 1868 by a surveyor for the Houston and Texas Central Railway on land donated by Robert Calvert during the Civil War. Over a decade later, after the Texas and Pacific extended its lines westward, Midland was laid out by railroad representatives in 1884, and Odessa in 1886. To Big Spring, the location of important railroad shops, an excursion train in 1884 brought prospective settlers for an auction of town lots. In South Texas ranching country, the Texas and New Orleans Railroad in 1881 created Marfa, and to the north the Gulf, Colorado and Santa Fe Railway advertised the sale on May 4, 1886, of town lots in Ballinger. Elsewhere, in the Panhandle, the Texas Townsite Company, a subsidiary of the Fort Worth and Denver Railroad, also developed several communities along the rails, including Washburn, which at one time was a thriving cattle-shipping center.[5]

To entice immigrants to its towns, the Texas and Pacific advertised public amenities. As early as possible, the construction of such improvements as courthouses, schoolhouses, and libraries was encouraged—although the first buildings often were not particularly noteworthy. In 1886 the sale of town lots in Odessa was advertised, with inducements including speculation that "a college will soon be built and a public library will be donated." The *Fort Worth Daily Gazette* announced in separate issues that a depot would be built in Mid-

[3] Rupert Norval Richardson et al., *Texas: The Lone Star State*, p. 259.

[4] Ibid., p. 260; Walter P. Webb and H. B. Carroll, eds., *The Handbook of Texas*, 2:752. To forty-one companies 32,153,878 acres of land were awarded (Gerald Sewell and Mary Beth Rogers, *Story of Texas Public Lands*, p. 30).

[5] Webb and Carroll, *Handbook of Texas*, 1:104, 273, 2:142, 302, 864; *Fort Worth Daily Gazette*, March 28, 1886; *Houston Daily Post*, April 15, 1884; A. W. Sledge, *Ballinger and Runnels County*, p. 3; Frederick W. Rathjen, *The Texas Panhandle Frontier*, pp. 246–247.

land as soon as lots were sold and that the town company agreed to donate "$3,000 toward a $30,000 courthouse."[6] In 1885 in Pecos City, the Texas and Pacific Railway announced that it would donate ten percent of the proceeds from the second-day sales to the construction of a schoolhouse and an artesian well. As another amenity and as an encouragement to the immigration of German Methodists from the northwestern states, the cities of Odessa and Big Spring forbade the sale of intoxicating liquors.[7]

The railroads had a phenomenal effect on the destiny of the Texas towns that had been established previously, as well as on new towns founded afterward by other entrepreneurs. In the 1870's, upon the arrival of the iron horse, Dallas and Fort Worth became thriving cities, in which populations increased and industry developed rapidly. In the Panhandle region, Amarillo was established in 1887, shortly after the area was reached by the Fort Worth and Denver City Railroad, and the town became a bustling cattle-shipping center after the arrival of the Santa Fe. Conversely, the population of the town of Boston declined after the railroad missed it in 1869, and New Boston was established adjacent to the route several miles away. Later both Mobeetie and Sherwood were virtually deserted after the railroads missed them; the citizens migrated to new communities located adjacent to the railroad rights-of-way. Recognizing the potential influence on their destinies, many communities raised cash bonuses or donated land to railway companies to promote the extension of tracks to them.[8]

Although, to attract buyers of lots, promoters of new towns certainly were eager to establish visual and social order, in the early years most fledgling communities along the railroads were not attractive places in which to

live. After the arrival of the Missouri, Kansas and Texas Railroad in 1872, Denison, according to one observer, attracted "professional ruffians, 'terminus' gamblers and the offscouring of society. . . ." All the lumber had to be hauled hundreds of miles to build the first rough structures, every third one of which "was a drinking saloon with gambling appurtenances. . . ." However, with the arrival of morals-conscious women with their families, and with the establishment of churches, the illicit prostitutes, gamblers, and ruffians were controlled, and the new communities improved morally and visually. The first crude buildings were either razed intentionally with wrecking bars or destroyed accidentally by fires and often were replaced by substantial wood or durable masonry buildings, the earlier ones with designs similar to those of antebellum buildings.[9]

Transportation also had a strong effect on patterns of growth in established communities, not just in new towns. In such coastal towns as Galveston and Houston, shipping activity attracted commercial development along waterfronts. While the public square generally had been the nucleus of the commercial districts of inland antebellum towns, the streets near the railroad depots became energetic centers of commercial activity in many postbellum communities. Depots attracted hotels and dining rooms, for the convenience of the weary travelers, as well as other commercial enterprises. This resulted in linear growth, first adjacent to the tracks, then along streets leading to the railroads—similar to today's strip development along prominent avenues and highways (figs. 66, 67). In such towns as Palestine, Colorado City, and Giddings, business buildings were located near the tracks, leaving the public squares with their courthouses to become parts of residential neighborhoods.

[6] *Fort Worth Daily Gazette*, March 28, 1886, April 15, 1884, and June 10, 1885.

[7] *Dallas Morning News*, October 16, 1885; Webb and Carroll, *Handbook of Texas*, 2:302.

[8] Webb and Carroll, *Handbook of Texas*, 1:39, 194, 2:220, 605.

[9] Edward King and J. Wells Champney, *Texas 1874: An Eyewitness Account of Conditions in Post-Reconstruction Texas*, p. 138.

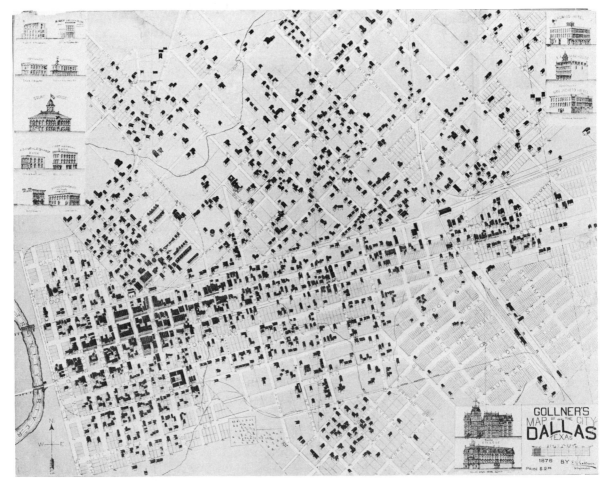

FIGURE 66. Dallas. Gollner's Map (1876). *From the collections of the Dallas Historical Society.*

The influence of the railroads on the growth pattern of the commercial district is apparent in this early map of Dallas. In the lower left-hand corner is the courthouse, surrounded by relatively small commercial buildings, apparently dating from earlier years. New, larger buildings, many of which certainly date from the 1870's, were located along the streets paralleling the Texas and Pacific Railroad and along the intersecting streets. Paralleling Pacific Avenue, the railroad restricted expansion to the north. Finally in 1925 the Texas and Pacific tracks were removed from Pacific Avenue, and the city became much safer.

In the towns planned by representatives of the railroads, the main streets ordinarily were laid out along the tracks. Theodore Kosse, chief surveyor of the Houston and Texas Central Railway, laid out Calvert with the commercial district parallel to the tracks. This divided the town in half, with the dwellings of the affluent class on one side, those of the laborers on the other.[10] Abilene was planned

[10] John S. Garner, "Calvert, Texas, 1868–1918: Rise and Fall of a Cotton Town," Abstracts of Papers Presented at the 31st Annual Meeting of the Society of Architectural Historians, San Antonio, Texas, April 5–10, 1978.

with two main streets, named North First and South First, paralleling the tracks on either side. Interestingly, in Pampa, a town laid out in 1888 along the Santa Fe Railroad, the hotel, fire station, city hall, and courthouse were all built in line on a row of narrow blocks extending at right angles from the tracks. In a good many towns, the passenger depot was situated between the tracks and a main avenue, thus serving as focus of the view from streets running at right angles to the railroad.

Town founding by various ethnic groups continued in the latter part of the nineteenth

FIGURE 67. Denison. View (1891). Courtesy *Amon Carter Museum, Fort Worth.*

Founded in 1858, Denison celebrated the arrival of the Missouri, Kansas, and Texas Railroad in 1872. Subsequently other lines passed through the town, and it became an important railroad center. Many railroad structures appeared, including roundhouses, water tanks, and so forth.

The impact of railroading was apparent in the development of the town, which is named for the then-president of the MKT. After the railroad arrived, the streets leading to the passenger station became lined with business buildings. Typical of many towns, the street layouts, as well as neighborhood development, obviously were influenced by the route of the tracks.

and early twentieth century, contributing further to the colorful composition of pockets of culture within the state. Among these new communities were the Norwegian settlements founded in Bosque County, where the quiet woods and clear streams reminded the settlers of parts of their homeland.

While the plans of most of these communities were simple grids, at some locations efforts were made to use utopian concepts in planning. In North Texas, within a German colony covering some seventy-five thousand acres, the town of Windthorst was laid out around a prominent hill. The eminence was

surrounded by a boulevard following an oval circuit; outside the boulevard were two systems of gridiron streets, one oriented to the cardinal points, the other, askew—however, only a few streets were ever realized. Nonetheless, as had been planned, this hill became a pedestal for the community church, thus expressing the religious and social focus of life by these Germans.

Blacks also established communities and planned neighborhoods. Kendleton, Pelham, and Galilee were all black communities. Within Austin, the Clarksville district was occupied by blacks and still retains much of its original character. In Dallas, Deep Ellum, a settlement originally composed of freed slaves, became a self-sufficient neighborhood.[11]

As Texas communities developed during the latter part of the nineteenth century, hierarchical neighborhoods evolved spontaneously as a result of the demand for building lots with prestigious locations. Main boulevards leading to governmental or commercial centers, streets running along eminent geographical features, and broad avenues featuring expansive yards attracted those with financial means who wished to announce their status. In Galveston well-to-do merchants, who owned large commercial buildings along the Strand, built elegant mansions along Broadway. In Fort Worth wealthy cattlemen as well as businessmen built along streets overlooking the Clear Fork of the Trinity River; while some ranchers built large dwellings at their rural headquarters, their showplaces were in towns. In San Antonio the King William district—named after King William I of Prussia—attracted successful German merchants. In the less prominent areas, the less well-off built their houses or rented dwellings or apartments.

Individuals selling goods or services preferred to cluster together within a given district, preferably near the focal points of daily community life—governmental or transportation buildings. Mutual benefits were derived when stables, mercantiles, markets, saloons, and hotels were conveniently located near a point of arrival—the town square or the railroad depot. Within this commercial district the intersections of streets formed the most prominent sites; corner locations were virtually universal preferences for banks, opera houses, and lodges—especially banks.

As an expression of cultural values, promi-nent sites off the public squares were often set aside for churches and schools. In the original plats of many communities, eminences or hills were reserved for educational purposes.

Town development in the nineteenth century also was influenced by various industries. The locations of these were ordinarily determined by the geography of the area and community features. Manufacturing plants requiring large amounts of water naturally located along rivers. Breweries in Fort Worth, Houston, and San Antonio—every large community had a brewery—all were situated near the rivers passing through the cities (fig. 68). Of course, waterworks, too, often appeared along the banks of rivers—for example, in Wichita Falls, where they were within four blocks of the courthouse, and in Fort Worth, where they were next to the river, northwest of the courthouse.

Geology occasionally determined the locations of some manufacturing plants, as well as some communities. For example, in 1880, the Alamo Portland and Roman Cement Company was established in San Antonio, where a large deposit of natural cement rock was discovered. The community of Thurber was founded in 1886 by the Johnson Coal Company near coal deposits but was abandoned in 1933, after which most of the buildings were wrecked. Terlingua was established near quicksilver mines in the Chisos Mountains, and Shafter was founded near a silver discovery in the Chinati Mountains.[12]

In some instances, commercial enterprises that were originally isolated became the nuclei of suburbs. Located north of the Trinity River, the Fort Worth stockyards district, for example, evolved into a complete community, with its own residential neighborhoods and commercial buildings.

During the last quarter of the nineteenth century, many of these prospering commu-

[11] Works Progress Administration, *Texas: A Guide to the Lone Star State*, p. 233; "Kendleton," "Pelham," and "Galilee," Historical Files, Institute of Texan Cultures, San Antonio; "Clarksville," Historical Buildings Files, Texas Historical Commission, Austin.

[12] "Alamo Portland Cement and Roman Cement Company," Historical Files of History of Engineering Program, Texas Tech University; Webb and Carroll, *Handbook of Texas*, 2:725, 729.

FIGURE 68. Houston Ice and Brewing Company, Houston (ca. 1890). *Houston Public Library.*

Incorporated in 1887, this company supplied ice and beer to many Houstonians. The plant was located on both sides of Fourth and Washington Streets. Included among the principal buildings were a five-story brewery and ice plant, a single-story wash house, a two-story boiler and engine house, a building for bottling, a stable, and an office building. The capacities of the plants were one hundred tons of ice per day and sixty thousand barrels of beer per year. Three artesian wells supplied water for the manufacturers. The beer, which won an international award, was sold under the label of Magnolia.

nities were ready for physical and aesthetic improvements. Fences of wood or decorative wrought iron were placed around courthouse squares to protect landscaping, which provided shade and beauty. Although near the end of the century a "swept lawn" of packed clay was installed around the Comal County Courthouse in New Braunfels—as well as around some residences in various parts of the state—most squares were planted with grass and trees, many of which have been removed during the twentieth century as the need for

paved parking areas has reduced the size of the square. Windmills, cisterns, water tanks, along with benches and bandstands, too, became parts of the settings.[13]

The avenues leading to these squares also received attention. Streets and roads, which were dusty when dry and quagmires when wet (fig. 69), were surfaced with a variety of mate-

[13] Contracts for improvements of public squares are recorded in commissioners court minutes of various counties. See, for example, Office of the County Clerk, County Commissioners Court Minutes, Comal County, vol. H (January 6, 1899), p. 399.

FIGURE 69. Congress Avenue, looking north, Austin (1876 view). *Institute of Texan Cultures, San Antonio.*

This view is representative of a typical town scene before significant street improvements were begun and before extensive electrical service became available. The condition of streets was often bad, as the ruts in this picture suggest. Drainage systems simply consisted of ditches located between streets and wooden sidewalks, which were often broken.

rials. In towns near the Gulf coast the streets often were covered with shells. In 1886, for example, the Galveston City Council contracted twenty-five thousand barrels of shells, at twenty cents a barrel, for street surfacing. The glare from the sunlight was objectionable, and horse and wagon traffic pulverized the crustaceans, creating white dust that filtered into everything. Because of durability, bois d'arc, a native hardwood known for its resistance to decay, was extensively employed over the streets in several towns, including Austin, Dallas, and Houston. Cypress sometimes was used, and San Antonio streets along with Alamo Plaza were paved with mesquite blocks. However, the absorbency of the surfaces of these and other woods was much criticized because it made them unsanitary under horse and mule traffic and because the blocks expanded and buckled in heavy rains.[14]

Limestone blocks and macadam (a compacted layer of small broken stones) were also tried, but eventually, after a number of visits were made to eastern cities to examine various types of paving, red bricks became the standard street surfacing in communities throughout the state.[15] Some of these handsome, albeit uneven, brick street surfaces have survived into the 1970's; among them are some of the streets in Canyon and Lubbock, Camp Bowie Boulevard in Fort Worth, and parts of the Mineral Wells–Weatherford highway. A few cities are now beginning to restore some of these warm-colored surfaces.

Attempting to improve community environments further, city councils passed a variety of ordinances restricting the development of hazards and requiring improvement of public areas. Ordinances restricting livestock within

the town were adopted early by most communities. Typical of these laws was an ordinance passed just after the Civil War requiring owners of lots along the prominent commercial streets of Galveston to construct sidewalks with curbs of wood, stone, or brick. Elsewhere contracts were let by cities to construct plank or brick walks, which were to be paid for by the owners of adjacent lots. As efforts to make cities safer, by the late 1860's both Houston and Galveston had developed fire zones in which wood construction was prohibited.[16]

Often prompted by public attitudes voiced through the local presses, city officials authorized many other improvements, which were made possible by developments in science and technology. Among the first technological community improvements were gas-lighting systems for public streets; subsequently such systems were introduced to buildings. As early as 1856 the Galveston Gas Company—the first in Texas—was chartered, and by 1859 it was thriving by converting coal from Liverpool into gas. Also in 1859 the San Antonio Gas Works was founded. Prior to the development of natural gas resources, various methods were employed to generate fuel. In 1869 the fixtures for lighting Jefferson were fueled by gas generated from burning pine knots in a kiln; in 1868 gas for lighting in Houston was generated from oyster shells and coal. During the 1880's many communities installed systems fueled by gas generated with coal shipped from the eastern states. After the turn of the century, of course, huge volumes of natural gas would be obtained from the ground.[17]

During the late 1880's and early 1890's gas piping was replaced by copper wires, as electrical power generators were installed in many communities. In 1881 the Brush Electric Light & Power Company was organized to supply dynamo-generated electricity for arc lights and

[14]Galveston Daily News, May 8, 1866; *San Antonio Conservation Society Newsletter* (September, 1979), p. 4.

[15]Brick street paving had only been in use in the United States for about twenty years before it was introduced into Texas, where it was first used on Congress Avenue in Austin (*Dallas Morning News*, January 2, 1905). A report was published in the *Galveston Daily News*, August 11, 1869, comparing shell street paving with macadam.

[16]*Galveston Daily News*, March 24 and April 5, 1866.

[17]*Galveston Daily News*, January 2, 1882; William Corner, *San Antonio de Bexar: A Guide and History*, p. 154; Works Progress Administration, *Texas*, p. 380; David G. McComb, *Houston: The Bayou City*, p. 21.

Figure 70. Elm Street, west from Akard Street, Dallas (view ca. 1895). *Dallas Public Library.*

During the last quarter of the nineteenth century, the developers of Dallas, like those of other cities across the nation, were quick to capitalize upon the new technology that made life easier and safer. Tall utility poles (which actually detracted from the character of ornately designed commercial blocks) carried telephone and electrical service to commercial districts and residential neighborhoods. Street-car rails embedded into the street paving contributed further to the confusion of the scenes.

motors in the commercial district of Galveston. By 1890 some electric companies were already expanding; in Dallas, for example, the Queen City Electric Light Company enlarged its plant with a new building 100 feet square.[18] Unfortunately, as electricity was developed, commercial streets of the cities became mazes of utility poles and wires (figs. 70, 71).

Within a short time, electricity also was employed by the street railways, which had given impetus to the development of suburbs and new neighborhoods. By the late 1860's streetcars were conveying passengers over bumpy tracks in some large communities. In 1866 the Galveston City Railroad was chartered and was in operation within two years; about fif-

teen years later there were sixteen miles of track and fifty-four cars in operation, all pulled by draft animals. In 1868 Houston also had horse-drawn cars, and in 1878 work was begun on streetcar tracks in San Antonio.[19]

However, as soon as electricity became plentiful, electric motors replaced mules to power the streetcar systems. After Fort Worth converted its streetcar system in 1889 (fig. 72), other communities rapidly followed suit. That same year Laredo constructed a large powerhouse for running its electrically powered streetcar line. In San Antonio the first electric motor was adopted in 1890, and in Houston the change came abruptly in 1891, ironically,

[18] *Galveston Daily News,* January 2, 1882; *Houston Daily Post,* January 15, 1890.

[19] *Galveston Daily News,* January 2, 1882; McComb, *Houston,* p. 41; Corner, *San Antonio de Bexar,* p. 6.

FIGURE 71. Main Street, north from Prairie Avenue, Houston. *From* Art Work of Houston, 1894, *Houston Public Library.*

Following the development of utility companies, many cities presented street scenes similar to this. In 1889 the Citizens' Electric Light and Power Company commenced operations and may have erected some of these power lines.

shortly after work had begun on a new two-story brick stable with "all the latest improvements" for the Bayou City Street Railway Company.[20]

Closely associated with electrical-energy-producing plants were ice works. In 1866 an ice factory was established in San Antonio, and as early as 1868 ice was manufactured in Jefferson. However, a decade passed before most communities were afforded the luxury of ice produced on a commercial scale.[21]

Electricity also made possible the development of telephone systems. During the 1880's, installations were made in cities across the state, including Fort Worth, where telephones were authorized in 1881.[22] These, of course, had a considerable effect on business efficiency as well as other aspects of life.

Business concentration in Texas cities was facilitiated by the introduction of the pas-

[20] *Houston Daily Post,* August 29, 1889; *Galveston Daily News,* January 2, 1887.

[21] Corner, *San Antonio de Bexar,* p. 162; Works Progress

Administration, *Texas,* p. 380. However, for San Antonio the *Historical and Descriptive Review of the Industries of San Antonio, Texas,* p. 76, gives 1870 as the date ice manufacture commenced in that city.

[22] *Daily Democrat* (Fort Worth), June 9, 1881.

FIGURE 72. Jennings Avenue, Fort Worth. (Photo ca. 1905). *Courtesy Fort Worth Public Library, Amon Carter Museum.*

The advent of electricity is quite apparent in this street scene. Overhead cables conducted power to street cars driven by electrical motors. In 1890 arc electric street lights were installed at several street intersections. After the turn of the century artificial lighting installed inside street cars also thrilled many passengers as they were conveyed slowly along bumpy tracks.

Except the Saint Patrick's Catholic Church, which was designed by J. J. Kane and built in 1888, all the structures in this view are gone.

senger elevator, which had been invented in 1853 and first used in 1857 in New York City. Although it had been practical for stairways to serve as many as four to six stories, the convenience—not to mention the novelty—of the elevator improved the rental potential of offices located on upper floors. During the 1880's elevators, consisting of open wrought-iron cabs and some fitted with leather seats, became attractive features. Propelled by steam or water power in the early years, then by electricity, these devices made slow ascents and descents—justifying decoration to entertain the riders as they waited for their stops. Of course, elevators made higher buildings possible, thus allowing a greater concentration of businesses within a given area.[23]

Other amenities for buildings included steam-heating systems, which made offices safer as well as more comfortable. During the 1880's steam heat became common in large houses and public buildings.

Also during the late 1870's and early 1880's, communities began installing waterworks and sewage systems. During this era, the large cities—for example, San Antonio—contracted for waterworks. As early as 1883 the small communities—for instance, Taylor—were calling for bids to construct works, which eliminated the need to haul water or install private cisterns and wells. All these public facilities were expanded rapidly; by 1890 the Houston Water Works, a corporation, had laid twelve-inch and twenty-inch mains, supplied

[23] Winston Weisman, "The Commercial Palaces of New York: 1845–1875," *Art Bulletin* 36 (1954):297. In 1893, the first electric elevator in Houston was installed in the Kiam Build-

ing, a fine Romanesque Revival work designed by Henry C. Holland, Olle J. Lorehn, and George B. Dickey, which still stands at the corner of Main and Preston Streets (Peter Rippe interview, Harris County, July 10, 1978).

FIGURE 73. Houston Water Works, Houston. *From* Art Work of Houston, *1894, Houston Public Library.*

During the last two decades of the nineteenth century, waterworks similar to these appeared in the large communities of Texas. Large standpipes augmented the water pressure in the lines.

The industrial-type buildings were designed with strict regard to function but nonetheless displayed subtle decorative features. Round and segmental arches and decorative cornice patterns enhanced the severe geometrical forms.

by artesian wells, in various neighborhoods (fig. 73). By the late 1880's Houston and other cities also had sewage systems, financed by taxes, thereby eliminating the need for the wooden backyard outhouses.[24]

All of these improvements—along with the developments in transportation—had a revolutionary effect on the development of Texas towns. Indeed, the relative effect of new technologies on cities and towns of the nineteenth century can be compared with the impact of twentieth-century transportation systems.

As these industries improving the quality of life were developing, new structures providing other civic benefits also appeared. These included market houses, where, beginning in the early 1870's, farmers could sell their products

at a central location, thereby eliminating the need for individual stands or house-to-house calling. The advantages of the market house were well expressed by a Fort Worth reporter: "Sanitary conditions of the city will be benefitted materially by this process of doing away with all the dirty meat markets and vegetable stands."[25] Although frequently simple one-story buildings were constructed, many of these markets were two-story frame or masonry structures housing other public functions on an upper level—conforming to eastern precedents.[26]

One market in Houston, constructed in 1872 following a study of facilities in large eastern cities, was a two-story building, which boasted twin towers enhanced with Classical

[24] Corner, *San Antonio de Bexar,* pp. 54–57; *Fort Worth Daily Gazette,* March 20, 1883; *Houston Daily Post,* April 10, 1895; McComb, *Houston,* pp. 127–130.

[25] *Fort Worth Democrat,* April 12, 1878.
[26] Cf. Padraic Burke, "To Market to Market," *Historic Preservation* 29 (1977):33–38.

FIGURE 74. Houston Market, Houston (1872).
From Thrall, History of Texas 1879.

Presenting a sophisticated appearance, this
market contained stalls for vendors, city offices,
and a theater. One tower supported a clock; the
other, a fire-alarm bell.

The city market also certainly had a significant
social impact on the communities. Like the market
square that preceded it, it provided a location
where a variety of people, races, and ages could
meet and visit.

decoration and housed public offices in the second story (fig. 74). The market that replaced
this structure was likewise a multifunctional
building with public facilities on the upper
floor (fig. 75). In the proposed Fort Worth
market of the 1870's, an opera house was projected for the upper story; in 1886 bids were
received in Temple on a similar type of building. In Galveston the city hall also was combined with the market, an arrangement admired by some, since it had the potential of
providing income to support the city offices
(fig. 76).[27] Although the Texas public market

has now nearly vanished, the Farmers' Market
in Weatherford survives into the 1980's, still
functioning much as the nineteenth-century
types did. Grocery stores, in which at one time
such staples as coffee, tea, and sugar were sold,
eventually made the city market obsolete.

Other public improvements included facilities for fire protection. During the nineteenth
century virtually every community experienced a major conflagration in which a number of buildings, even entire blocks, were destroyed. For example, in 1885, under the
headline "A Night in Hell," the *Galveston
Daily News* reported that four hundred dwellings had burned, leaving one thousand families homeless.[28]

Early measures to provide protection—
such as street cisterns and Fort Worth's ordinance requiring that each merchant keep two
full barrels of water on hand at all times—
were superficial and completely ineffective.
Near the end of the century continuing efforts
to improve protection resulted in the establishment of volunteer, then professional, fire departments and in the construction of buildings
to house fire-fighting equipment. Early in the
1890's, Dallas, for example, had developed a
volunteer fire department of about one hundred men. Hose carriages and hook-and-ladder trucks were pulled by hand, a steamer by
horses. However, such organizations sometimes were less than effective. When fire broke
out in Harrison County's Victorian-styled
courthouse, the fire department, located
across the street, responded but overturned
the engine. Then, when it was righted and finally did arrive, the firemen found that the
cisterns that were expected to supply the water
were dry.

Nonetheless, by the end of the century many
substantial halls containing spaces for firemen
and equipment had appeared. Central Fire
Hall in Fort Worth (1899) epitomized the durably built stations (fig. 77). Some others displayed charming decoration (fig. 78).

[27]McComb, *Houston*, pp. 72, 79–80; *Houston Daily Post*,
December 17, 1891; *Fort Worth Daily Gazette*, November 25,
1886; Howard Barnstone, *The Galveston That Was*, pp.
155–156.

[28] *Galveston Daily News*, November 14, 1885.

FIGURE 75. Houston Market, Houston (1891?). *From* Art Work of Houston, *1894,* Houston Public Library.

After a fire destroyed the 1870's market, this spacious new multifunctional structure, occupying an entire block, was built. The first floor was divided into stalls and booths. The second story contained the offices of city government, including council chambers, and a library. In addition there was a large hall for the general use of the public. Built of stone, it was designed to be a permanent structure. However, in the twentieth century, the block became a parking lot; then in 1977 the asphalt was removed, and the block was developed into a landscaped open space.

Like the city markets, the buildings serving as stations for fire-fighting equipment often were multipurpose. In 1876 Fort Worth erected a two-story brick building to house the mayor's office, jail cells, and fire engine.[29] Plans for the Denison Fire-Engine House (1885) detailed a two-story building with room for engines and horses on the lower level and offices on the upper, a common arrangement. Another representative example was built in Sherman (fig. 79).

Although, as mentioned, city hall offices were frequently combined with other facilities, structures containing only city governmental functions were often constructed. In

[29] *Fort Worth Democrat,* October 20, 1876, November 22, 1885.

such cities as Victoria, San Antonio, and Laredo, facilities for city fathers were housed in large buildings with imposing forms; Dallas and Fort Worth, too, had specialized buildings (figs. 80, 81). However, many of these city halls no longer stand; others have been much altered by additions and by the removal of details.

Other functional kinds of structures providing for the public welfare included health-care facilities. Financed by individual physicians, community funds, religious orders, or railway companies, many hospitals were built during the last three decades of the nineteenth century. Among these was the San Antonio Hospital, a Catholic institution originally located opposite the courthouse on a site that had for-

FIGURE 76. Galveston City Hall (1888). Alfred Muller, architect. *From* Harper's Weekly.

Elaborate stylistic features distinguished the French Renaissance Revival building. A grand stairway provided access to the city offices. At the corners, the oriels were distinguishing features. A high tower with a clock rose skyward, providing a lofty podium for four romantic statues representing patriotism, honor, courage, and devotion.

The building was severely damaged in the 1900 storm. Subsequently numerous features were removed: the tower and third story were taken off, along with the stair and most of the decorative features. Following the completion of a new city hall in 1916, the structure housed the police department and served as a fire station. The building was demolished in 1966.

FIGURE 77. Central Fire Hall, Fort Worth (1899). *Courtesy Fort Worth Public Library, Amon Carter Museum.*

Located on Throckmorton Street, this fire hall was an interesting structure, built of stone. The Roman arches and roll moldings enframing the openings, the tower, and the turret all contributed to the character of the building. Window planters supported on corbeling softened the hard edges of the composition.

On display for the photographer was an interesting array of equipment. Although mechanization is apparent, horses were still in use to draw the engines. After this view was taken, the hall was enlarged; then in 1938 it was razed.

FIGURE 78. Mission Hose Company No. 4 Building, San Antonio, (ca. 1880). *From* Art Work of San Antonio, *Daughters of the Republic of Texas Library, San Antonio.*

Built with walls of masonry, this building displayed fanciful details. Decorative barge boards, gingerbread, and patterns of woodwork added picturesqueness to this work designed to house fire-fighting equipment.

FIGURE 79. Sherman City Hall and Central Fire Station, Sherman (ca. 1885). *From postcard in possession of the author.*

The Sherman fire station was typical of many late-nineteenth-century buildings with similar functions. On the first floor of this building were spaces for a fire engine, hose carriage, and hook-and-ladder truck, along with stalls for the horses. At one end of the second story was located the firemen's hall. Above the mass of the building rose a tower with an alarm bell and an observatory—universal features on buildings of this type.

merly been occupied by a priest's house. Others included the Galveston City Hospital (1875), a "frame building of domestic cottage style architecture," and the Sisters of Charity Hospital (1875), a brick work in the style of the "Renaissance with Mansard roof. . . ." Both Galveston buildings were designed by Nicholas J. Clayton. In Fort Worth the Missouri Pacific Railroad Hospital was built around 1883, destroyed by fire in 1885, and then rebuilt. While the Houston Infirmary also was a frame building (fig. 82), St. Paul's Sanitarium in Dallas was built of masonry, in Romanesque Revival style (fig. 83).[30]

During these developmental years following the Civil War, the interest in cultural refinement that had bloomed during the antebellum period continued. The continuing success of societies founded earlier to encourage interest in the arts and the organization of new groups demonstrated further cultural aware-

[30] *San Antonio Express,* January 6, 1870; *Galveston Daily News,* October 3, 1875; *Fort Worth Daily Gazette,* July 20, 1883; *Dallas Morning News,* November 15, 1896.

FIGURE 80. Dallas City Hall, Dallas (1889). A. B. Bristol, architect. *From the collections of the Dallas Historical Society.*

Located on the present site of the Adolphus Hotel, this building housed the city government offices, as well as the public library. The third city hall constructed by Dallas, it was used for about twenty years before it was razed to make room for the Adolphus Hotel.

FIGURE 81. Fort Worth City Hall (1892–1893). A. N. Dawson Architectural Company, architects. *From postcard in possession of Mrs. Laura H. Portwood, Fort Worth, courtesy Amon Carter Museum.*

Located at Monroe Street and Tenth Avenue, this edifice was designed to house city governmental offices. Included on the ground level were offices for the waterworks department, tax assessor and collector, city marshall, police, city courtroom, city judge's and clerk's offices, city prison, and council chamber. Contained on the second level were the offices of the mayor, city attorney, city auditor, and city engineer and a blueprint room. On the third level was a circular auditorium. According to one reporter, the building was well ventilated through windows and corridors that extended from each side, and all the offices were well lighted.

FIGURE 82. Houston Infirmary, Houston (ca. 1880) *From* Art Work of Houston, *1894,* Houston Public Library.

The early infirmaries and hospitals often were of frame construction; hence they often burned. In this building simple wooden decorative features and a small amount of cresting provided interest on a rather plain design. The street passing near the infirmary was surfaced with planks.

FIGURE 83. St. Paul's Sanitarium, Dallas (1896–1898). J. Riely Gordon, architect. *Photo*, Art Work of Dallas, *1910*, *Archives and Research Center for Texas and Dallas History, Dallas Public Library*; *drawing*, Sketches from the Portfolio of James Riely Gordon, *Dielmann Collection, Daughters of the Republic of Texas Library, San Antonio.*

Although the completed building was somewhat simpler than the proposed design, the sanitarium was nonetheless a fine Romanesque Revival work. The tower extended through all the stories and provided ventilation for the hallways. Below the main entrance was a driveway by which sick individuals arrived and the remains of deceased were removed—without being seen by the public.

The building, which was ornamented with red Pecos sandstone, was demolished in 1963, when a new hospital was opened.

ness. Also, as in previous years, a cultural association between morals and art continued to be proclaimed by some local social critics. The growth of theater arts, for example, was encouraged by the press, but not all believed it to be beneficial. Some apparently considered the theater immoral; others considered this form of entertainment to be ". . . of a refined and refining character."[31] Further, some argued that the theater would improve intelligence and taste and would be good for the business of a community. Other associations between morality and art were suggested in an article the *Houston Daily Post* published considering the "moral monstrosity" of New York architecture.[32]

While there was concern about the effects of art and architecture on the moral conditions of the state, little was said about the immorality of technology during these years. Although it seems likely that some Texans read Englishman John Ruskin's *Seven Lamps of Architecture* and some may have been familiar with English critic William Morris' objections to the machine, few recorded negative reactions to mass-produced art in Texas. While Ruskin viewed cast iron as a "dishonest material," in Texas, as in other parts of the United States, the use of this new material in commercial architecture was considered an indication of architectural progress. Technology naturally was associated closely with growth and prosperity; moreover, mass production, regardless of quality, made more things available to more people than had ever been possible before in history. Even the middle classes now could afford to acquire taste.[33]

During the 1870's, community prosperity and progressiveness were quite apparent in

commercial architecture. While mercantiles, hotels, and other commercial enterprises in newly established communities continued to occupy wood-fronted and arcaded, masonry-fronted buildings, similar to structures of antebellum days, in the rapidly growing cities increasing population and thriving business were evidenced by the greater floor areas and higher facades of commercial enterprises. Many of the commercial buildings of the latter part of the nineteenth century were designed with one or more floors for display or storage. Often the second and third floors contained additional displays or large halls for meetings. To enhance the masonry-fronted buildings, a variety of patterns of brick and stone was used; on the stonework different textures and tool marks provided additional interest. To shade the fronts and openings, porches, supported by thin columns, were frequently projected over sidewalks.

Along with commercial developments and improved transportation came new architectural technology in the form of cast-iron and plate-glass fronts. Cast-iron building components had been employed in Texas prior to the Civil War, but, due to the difficulty weight posed for transportation, their use had been restricted to the coastal towns.

Federal buildings from the 1850's incorporated masonry and cast iron as a means to promote the infant yet rapidly developing new metal industry. The Old Federal Building in Galveston, originally the Galveston Custom House and Post Office—now a national landmark—was completed in 1860 according to the plans of Ammi B. Young, supervising architect of the treasury. It incorporated columns, balustrades, and window details of cast iron manufactured in New York. On the interior, iron stairs provided communication between the post office on the ground floor and the courtroom on the second.

The use of cast iron in this Galveston federal building was contemporaneous with developments in the East—culturally, Galveston was linked to the East, via the sea. The advantages

[31] *Galveston Daily News*, September 6, 1868.
[32] *Houston Daily Post*, November 5, 1887.
[33] Several editions of John Ruskin's *The Seven Lamps of Architecture* were available in the United States. The first appeared in London (published by Smith, Elder & Co.) in 1849. Subsequent editions appeared throughout the last half of the century. Morris' thought is discussed in Herbert L. Sussman, *Victorians and the Machine: The Literary Response to Technology*, pp. 104–134.

of iron included fire resistance, plasticity, and economy. Resistance to flames and the capacity to bear heavy loads had given impetus to the development of functional iron structural systems for mill buildings in England at the turn of the nineteenth century. Then manufacturers abroad and in the United States discovered the aesthetic and economic potential of the material. With iron, complex details imitating forms that originally had been time-consuming products of the stonecutter's chisel could be cast efficiently, once molds had been formed.

Because of the economy inherent in mass production and the relative ease of manufacture of metal components with complex forms and details, iron prefabrication had been exploited by such eastern manufacturers as Daniel Badger and James Bogardus. During the 1840's prefabricated iron components were used extensively in American facades; between 1850 and 1880—sometimes called the cast-iron age—commercial buildings with iron fronts appeared throughout the United States.[34]

Catalogs illustrating a variety of details provided Texans with opportunities to become familiar with the type of cast-iron architecture that lined the streets of such cities as New York, Savannah, and St. Louis. From these catalogs they could select and order their own assemblages (fig. 84). As early as 1841, articles in Texas newspapers describing iron buildings in Europe and the East must have created awareness of the new material. Then in 1854, publication in local papers of detailed descriptions of the construction of Harper's Building, New York City, an important iron-fronted and iron-structured work, may have increased interest.[35]

Eastern manufacturers of cast iron advertised their products to Texans. In 1858 the Builders' Foundry of Philadelphia advertised the availability of a wide variety of architectural components in the *Texas Almanac* (fig. 85). By this time some of the products had already been used in Texas; the firm listed several references in Galveston, including Ball Hutchings & Co. In 1870, in the *Galveston Daily News*, Robert Wood & Co., also of Philadelphia, advertised ornamental iron products, which included "cemetery adornments . . . chairs, summer house, iron stairs, . . ." and storefronts.[36]

Although the use of metal building components in the inland communities would await the development of the railroads, even prior to the Civil War iron was employed in a number of commercial buildings in Houston and Galveston. Among the fine examples of commercial cast iron is the Pillot Building in Houston, a structure that was completed sometime between 1857 and 1869, was nearly lost during Houston redevelopment, but still stands. Another was the Willard Richardson Building, Galveston, which was demolished in 1962. The Edmund L. Ufford Building in the Island City, with its iron window hoods and street fronts, survived until a fire destroyed it in 1978 (fig. 86).

While the ironwork used in antebellum storefronts was imported from eastern foundries, locally produced architectural iron became available following the Civil War. During the late 1840's, 1850's, and Reconstruction, Texas ore had been processed into iron bars by charcoal-fired furnaces. However, at that time, most of the iron was molded into household items, machinery, and farm implements. In 1845 a foundry to produce ironwork was established in Galveston, and in 1851 one was opened in Houston. In 1870 Kelly's Iron Foundry near Jefferson was man-

---

[34] Sigfried Giedion, *Space, Time, and Architecture*, p. 200. However, the use of cast iron continued well into the twentieth century. It reached its height probably in the 1880's.

[35] The *Telegraph and Texas Register* (Houston), August 4, 1841, described a church in London, England, built entirely out of cast iron. The *Standard* (Clarksville), October 7, 1854, described the Harper's Building. Texans also may have read about

the building in *Harper's New Monthly* 32 (December, 1865–May, 1866):1–31.

[36] *Galveston Daily News*, August 24, 1870.

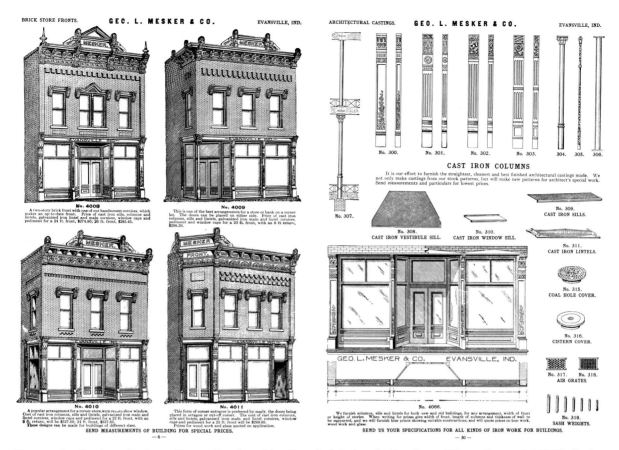

FIGURE 84. Designs for Store Fronts Produced by Geo. L. Mesker & Co. *From "Store Fronts,"* APT Bulletin, *no. 4, 1977.*

In its plant in Evansville, Indiana, George Mesker's company manufactured architectural iron components for buildings that were distributed throughout the United States. Builders of commercial structures could obtain entire fronts or individual items such as cast-iron sills, columns, and lintels and galvanized-iron fronts, cornices, window caps, and ceilings.

According to the manufacturer, the components could be combined in various compositions and arranged on buildings of any width and height. The manufacturer also furnished the show windows, sashes, doors, and glass.

Included among the many widely dispersed Texas communities where Mesker fronts appeared were Meridian and Canadian.

ufacturing such products as "gin gearing, hollowware, wash kettles, sugar mills, evaporators, andirons, etc." [37]

Apparently, it was not until after Reconstruction that local foundries began producing building components. During the 1880's a number of Texas foundries were built to man-

ufacture architectural iron in competition with eastern firms. Early in the decade, for example, the Phoenix Iron Works, Houston, advertised its commercial products in *Burke's Almanac*. Also in the early 1880's a plant had been developed at Rusk to be operated by the state prison. At this foundry about eight hundred tons of iron were cast into columns, pedestals, bases, and stairs for the present Texas capitol. In 1882 the Vulcan Foundry and Machine Works, Fort Worth, claimed the man-

[37] S. O. Young, *A Thumb-Nail History of the City of Houston, Texas*, p. 132; Raymond E. White, "Cotton Ginning in Texas to 1861," *Southwestern Historical Quarterly* 61 (October, 1957):266; *Galveston Daily News*, August 23, 1870.

BUILDERS' FOUNDRY,

PHILADELPHIA.

IRON FRONTS AND BUILDING WORK,

In all its varieties, furnished at the shortest notice. Also,

Mettam's Patent Revolving Iron Shutters,

Castings for Machinery, and Jobbing of all kinds.

The undersigned are prepared to furnish, at the shortest notice,

Iron Fronts, of any design,

With or without Mettam's Patent Revolving Iron Shutters, a new and superior article.

GIRDERS, of all kinds and sizes.

COLUMNS, SHUTTER BOXES AND LINTELS,

ORNAMENTAL WINDOW HEADS AND SILLS,

Caps and Bases for Pilasters and Columns,

BRACKETS FOR CORNICES,

ENRICHED MOULDINGS AND ORNAMENTS,

AND EVERY VARIETY OF

BUILDERS' CAST IRON WORK.

They would refer to E. S. Wood, Ball, Hutchings & Co., H. Rosenberg, and Richardson & Co., Galveston; L. P. Blair & Co., Baltimore; A. J. Bowers, Richmond, Va.; J. K. Goodwin & Bro., Selma, Ala.; and to Architects and Builders generally throughout the United States.

Estimates furnished to parties applying personally or by letter.

SANSON & FARRAND,

Corner of 12th and Willow Streets,

PHILADELPHIA.

E. S. WOOD, Agent, Galveston.

FIGURE 85. Advertisement, Builders' Foundry (1858). *From* Texas Almanac, *1858*.

Advertisements such as this appeared in various publications. Although a number of advantages were claimed for the material—including safety from being struck by lightning and fire resistance—this ad primarily appeals to interest in structural and decorative uses.

Evolution in Technology and Taste

FIGURE 86. Edmund L. Ufford Building, Galveston (1860). *Galveston Historical Foundation, Galveston.*

Such cast-iron fronts as this, with its finely detailed ironwork, attested to the prosperity and progressiveness of Galveston during the 1860's and 1870's. Constructed by John Brown, a local builder, these commercial blocks had upper-story windows with cast-iron lintels and ground-level columns of cast iron enclosing brick piers. The doors were originally French type.

The Ufford was destroyed by a fire of suspicious origin in 1978. Advertised in the 1866–1867 *Galveston City Directory* as "Ufford's Iron Front Fire-Proof Building," it had survived several other fires prior to 1978.

ufacture of the heaviest iron front "ever made south or west of St. Louis."[38]

The "ironclad" became a hallmark of commercial progress. Newspapers frequently extolled the beginning of work on a new metal and glass facade. In the 1870's and early 1880's many iron and plate-glass fronts appeared in San Antonio, Dallas, Fort Worth, Galveston, and Houston (fig. 87). The common use of iron and glass, along with the uniformity imposed by equal lot widths, provided unity, yet variations in height and details added interest (fig. 88).

The iron front was as functional as it was fashionable. Large areas of plate glass sepa-

rated by thin columns allowed light to penetrate more deeply into the deep interior spaces than did the antebellum arcaded masonry fronts with French doors. Moreover, these show windows allowed for the development of sidewalk displays—although some natural ventilation was sacrificed with the elimination of doors. Moreover, in Texas as elsewhere, the iron columns provided an economical medium for new types of decorative features, for which the demand began developing during the 1870's.

The complete iron front, sometimes found in the East, was infrequently used in Texas. The typical Texas design consisted of slender iron columns, usually bearing a foundry imprint, painted white or brown to inhibit rusting, and supporting an iron or wooden beam

[38] James Burke, Jr., *Burke's Texas Almanac and Immigrants' Handbook*, p. 226; *Houston Daily Post*, December 29, 1889; *Fort Worth Daily Democrat-Advance*, March 16, 1882.

FIGURE 87. Masonic Lodge Building, Houston (1868). *From* Art Work of Houston, *1894,* Houston Public Library.

Metal components were used in the front of this handsome building. Iron columns supported the ground-story girders spanning the glass openings. Above, galvanized iron features apparently were employed for the several different designs of the window caps. A wide cornice, also of sheet metal, boldly terminated the composition.

spanning the plates of glass, which ordinarily were held by wooden mullions. Above this rose a heavy masonry front, perforated by window openings with metal lintels or hoods, and a sheet-metal cornice, all modeled after Classical architectural features and ordinarily painted in colors contrasting with the brick or stone. By the 1880's the popularity of the thin iron column was such that in the Land Title Block, Fort Worth (1889), wood was used to imitate metal supports for girders that were actually supported by masonry walls.

In addition to cast iron, a number of firms were established to produce galvanized-iron sheet-metal architectural components. Specializing in galvanized-iron cornice manufac-

ture, Harry Brothers of Fort Worth included in their listings "corrugated iron roofing and siding, and the patent-corrugated iron ceiling, metallic shingles, etc." In addition they made sheet-iron "weatherboarding," which they claimed was fireproof. Economically mass-produced and light weight, galvanized-iron components became widely popular throughout the state.[39]

Galvanized iron, then, was used for a variety of details on both interiors and exteriors. Cornices with bold projections, brackets, modillions, and so forth, terminated the facade compositions of innumerable commer-

[39] *Fort Worth Daily Gazette,* August 8, 1885.

FIGURE 88. Main Street, south from Franklin Avenue, Houston (photo ca. 1890). *From* Art Work of Houston, *1894,* Houston Public Library.

Excepting the three-story T. W. House Bank building in the foreground, this street scene presents the popularity of prefabricated metal components in commercial architecture. Most of the buildings have cast-iron supports at the ground level. Above this the window openings are decorated with galvanized sheet-metal caps. Finally cornices, complete with a full panoply of Renaissance features, finials, and flagpoles, complete the compositions. However, the small brick two-story building in the near foreground epitomizes the appearance of commercial blocks before metal became available and popular. Virtually all the metal-component structures are gone.

cial buildings and courthouses. A wide variety of standard patterns was available from several catalogs. For exterior work, in addition to cornices, there were available window hoods—in the form of stilted, segmental, and round arches—and wall coverings, all imitating stone. On interiors, metal stamped with delightful, intricate patterns replaced beaded tongue-and-groove board ceilings.

While a simple application of sheet metal consisted only of a galvanized-iron cornice, in some instances entire fronts (except the ground-level columns and plate glass) were sheathed with the material, attached to a light wooden framework. As eastern manufacturers of cast-iron fronts had done in previous decades, Texans often designed sheet-metal decoration using details from European Classical buildings of the past. However, in some cases components for false fronts were ornamented only with repetitive geometrical designs.

Although iron was fire resistant, it was not fireproof. The numerous conflagrations that occurred during the last half of the nineteenth century demonstrated again and again that unprotected iron exposed to intense heat deformed drastically, causing many structures to collapse. Although builders continued to use iron without fireproofing in small communities well into the twentieth century, by the late 1880's architects in the large cities commonly specified that iron be protected by enclosing it with terra cotta, bricks, or plaster, as was being done in Chicago and New York City.

Other developments in iron technology were related to transportation. In the rural regions as well as the urban areas, new metal bridges spanned streams, rivers, and passes, replacing the ford and the ferry. The construction of many new iron-trussed bridges was contracted as the wealth of the counties increased. These new metal bridges superseded wooden designs that had appeared earlier, although works of timber were also built in later years. The tradition of building with wood included several covered bridges that no longer stand. A fine example of the all-weather crossing spanned Wilson Creek, on the Old Dallas Road southwest of McKinney; another was built across the San Marcos near Gonzales.

Although the trussed bridge was most common (fig. 89), suspension bridges also were used in rural areas—they were light and easy to transport. In Fayette County there remain several suspension bridges, and throughout the state a large number of trussed iron bridges are still in use. Hunt County had at least eight wire-cable bridges.[40] In the early 1890's, a significant number of cable bridges were contracted. One of the most graceful of the suspension bridges, built somewhat later, was the bridge across the Colorado at Bend (fig. 90).

With spans ranging from about 50 feet to about 200 feet, other suspension bridges crossed rivers in the mid-easterly sections of the state. Among the important spans, a suspension bridge was built across the Brazos River at Waco in 1868–1870—commenced a year before the famous Brooklyn Bridge was begun in New York City. Spanning some 475 feet with fourteen cables one and a half inches in diameter, it still survives, although the supporting brick piers have been plastered and many of the decorative features have been removed. The wire cables were manufactured by August Roebling of New York.[41]

The railway companies that made possible the economical transportation of iron building and bridge components also themselves exploited the capabilities of iron. Although the use of wooden trestles to support rails across ravines and rivers was continued, daring spans with iron trusses also were realized.

In addition to the bridges, trains required other types of structures, few of which remain today. Service structures were erected for repair and maintenance of rolling stock. Then roundhouses, with their turntables, built on circular, segmental plans, were constructed in many towns, including Denton, Sweetwater, and El Paso (fig. 91). Cypress water tanks filled by pumps or windmills to supply the massive steam engines have also virtually disappeared. Also near the railroad tracks, grain elevators, built with compartments of wooden planks laid up flatwise, began appearing at the end of the century—almost none remain.

Within the towns they served, the railway companies built terminal buildings on a scale that reflected the activity of the community. In places with small populations, these were simple and repetitive in form; the companies apparently used standard designs. They consisted of frame buildings with broad, overhanging eaves, occasionally incorporating a few decorative brackets or patterns of wood

---

[40] *Fort Worth Daily Gazette*, April 19, 1888.

[41] Roger Norman Conger, "The Waco Suspension Bridge," *Texana* 1 (1963):193–196.

FIGURE 89. Galveston Highway Bridge (1892–1893). *From* Art Work in Galveston, *Texas Collection, Barker Texas History Center, University of Texas at Austin.*

Built near the end of the century, this bridge provided communication between the coast and Galveston Island. A series of bowstring arch-trusses, mounted on concrete piers, supported the roadway. However, the bridge was destined for a short life; the devastating hurricane of 1900 demolished the work.

FIGURE 90. Bridge across the Colorado at Bend (1902). *Texas Highway Department, Austin.*

Connecting the counties of San Saba and Lampasas at Bend, this was a graceful work that served for nearly three-quarters of a century. To assist in the construction of the work, a falsework of pine and cedar was set up. The cables were then installed, and the steel was placed and riveted. This was the only suspension bridge ever maintained by the Texas Highway Department.

Designed for horse and wagon traffic, the bridge became unsafe for heavy vehicle loads. Consequently it was taken down in the early 1970's. A new plate girder bridge built upstream now connects the two river banks.

FIGURE 91. Atchison, Topeka and Santa Fe Railway Roundhouse, El Paso (1881). *Atchison, Topeka and Santa Fe Railway, Chicago.*

Roundhouses similar to this were common sights in cities containing railroad service yards. Laid out on a circular plan, they contained stalls for servicing steam locomotives. The engines were brought onto a turntable that revolved until the track to the appropriate service area was reached. The locomotive was then driven into the service shed.

siding. In form, buildings were long and narrow, containing passenger services at one end and a freight storage room at the other. While many of these have been lost, many others have been moved from their original sites and converted into homes, antique shops, and so forth. Nonetheless, a good many extant stations remain unused in small communities throughout the state.

During the developmental years of railroading in the cities served by more than one line, each company built its own terminal. However, during the golden era of railroading, early in the twentieth century, these were all replaced or supplemented by union terminals serving all lines—few of the nineteenth-century individual terminals remain in the large cities.

In Texas, as often happens with major historical events, the Civil War marked a turning point in taste. Although the use of Greek details continued for about a decade thereafter,

the public was developing a fondness for picturesqueness. Then too, a natural desire for change contributed further to an admiration of ornateness.

This shift toward the picturesque was particularly apparent in buildings associated with cultural advancement, where features reflecting the aesthetics of other sections of the country were incorporated. During the latter part of the nineteenth century, trends in architectural style appearing in prospering Texas cities connected to the East by the railroads certainly were influenced by the popular tastemakers of the period. Both *Godey's Lady's Book* and *Frank Leslie's Illustrated Newspaper* published a number of items on taste in architecture and furnishings that must have been read in postbellum days by many people in Texas. In addition, many Texans probably read some of the popular books on taste, including one of the seven American editions (1872–1883) of Sir Charles Eastlake's *Hints on Household*

Taste. Such architectural journals as *American Architect and Building News,* like the journals of today, greatly influenced those who practiced architecture.

Progressive Texans living in the state's commercial centers were inclined to demonstrate through fashionable architectural designs that they were on a par with the established sections of the United States. Substantial buildings clothed in elaborate decoration conforming to historical styles that were fashionable in the cultural centers of the East provided psychological security, assuring residents, investors, and prospective immigrants of the progressiveness and stability of the cities. Provincialism was considered a sign of economic and cultural stagnation.

Local newspapers printed laudatory descriptions of cities and of projected and realized buildings, extolling architecture as an indication of cultural advancement. Similar to those published in other cities of the West, artwork books, with minimal text and a number of handsome photographs of buildings, were further manifestations of this spirit. Typical public pride in architecture was expressed by the *Fort Worth Democrat,* which described the 1876 Tarrant County Courthouse as "an ornament and a credit to the county." Over a decade later the same spirit prompted the proclamation in Houston that "House's bank building will be one of the handsomest and best appointed bank buildings in the South." In Fort Worth a new high school was lauded as "an ornament to the city . . . and . . . one of the most elegant buildings in the state."[42] In Houston, the proposed Masonic Temple (built in 1868) was expected to become "the most imposing structure in the state." In 1877 a reporter wrote that the public buildings in Fort Worth "testify of the spirit of enterprise that pervades our people, and are typical of the solidity and substantial character of the city to

which they belong." Still later, the *Houston Post* reported that the North Texas Insane Asylum, Terrell, was "a fair reflex of modern architecture typical of the advanced civilization of the age."[43]

The transition from provincial and antebellum styles to contemporary postbellum fashions commanding this public esteem occurred gradually, particularly in the rural regions, where either traditions had become strong or isolation and primitivism slowed shifts in taste. In any event, this transition at first consisted of the application of fanciful decoration to traditional forms. For houses, Greek Revival plans were retained, but the Classical orders of antebellum porches were replaced by jigsaw and spindle work, and finials and crestings were placed on roof ridges. Often these details were added years after a building was originally finished, when enlargements or remodelings took place.

Many houses in the state displayed these transitional trends. Among those now gone were the F. Groos House (1872) in San Antonio (fig. 92) and the James Rives House (1875) in Mission Valley (fig. 93).

The change in taste from an appreciation of simple Greek Revival details to a delight over more intricate arrangements also appeared in the public buildings of the late 1860's and 1870's. The Texas courthouse of this era was on the traditional Greek Revival plan but, in some cases, was larger and incorporated more complex decorative features than had appeared previously—a development stimulated by an improving economy accompanied by a desire for newness and change.

The plan of the Bosque County Courthouse, Meridian (1873), built by A. J. George, was representative. According to the specifications, the edifice was to be forty-six feet square, with walls twenty-four feet high and two feet thick. Corridors were to divide the ground story into four offices, sixteen feet

[42] *Fort Worth Democrat,* September 27, 1876; *Houston Daily Post,* June 1, 1889; *Fort Worth Weekly Gazette,* November 14, 1889.

[43] *Dallas Herald,* June 27, 1868; *Fort Worth Democrat,* March 25, 1877; *Houston Daily Post,* October 3, 1883.

FIGURE 92. F. Groos House, San Antonio (1872). *Daughters of the Republic of Texas Library, San Antonio.*
    Built on Alameda (now East Commerce) Street by a successful banker, this house was on a large scale. The porch columns, along with their complete classical entablature, were massive. By the time it was erected, the Greek Revival was no longer fashionable in eastern cities, and the attenuated design of details and lack of a projecting two-story portico indicated that by this time the romantic meaning of the Greek mode had lost its impact in Texas. The triangular pediment with its modillions suggests the Italianate mode, which had become fashionable in the state.

FIGURE 93. James Rives House, Mission Valley (1875). *Historic American Buildings Survey, Library of Congress, Washington, D.C.*

With its five-bay front, gable ends with chimneys, and center-matched siding under the porch, this house displayed typical Greek Revival details. However, changes in taste that brought admiration for applied decoration show in the balustrade—a Classical feature—and the use of thin columns supporting a lintel trimmed with scallops—Victorian features.

square. The second floor contained the courtroom and three offices, each ten feet wide. On the exterior, the doorways were spanned by semicircular arches, which were not used in Greek Revival architecture, and on the east, for public announcements, a door opened onto the portico from the second floor. The whole was crowned with a "6×6 observatory in the center, banistered. . . ."[44]

The transition in style was apparent in many Reconstruction courthouses, but none of these remain.[45] With a form similar to many antebellum works, the Coryell County Courthouse, Gatesville (1872), was a square, five-bay building, with a hipped roof accented by chimneys (fig. 94). The 1873 Comanche County Courthouse, Comanche, was similar, but it was three bays by five. The Ellis County Courthouse, Waxahachie, of the 1870's, likewise was on a traditional antebellum plan; however, Italianate details, including a bracketed cornice, quoins, and windowcaps, which had become popular in the East several decades before, were incorporated into the form (fig. 95). In similar spirit the Dallas County Courthouse, Dallas, represented a continuing development of this trend and was one of the finest Italianate buildings of the period (fig. 96).

[44] Office of the County Clerk, County Commissioners Court Minutes, Bosque County, vol. A (May 29, 1873), pp. 497–498.

[45] The oldest courthouse still in use is in Cass County. Although remodeling has rendered the old part unrecognizable, it is believed that one extant section was constructed in 1866. The oldest courthouse in use with an original section visible is the Kendall County Courthouse, Boerne, which was built in 1869.

An addition was made in 1909, after the plans of Alfred Giles, and remodelings have been done in recent years.

FIGURE 94. Coryell County Courthouse, Gatesville (1872). *Texas Historical Association, Austin.*

Replacing a one-story wooden building, this limestone courthouse epitomized those erected in the rural county seats with relatively small populations. The rhythm of openings in the facade, as well as the plans, with offices on the first floor and courtroom on the second, was similar to that of many antebellum courthouses. However, change in taste is indicated by the round-arched openings providing access to the breezeways and the windows with fanlight transoms in the second story. This building served county functions until 1897, when a new structure, designed by W. C. Dodson, was erected.

FIGURE 95. Ellis County Courthouse, Waxahachie (1870–1873). *Sims Public Library, Waxahachie.*

The third courthouse of Ellis County, this distinctive edifice replaced a two-story frame building, twenty-four by thirty-six, built by David P. Fearis. This new courthouse, sixty feet square, was built of limestone, on a traditional plan. Four spacious offices were created by the corridors that divided the ground floor into quadrants. On the second floor was located a courtroom with a high ceiling. The cost was about $40,000, a large sum at the time.

The building was distinguished by fine details. A bracketted cornice and a handsome cupola provided character felt to be appropriate for the county government. In 1894 this building was reduced to ruins to make room for the present courthouse, designed by J. Riely Gordon.

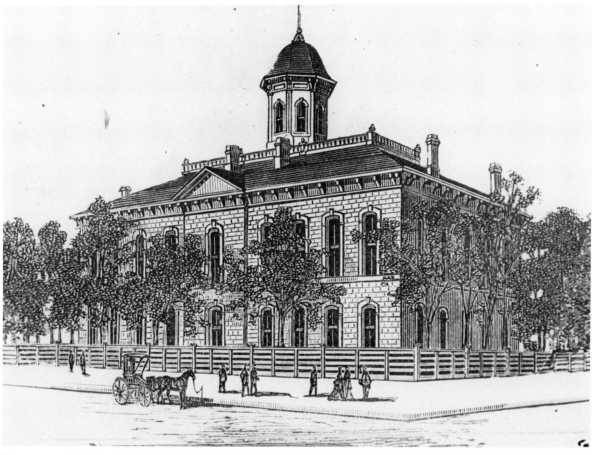

FIGURE 96. Dallas County Courthouse, Dallas (1871–1873). *Dallas Public Library.*

After the antebellum Greek Revival courthouse was condemned and sold, this fine edifice was constructed; it was the third for the county. The walls were limestone, quarried within the county. Less than ten years after it had been completed it burned, but the walls remained. These were incorporated into a new, more elaborate structure (fig. 98).

The reflection of other trends from other sections of the country also indicated a strong demand for new character. Although it never became popular, the octagonal style, which had previously appeared in a few residences elsewhere in the United States, appeared in Bosque County in the Johnson-Bridges house (ca. 1861), which incorporated two octagonal rooms, with walls of concrete separated by a breezeway, all under one roof, similar to the arrangement of a double log cabin. Although falling to ruins, this structure still stands. The octagonal style also was embodied in the Tarrant County Courthouse of 1876 (fig. 97),

which was destroyed before the turn of the century in order to make room for the present courthouse. Another octagonal building, also gone, was erected at Baylor University when the campus was located at Independence.[46]

A change in taste from Classical repose to Romantic picturesqueness was apparent

[46] The octagon mode was popular in the United States during the 1850's and was promoted by Orson Squire Fowler, a phrenologist. According to Fowler, a floor plan in the shape of an octagon enclosed more area for a given length of perimeter. It also was considered more beautiful than rectangular forms. Examples of octagon houses in Texas included the E. S. Perkins House, Houston (ca. 1850), with Classical details, and the President's House, Baylor University, Independence (ca. 1860).

FIGURE 97. Tarrant County Courthouse, Fort Worth (1876). Thomas and Warner, architects and builders. *From Thrall*, A Pictorial History of Texas.

After flames consumed the antebellum courthouse of Tarrant County, the county commissioners contracted this unusual building in octagonal style. Projecting from alternating sides of the octagonal mass toward the four corners of the public square, the wings contained county offices, judges' quarters, and jury rooms. Courtrooms occupied the lower and upper floors of the main mass. On the exterior, the walls of stone were finished with stucco, to simulate a brownstone finish. The architects were praised by the *Fort Worth Democrat* for being "brave enough to get out of the beaten track, and present the people of Fort Worth and the county a model which is likely to be largely copied in public building" (March 25, 1877).

FIGURE 98. Dallas County Courthouse, Dallas (remodeled, 1881). James E. Flanders, architect. *From the collections of the Dallas Historical Society.*

After the third Dallas County Courthouse was partially destroyed by fire in 1880, the building was rebuilt with more space and more elaborate stylistic features, as shown here. A third story was incorporated under a Mansard roof and a high tower with Classical features was added to crown the composition. All this provided a more fashionable architectural statement. Located nearby was a jail, which was connected to the courtroom level of the courthouse by a bridge.

In 1890 the courthouse again burned. Subsequently, the Romanesque Revival building that today stands on the public square was erected.

too, with the growth of admiration for buildings incorporating the Mansardic roofs of the Second Empire style. This mode, which included Renaissance features made popular in the France of Napoleon III, became fashionable throughout the United States during the 1870's and was considered—in part, at least, because of the influence of the Louvre—to be an ideal form for public buildings. Alfred B. Mullet, supervising architect of the treasury, utilized that style in the design of the State, War and Navy Building, Washington, D.C. (1871–1875). This influential governmental building apparently was much admired in Texas; about a decade after its completion, one prominent Texas architect proclaimed in an address to fellow professionals that it was "one of the most beautiful on the continent." [47]

After the Civil War in Texas, building remodelings incorporating Mansard roofs indicated the popularity that had developed for the Second Empire style. A Mansard roof was

[47] *Houston Daily Post*, January 18, 1888.

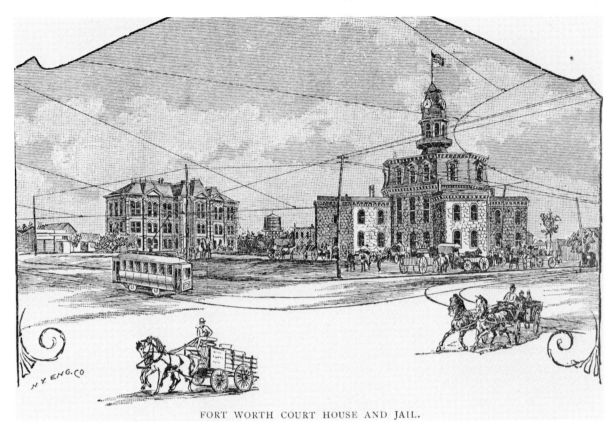

FORT WORTH COURT HOUSE AND JAIL.

FIGURE 99. Tarrant County Courthouse and Jail, Fort Worth (remodeled, 1881). J. J. Kane, architect. *From The City of Fort Worth and the State of Texas, courtesy John W. Hackney and Amon Carter Museum.*

Perhaps due to increasing county growth, as well as progressive attitudes, the county courthouse that had been completed in the latter part of the 1870's was remodeled only a few years later. Nonetheless, by 1891 agitation for a new courthouse had begun. In 1895 the present courthouse with pink Burnet granite walls in Renaissance Revival style was completed.

installed over the Greek Revival Main Building at Austin College, Huntsville (1851–1852), although the original lines have now been restored. After it partially burned in 1880, the Italianate-style Dallas County Courthouse was rebuilt, and an imposing Mansard roof and large tower were added (fig. 98). Likewise the Tarrant County Courthouse was remodeled, with the addition of Mansardic roofs over the wings and center octagon; even the lines of the tower roof were altered to fit the style (fig. 99). Since both the Italianate and Second Empire modes included Classical Renaissance details in their vocabularies, these remodelings could be realized in an organic manner.

The Second Empire style also became fashionable for new buildings. In Austin and other cities where residents were knowledgeable of eastern taste, public buildings were erected in full-blown architectural styles in vogue in other sections of the country. On the Baylor University campus in Independence, a new hall was crowned with a Mansard roof (fig. 100). In Austin, several years after the railroad arrived, work was underway on a new Travis County Courthouse (1875–1876) in the then-popular French style (fig. 101). This edifice was finished shortly after the completion of the State, War and Navy Building and the beginning of the work on Philadelphia City Hall (1871–1881), the latter of which also had a

FIGURE 100. Tryon Hall, Men's Campus, Baylor University, Independence (1860's). *Texas Collection, Baylor University, Waco.*

Excavations for the foundations of this hall were commenced in the 1860's; however, work was sporadic and the building had not been finished when Baylor was moved to Waco in 1886. The central-hall-type plan that was used was quite consistent with antebellum traditions, but the details reflected changing taste. The pronounced stringcourse, stilted-arched openings, and Mansard roof with dormers were all characteristic of the fashionable Second Empire style.

FIGURE 101. Travis County Courthouse, Austin (1875–1876). Jacob E. Larmour, architect. *From* Art Work of Austin, *Austin–Travis County Collection, Austin Public Library.*

Designed by a prominent Austin architect, this edifice displayed both straight- and convex-profiled Mansard roofs—hallmarks of the Second Empire style. Corner pavilions crowned with crestings contributed to the picturesqueness of the structure.

FIGURE 102. Lamar County Courthouse, Paris (1874–1875). *From Thrall*, A Pictorial History of Texas.

By the 1870's the antebellum courthouse that had been built for Lamar County in 1846–1847 was in poor physical condition. Late in 1873 Charles Wheelock of Sherman submitted to the commissioners court plans for a new building. Construction by contractor John McDonald was subsequently authorized, and the old courthouse was destroyed.

Wheelock designed a monumental work. The Second Empire style incorporating flat-sided Mansard roofs provided an up-to-date appearance that was much admired in the 1870's. This building served for two decades, after which it was declared unsafe and was demolished to make room for another new courthouse.

FIGURE 103. Gregg County Courthouse, Longview (1879). F. E. Ruffini, architect. *Archives Division, Texas State Library, Austin.*

Built in a county organized only in 1873, this courthouse also displayed Second Empire features. Noteworthy details included both Roman and stilted arches, pilasters of colossal order with carved capitals, and cut stonework around the entrance. A strongly profiled stringcourse at the base of these pilasters created a base for the first story. Pilasters below this were rusticated, as if to create the effect of stone construction.

This courthouse was demolished in 1897 to make room for a new brick structure. This latter building also was replaced—in 1932 by the present courthouse.

FIGURE 104. Galveston County Courthouse, Galveston (1875). Nicholas J. Clayton, architect. *From Art Work in Galveston, Texas Collection, Barker Texas History Center, University of Texas at Austin.*

This building was a monumental cubical design, with massing that recalled some of the courthouses built about the same time in some New England cities—for example, Providence, Rhode Island. The entrance was emphasized by a pavilion, surmounted by a triangular pediment and convex Mansard roof. A broad cornice, high chimneys, delicate roof cresting, and window hoods, with designs that varied at each floor, provided stylistic distinction.

strong influence on taste in public-building design. The Lamar County Courthouse, Paris (1874–1875), and the Gregg County Courthouse, Longview (1879), also were in this style (figs. 102, 103). A large-scale application of the style appeared in the Galveston County Courthouse (fig. 104).

Mansard roofs even crowned many commercial works, albeit the Second Empire style was best employed in freestanding structures, where facades with advancing and receding planes could be developed plastically. Nonetheless, pilasters, chimneys, and dormers all could be incorporated into designs to produce richness of effect. Exemplifying this were both the City National Bank, Fort Worth (fig. 105), and the A. E. Kiesling Drug Store, Houston (fig. 106). The Tremont Opera House, Galveston (1871), another fine example of the Mansardic mode, has been gone for many years (fig. 107).

Transitions in taste likewise were apparent in the ecclesiastical edifices of the period—a trend that had begun before the Civil War. There were churches built in the Gothic Revival style before the Civil War—for example the Catholic Cathedral, Galveston (1847–1848), which still stands. After the war, though, more Classical building forms began displaying Gothic stylistic elements. In Jefferson, the Catholic church (1867), also extant, was a typical Classical form, although pointed-arched openings continued to reveal a decline in the authority of the Greek Revival. In Texas, public taste was coming to favor more picturesqueness and architectural complexity than the reposed Greek provided.

Opportunities for professional architects developed along with needs for large and complex buildings incorporating new technology and fashionable design. Most architects practicing during the latter part of the century had prepared for the profession by serving apprenticeships with other firms or by gaining experience with building contractors. Not until the doors of Texas A&M were opened in 1876 were there opportunities for state residents to

FIGURE 105. City National Bank Building, Fort Worth (ca. 1885). Haggart & Sanguinet, architects. *From* The City of Fort Worth and the State of Texas, *courtesy John W. Hackney and Amon Carter Museum.*

Representative of the Second Empire style in commercial work, this bank building featured a Mansard roof, stilted arches, and Classical columns. Through the scale provided by the people in the street, the artist depicted the structure as being somewhat larger than it actually was.

obtain academic preparation in both architecture and building construction. By the turn of the century (1904–1905) a curriculum in architectural engineering at A&M provided training that included courses in design, lighting, structures, heating and ventilation, and sanitary engineering. However, even with the new educational opportunities, during the nineteenth century immigrant architects composed the greater part of the qualified profession. Many of the most skilled individuals

FIGURE 106. A. E. Kiesling Drug Store, Houston (1875). Eugene T. Heiner, architect. *Harris County Heritage Society, Houston*.

This is another fine example of Second Empire commercial work. The window hoods, thick cornice, and Mansardic roof with dormers all combine to create an opulent effect. Today the building is occupied by a fried chicken food service, and only the cornice and its consoles are recognizable.

moving to Texas arrived during the 1870's.[48]

Toward the end of the century many of those rendering professional services became sensitive to the need to establish restrictions on the practice of architecture. Consequently, a number of associations were organized—a trend that was consistent with the national movement wherein trades and professions developed organizations to provide mutual benefit and protection of members.

The practice of architecture at the turn of the century was accompanied by many hardships. It was often necessary to travel long distances to compete for a commission or to supervise a building underway. While travel by

[48] Several important and talented architects immigrated to Texas in the 1870's. In 1872 Nicholas J. Clayton moved to Texas as employee of the Memphis firm of Jones and Baldwin to supervise construction of the Tremont Hotel and the First Presbyterian Church in Galveston; he remained and became one of the outstanding architects of the state. Eugene T. Heiner established a practice in Houston in 1876, where he had moved from Terre Haute, Indiana. A native of England, Alfred Giles moved to Texas in 1873. Frederick Ernst Ruffini, a native of Cleveland, Ohio, moved to Austin in 1876. James E. Flanders arrived in Dallas in 1875.

FIGURE 107. Tremont Opera House, Galveston (1870). *Courtesy Rosenberg Library, Galveston, Texas.*

Similar to many commercial buildings dating from the 1870's, this opera house had a ground-floor facade of iron and glass and upper stories of masonry with openings spanned by iron lintels. The cornice was galvanized iron. The Mansard roof, of course, was a fashionable feature of the period.

Located at Market and Tremont streets, it was built by Willard Richardson. A grand entrance was located on Market Street, adjacent to commercial rental space. Accessible by a grand stair and through a lobby, the auditorium was situated on the second floor. Among the acclaimed features were the stage, with modern machinery and gas footlights in white, red, and blue colors. In 1895 Nicholas J. Clayton remodeled the structure, but it is now gone.

train was safe enough, robbers and the natural elements presented hazards to those traveling by horseback or buggy. Illustrating these dangers, a stagecoach on which Alfred Giles was traveling was held up, and the architect was forced by the robbers to help rifle the mail.[49] Distances added to the difficulties of practice. There were about 160 miles, as the crow flies, between Paint Rock, where the Concho County Courthouse was built, and Austin, where its architect, F. E. Ruffini, headquartered. From Sweetwater, the site of the

Nolan County Courthouse, to Dallas, where its architect lived, was well over 200 miles. Eugene Heiner of Houston had to travel by rail or trail over 300 miles to Ballinger to present plans for the Runnels County Courthouse.

The offices of these architects were usually located on an upper floor of a commercial building, and the decor reflected the taste of the times. Successful firms employed several draftsmen. Offices were often compartmentalized, apparently for privacy, and were decorated with the plants that were so popular then.

[49]Mary Carolyn Hollers Jutson, *Alfred Giles,* p. 4.

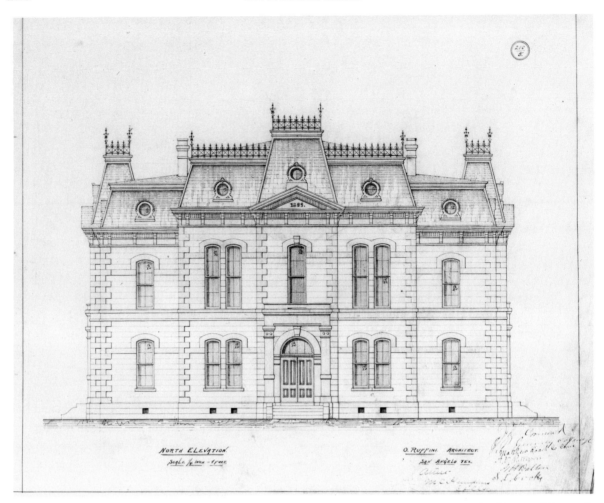

FIGURE 108. Plans for Mills County Courthouse, Goldthwaite (1889–1890). Oscar Ruffini, architect. *Archives Division, Texas State Library, Austin.*

These plans are characteristic of architectural drafting during the last half of the nineteenth century. Accurate, large-scale drawings with minimal detail provided the contractor the information essential for construction. Dimensions on plans were sparse, but information could be scaled from the large drawings. Of course, building spaces were much simpler than today, hence the plans were less complex.

With wooden T squares and triangles, draftsmen produced beautiful, large-scale drawings on linen or paper; dimensions and details were few. Watercolors applied to the plans indicated materials: yellow for wood, red for brick, blue for stone, brown for metal (fig. 108). Specifications, of course, were written by hand. Since, in the early years, the means to reproduce drawings was limited, typically only one set existed, and it always remained the property of the architect. Rarely,

special arrangements were made by the owner for two sets of drawings—as in the case of the Shackelford County Courthouse, where duplicate sets were requested by the county commissioners.[50] However, by the 1890's, offices were producing multiple copies of blueprints from tracings (fig. 109).

During the nineteenth century architects

[50] Office of the County Clerk, County Commissioners Court Minutes, Shackelford County, vol. 1 (April 1, 1883).

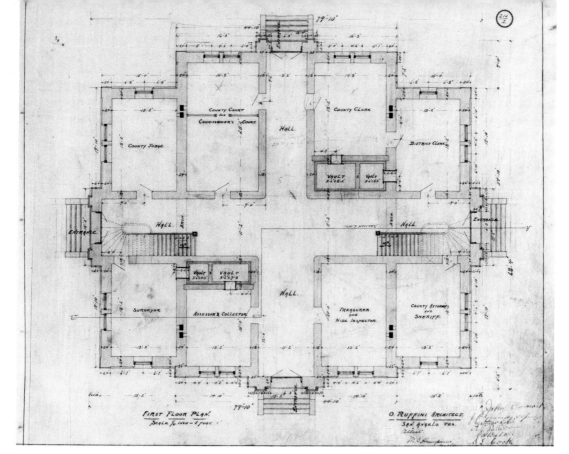

FIRST FLOOR PLAN.
Scale ⅛ inch = 1 foot.

O. RUFFINI ARCHITECT.
SAN ANGELO, TEX.

COUNTY JUDGE.

COUNTY COURT and COMMISSIONER'S COURT

HALL

COUNTY CLERK

DISTRICT CLERK

VAULT

VAULT

ENTRANCE

HALL

HALL

ENTRANCE

SURVEYOR

ASSESSOR & COLLECTOR

VAULT

VAULT

HALL

TREASURER and HIDE INSPECTOR.

COUNTY ATTORNEY and SHERIFF.

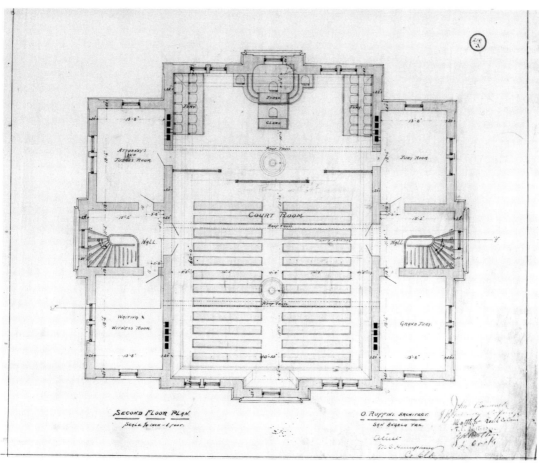

SECOND FLOOR PLAN
Scale ⅛ inch = 1 foot.

O. RUFFINI ARCHITECT
SAN ANGELO, TEX.

JURY

JUDGE

CLERK

JURY

ATTORNEY'S and JUDGES ROOM

JURY ROOM

HALL

COURT ROOM

HALL

WAITING & WITNESS ROOM.

GRAND JURY.

ROOF TRUSS

FIGURE 109. Office of Waller & Field, architects, Fort Worth. *Courtesy Fort Worth Public Library, Amon Carter Museum.*

This scene epitomizes the architectural office at the turn of the century. In relatively dark spaces draftsmen produced handsome watercolor renderings. Working drawings were produced with wooden triangles and T squares. In the back right-hand corner is the equipment for blueprinting.

promoted their practices through several avenues. Of course, then as now, they solicited work through references and by cultivating influential and wealthy people. They also frequently advertised in newspapers and city directories (fig. 110). For private work, at least, these means were effective.

However, architects of public buildings were often selected through competitions—a procedure dating back at least to the national Capitol competition won by William Thornton in 1792 and one which should have encouraged the development of good designs. Building committees and county commissioners, by advertisements in newspapers and architectural journals, invited interested professionals to submit drawings. Then the committee, usually without professional judgments, selected the design it preferred and awarded the commission. Familiar names

often competed; J. Riely Gordon and W. C. Dodson, for example, traveled considerable distances many times to vie for commissions.

However, winning a competition did not always assure work. For unrecorded reasons, some architects, once selected, were replaced by competitors after the commission was awarded. J. Riely Gordon was originally selected by county commissioners to design the present Denton County Courthouse but was replaced by W. C. Dodson. Dodson was originally awarded the commission for the 1895 Van Zandt County Courthouse—now gone—in Canton but was replaced by J. Riely Gordon.[51] Interestingly, Dodson and Gordon

[51] Office of the County Clerk, County Commissioners Court Minutes, Denton County, vol. C (July 2 and August 9, 1895); Office of the County Clerk, County Commissioners Court Minutes, Van Zandt County, vol. 4 (August 14 and September 4, 1894).

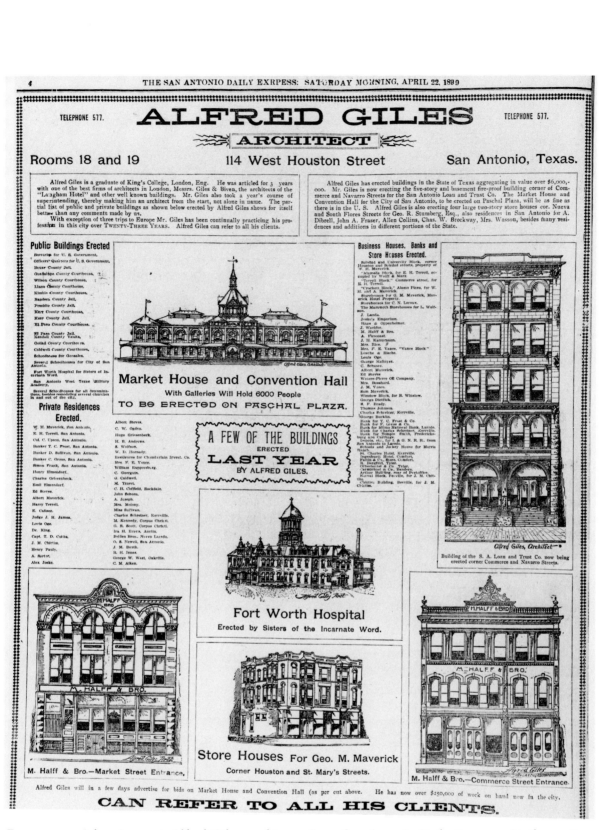

FIGURE 110. Advertisement, Alfred Giles, architect. *From* San Antonio Daily Express, *April 22, 1899, courtesy University of Texas at Austin.*

Alfred Giles, like many of his peers, advertised freely in the local newspapers. Although advertisements frequently consisted of only the publication of a business card in the professional listings of the paper, occasionally such large, well-illustrated layouts as this appeared.

collaborated on the McLennan County Courthouse (1901–1902) in Dodson's hometown;
after being appointed "expert architect" by
county commissioners, the Waco architect recommended plans by Gordon, which were accepted. Dodson supervised construction.

Given the number of competitions and the
number of competitiors, it is not surprising
that many architects used set designs, with
variations made only to fit the budget and
tastes of the commissioners of a particular
county. Interestingly, precise functional requirements were not often published in competition announcements; only an approximate
budget and general needs would be stated.

Contractors also competed with architects
for commissions. Sometimes they employed
architects to prepare plans for them, but more
often one of the principals of the firm developed the designs. In the northern section of the
state J. H. Britton designed and built a number
of structures, including the 1870's courthouse
for Denton County. R. F. Sayers built the 1881
courthouse for Wise County. The firm of
Lovell and Hood was quite active during the
1880's. Martin, Moodie, and Johnston, headquartered in Colorado City, produced many
plans and specifications for structures, which
they also built.[52]

Associations between architects and builders were developed in several instances. In 1877

Joseph Kane and J. J. Kane advertised as "architects and contractors," with shop and office
on Belknap Street in Fort Worth. The Goliad County Courthouse, Goliad (1894), and
the Caldwell County Courthouse, Lockhart
(1893), were virtually identical designs, which
Alfred Giles claimed as his. However, all transactions over the buildings involved only the
contractors—Martin, Byrnes, and Johnston,
as the firm had become known—and the
county commissioners. Likewise, the Gonzales
County Courthouse, Gonzales (1894–1896),
was almost certainly designed by J. Riely Gordon, but official transactions involved only the
county commissioners and the contractor,
Otto P. Kroeger. And the jails in both Brownwood and Comanche appear to have been designed by Gordon, but the contractors, Martin
and Moodie, were credited with providing the
plans and construction.[53]

Thus during the middle decades of the last
half of the nineteenth century, significant developments occurred in building technology,
and noteworthy changes occurred in architectural taste. The improvements in life made possible by technology created a need for buildings of new functional types, which previously
had been unknown in the state. At the same
time the demand to express attainment provided the setting for the development of the
architectural opulence of the Victorian era,
from which some of our most lamentable
losses have occurred.

[52] *Houston Daily Post*, December 2, 1891; Office of the
County Clerk, County Commissioners Court Minutes, Denton
County, vol. A (May 31, 1876); Office of the County Clerk,
County Commissioners Court Minutes, Wise County, vol. 1 (De-
cember 15, 1881). Among the fine works of Lovell and Hood was
St. John's Episcopal Church, Brownwood (1892). Martin and
Moodie built, for example, the 1876 Grayson County Court-
house and the 1876 Comanche County Courthouse.

[53] *Fort Worth Democrat*, March 15, 1877.

5

Lost from the Era of Elegance: Houses and Commercial Buildings

THE architect practicing in Texas during the last two decades of the nineteenth century worked for the most part during an era of prosperity. He had at his disposal an abundance of building materials, both natural and manufactured. The healthy economy created by cattle, cotton, and lumber, as well as by new industries and investments, all combined to provide the wealth essential for the construction of large, opulent private and public buildings. Nature provided a wide variety of local woods for structures and finishes and different colors of stones for support and decoration. When more variegation or elegance was demanded than could be provided by the land, the railroads imported such materials as pressed brick from Philadelphia, floor tile from New York, and encaustic floor tile from Indianapolis. Iron columns for support, slate for roofing, and colored glass for windows were among the other materials imported.

While Victorian Texans, like others in the country, were much charmed by lavish building exteriors, they also gave considerable attention to the inside spaces. Throughout the last two decades of the century, interior volumes became more complex and interesting. Appropriate spatial transitions between exteriors and interiors were developed, and such interior circulation spaces as halls and stairways were refined in form and decor.

At the same time, architectural designers continued to plan spaces to ameliorate life in adverse climatic conditions. Broad porches in the shadows of buildings provided cool outdoor areas for relaxation on hot days; high ceilings and stair towers allowed uncomfortable hot air to rise; and the extensive use of double-hung windows allowed good cross ventilation. Then too, the use of wide hallways provided for efficient air circulation. Openings between floors not only improved ventilation but also created aesthetically pleasing spaces. While canons on taste came from the East, adaptation to the environment occurred at home.

Texans living during the era of elegance—times of rapid architectural change—developed an appreciation for picturesqueness. To provide the required interest, various fashions and combinations of styles became popular—following the trends set earlier by eastern tastemakers—although they often were adapted into original compositions at home. Virtually any historical style that provided irregular forms and intricate details could satisfy the love for ornateness. Contemporary writings reveal that Victorians loved distinctive character in buildings, particularly buildings with respected functions. As a complementary enhancement of picturesque forms, polychromy provided by the natural colors of materials was much admired. The craftsmanship of fine stonecutting and handsome wooden panel work contributed further to the beauty of Victorian architecture.

In the details forming part of the vocabularies of fashionable styles, Texans could appreciate several types of decoration. For those who enjoyed the beauty of plants, there were naturalistic forms, which appeared prominently on column capitals in many building types. For those who appreciated representation, there were symbolic features, displayed prominently in ecclesiastical edifices. For those who liked abstract patterns, there were geometrical configurations, which commonly were placed around entrances and towers of courthouses, as well as other structures.

The availability of talented "mechanics," of course, contributed to the distinctive detailing of buildings; these artisans made possible fine construction with handcrafted decoration. During this era German masons and carpenters became well known for fine workmanship, and many masons immigrated from Scotland. In addition, countless fine Anglo-American woodworkers either came from other states or learned their crafts at home. Nonetheless, much of the decoration that was so admired was machine produced.

The expansion of industry after the Civil War contributed immeasurably to the capability to mass-produce the components that provided the character so much desired. Although factories of the antebellum and Reconstruction periods already had provided some builders with such standard items as stair balusters and fireplace mantels, increased production resulted in more economy and in an availability of a greater variety of building details and furnishings than previously. Mechanization made possible economical exploitation of gingerbread by the jigsaw, spindle work by the lathe, shingles by the bandsaw, and sheet-metal work by the press—all of which could be easily transported by the railroads.

The application of this gingerbread and spindle work to porches and eaves, patterns of shingles to walls, and metalwork to ridges and cornices produced an ornamental delicacy that became characteristic of the Victorian era. Generally, Victorians preferred a great profusion of details—just as they loved ornateness in dress, furnishings, and other items. Yet the details ordinarily remained subservient to the whole, an effect resulting from the small size and uniform character of the features contrasted with the large, plain-surfaced building masses.

Many of the decorative features that became popular recalled components of furniture designed by the English tastemaker Sir Charles Eastlake. Spindle columns supporting porches resembled legs of furniture, and geometrical cornice decoration was reminiscent of ornamental borders on beds and mirrors. All this brought about the stylistic label of *Eastlake* for buildings incorporating these features, in spite of their being associated with a taste in architecture with which the English furniture designer had no sympathy.[1]

Frame houses with walls covered by clapboards and with picturesque wooden and metal decoration became very popular in the thriving sections of the state, although most are now either destroyed or have lost many of their details. Large dwellings, often designed by architects, frequently were elaborate displays of spindle work, shingles, gingerbread, and metalwork. A representative example, now gone, was the R. S. Bowan House, Coleman, designed by Oscar Ruffini of San Angelo (fig. 111). Variations on the theme were virtually infinite, as illustrated by the H. Elmendorf House, San Antonio (fig. 112), the Alexander Sanger House, Dallas (fig. 113), the G. A. Mistrot House, Houston (fig. 114), the S. K. Dick House, Houston (fig. 115), and the T. W. House dwelling, Houston (fig. 116).

Contributing further to the picturesqueness of frame dwellings of this period were irregular house plans. Variations of asymmetrical massing were developed through an assort-

[1]Harold Kirker, *California Architecture*, p. 106.

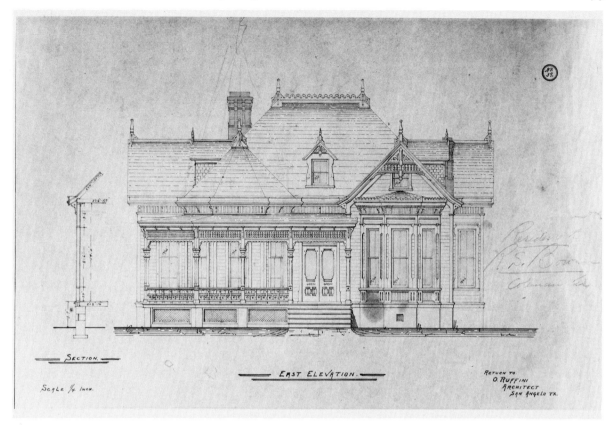

FIGURE III. R. S. Bowan House, Coleman (ca. 1880). Oscar Ruffini, architect. *Archives Division, Texas State Library, Austin.*

This dwelling incorporated many of the wooden decorative features that were fashionable during the 1880's. Porch columns were thin and delicate—like table legs. The cresting and decorative trim along the dormer cornice and the porch railing all seemed to express an Eastlake philosophy, which held that ornamentation should be subservient to the general design.

ment of forms and the placement of porches and rooms. Picturesque massing and intricate decorative work even became widely fashionable for modestly scaled dwellings. These often displayed simple decorative details that produced a uniformity of character (fig. 117).

The middle classes could now afford taste not only in such mass-produced items as furniture and wallpaper but also in architecture. Newspapers of the period commonly published columns illustrating plans and elevations of small "tasteful" and "artistic" dwellings designed for the middle classes.[2]

[2] See, for example, *Houston Daily Post*, July 10, 1889, for plans and perspectives of "neat" and "artistic" dwellings.

Asymmetrically planned, these dwellings, if they had more than one story, usually had a stair hallway located at one side. Typically, on the ground floor there were only a living room, sitting room, and pantry. On the second floor were bedrooms and often a sewing room to accommodate clothes-making activities of the middle-class homemaker.

Although architects designed many large houses, other home builders obtained designs from one of the many plan books that were available. Moreover, many professional designers in Texas themselves certainly used the available pattern books to obtain graphic information on "modern" styles, details, and

FIGURE 112. Henry Elmendorf House, San Antonio (1881–1882). Alfred Giles, architect. *From* Art Work of San Antonio, *Daughters of the Republic of Texas Library, San Antonio.*

For Henry Elmendorf, Giles designed a cubical house with masonry walls. A two-story porch with attractive details enhanced one side, which faced Alamo Street.

Later additions planned by an unknown architect were made to enlarge the house to the form illustrated here. Intended to delight the eye, delicate woodwork graced the porches, where evenings could be spent in the shade. The fence surrounding the property complemented the character of the dwelling.

FIGURE 113. Alexander Sanger House, Dallas (ca. 1895). *From* Art Work of Dallas, 1895, *Archives and Research Center for Texas and Dallas History.*

Formerly located at South Ervay Street, this fine house displaying intricate detailing was built by a prominent merchant. Sanger and his brother Philip developed the famous Sanger Brothers wholesale and retail dry goods store into one of the most prominent commercial establishments in the Southwest. The structure displays a delightful composition of delicate features. Noteworthy are the lattice work, spindle columns, shingle patterns, and crestings. Porches and verandas reflected a residential function.

FIGURE 114. Gustaf A. Mistrot House, Houston (ca. 1885). *From* Art Work of Houston, *1904,* Houston Public Library.

Built by a merchant who handled dry goods and notions, this house exhibited characteristic Eastlake features. Porches supported by thin columns, spindle work, and other decorative features all contributed to the charm of the building. Surrounding a large yard, an ornamental iron fence enhanced the setting. The house was formerly located at 1504 Clay Street, which is now occupied by an auto parts dealer.

FIGURE 115. S. K. Dick House, Houston (ca. 1885). George E. Dickey, architect. *From* Art Work of Houston, *1894,* Houston Public Library.

Designed by a prominent Houston architect who had had about fifteen years of experience by the time this house was built, the Dick house exhibited a variety of fanciful details. High brick chimneys, roof crestings, numerous gables, and strong relief in the brickwork all contributed to the picturesqueness of the building. The porches supported by thin columns with elaborate spindle work were characteristic of Eastlake style.

FIGURE 116. Thomas W. House House, Houston (ca. 1885). George E. Dickey, architect. *From* Art Work of Houston, *1904,* Houston Public Library.

Yet other variations of composition and detailing were expressed in this dwelling. Porches in Eastlake style, a corner turret, and a dominant arched opening containing a balcony provided variations on a theme familiar during the latter part of the nineteenth century. Then, as now, architects worked with standard components but combined them in a variety of ways.

FIGURE 117. Holmes Street, Dallas. *From* Art Work of Dallas, *1895,* Archives and Research Center for Texas and Dallas History, Dallas Public Library.

At one time countless houses similar to these existed in communities throughout the state. However, as the large cities grew, they rapidly disappeared. Nonetheless, many of this style still exist in small towns with populations that have remained stable over the years. Rows of porches, where occupants spent warm evenings visiting, had an important social function.

materials.[3] Like today's magazines and journals, these books contained perspectives of the dwellings in various styles, along with floor plans, which were often modified by builders. Among the authors of plan books was George F. Barber of Knoxville, Tennessee, who published books of designs that were used in Texas.[4] Some builders may have ordered plans—and they certainly ordered building components and furniture—from the Sears and Roebuck Company mail-order house in Chicago.

The decorative attributes of most of the frame buildings were colorfully highlighted with patterns of painted trim. Using greens or browns—probably the most popular colors during the last decades of the nineteenth century—builders painted cornerboards, window casings, columns, and so forth dark colors. To provide vivid contrast, the walls were painted with white or a light value.

The desired picturesqueness in house design was provided by several styles, among them the Queen Anne, a mode imported from England but innovated upon in America. Abroad, Queen Anne buildings had been characterized by ground-story walls of brick, upper-story walls of half-timbering, high brick chimneys, and casement windows. In Texas, as in other states, the English elements (made popular through both publications and the British buildings at the 1876 Centennial Exposition in Philadelphia) were sometimes retained even when other picturesque elements were added. They were freely rearranged into a variety of compositions incorporating brick and stone and frame walls surfaced with shingles and clapboards. Turrets, gables, and bay windows in a variety of configurations added to an irregular silhouette. The Queen Anne–style W. H. Abrams House, Dallas (ca.

1888), now gone, had lower-story walls finished with clapboards, upper walls with shingles (fig. 118). The W. B. Chew House, Houston (ca. 1892), was a picturesque composition with brick and shingles as the primary exterior materials (fig. 119).

Wall patterns resembling those created by the English half-timber buildings characterized the mode twentieth-century historians call the Stick style. In Texas many residences were built with balloon-framed walls articulated into rectangular and triangular panels by thin boards—a kind of wooden wall framing. Within the geometrical divisions defined by these wooden strips were located panels of weatherboards. Excellent examples of the Stick style in Texas, both now gone, were the E. P. Turner House in Dallas (fig. 120) and the C. Lombardi House in Houston (fig. 121).

Modes incorporating wood as a primary material also included the Shingle style. The Queen Anne had formed a point of departure for the evolution of this style on the East Coast. In America the half-timbering and tile work of the English Queen Anne were replaced by shingles, and first floors were often enclosed with stone walls, as in the H. E. Barnard House, San Antonio (fig. 122). Ultimately the style evolved into a mode wherein buildings were covered completely with shingles. Balconies, porches, and other picturesque components also were incorporated into compositions, as seen on the J. C. Weaver House in Dallas (fig. 123). In Austin, E. M. House built a handsome Shingle-style dwelling, which also has been razed (fig. 124). Shingles even gave individual character to residences of modest size when the gables above clapboarded walls were covered with a wide variety of patterns, apparently according to the whim of owners and carpenters.

While buildings with Queen Anne forms frequently were finished with shingles, other styles, too, incorporated wholly or partially, shingled walls. The Romanesque Revival style, a mode most satisfactorily expressed with ashlar masonry walls, also provided

---

[3]See, for example, A. J. Bicknell, *Detail, Cottage and Constructive Architecture*; W. T. Comstock, *Modern Architectural Designs and Details*. Both were reprinted in 1978 by the Atheneum Library of Nineteenth Century America.

[4]Geo[rge] F. Barber, *Modern Artistic Cottages or the Cottage Souvenir*; idem, *The Cottage Souvenir Revised and Enlarged*.

FIGURE 118. Edwin P. Cowan House (William H. Abrams House), Dallas (ca. 1888). *From* Art Work of Dallas, *1895,* Archives and Research Center for Texas and Dallas History, Dallas Public Library.

The scale and style of this house were characteristic of the dwellings erected by successful businessmen. Contrasting forms and configurations of materials all contributed to the architectural variety that was in vogue at the time. Delightful patterns of shingles and compositions of historical details provided the elegance that was esteemed. The house was purchased by William H. Abrams in 1893 and was razed in 1930.

FIGURE 119. W. B. Chew House, Houston (ca. 1892). J. A. Tempest, architect. *From* Art Work of Houston, *1894,* Houston Public Library.

Picturesque composition of forms and a variety of details and materials all expressed the worldly success of the builder of this large house. Characteristic Queen Anne features included the polygonal turret, projecting attic gable, verge boards, and a version of the Palladian type window. The site of the Chew house is now a parking lot.

FIGURE 120. Edward P. Turner House, Dallas (ca. 1890). *From* Art Work of Dallas, *1895,* Archives and Research Center for Texas and Dallas History, Dallas Public Library.

Fashionable, up-to-date styles evidenced the prosperity of many immigrant businessmen. A native of Iowa, Turner moved to Texas and served as a ticket agent for the Texas and Pacific Railroad. By the time this "modern" house was built, he had acquired considerable valuable real estate. The building was located at 147 Ewing.

This house was a wonderful example of Stick-style architecture. Characteristic features included the division of the wall surfaces into panels filled with various patterns. The lofty turret and high porch seemed to announce status.

FIGURE 121. C. Lombardi House, Houston (ca. 1890). *From* Art Work of Houston, *1894,* Houston Public Library.

While it incorporated details that also appeared in other styles, this house was a fine example of the Stick style. Characteristically, the walls were divided into panels surfaced with either shingles or clapboards. However, porch details were typical of Eastlake and, the chimneys were typical of the Queen Anne. Balconies, dormers, and gables added further interest.

FIGURE 122. H. E. Barnard House, San Antonio (ca. 1890). *From* Art Work of San Antonio, *Daughters of the Republic of Texas Library, San Antonio.*

    Historical stylistic features and warmth of materials distinguished this medium-size house. The Queen Anne style provided a form vocabulary, while the shingles and masonry were composed into interesting textures. Picturesqueness was provided by lofty chimneys, steep roofs, and a cylindrical turret.

FIGURE 123. John C. Weaver House, Dallas (ca. 1890). *From* Art Work of Dallas, 1895, *Archives and Research Center for Texas and Dallas History, Dallas Public Library.*

    Formerly located at 435 Fairmont Avenue, this was a fine example of the Shingle style. Incorporating Queen Anne forms, the house was entirely surfaced with shingles, producing warmth and fine scale. In this building, as was often typical of the style, a variety of shingle patterns was employed. The gable and turret create an asymmetrical balance about the entrance, which is boldly announced by steps and another gable. The building was demolished in 1969.

FIGURE 124. Edward Mandel House House, Austin (1892). Frank Freeman, architect. *From* Art Work of Austin, *Austin–Travis County Collection, Austin Public Library.*

This house incorporated broad porches, porte cochere, and balconies. To obtain a suitable architect, the owner traveled to Brooklyn, New York, where he commissioned Frank Freeman to do the design. By hiring a successful eastern architect, the owner imported first-hand, up-to-date taste.

a form vocabulary for wood construction. In some cases, the ground-level walls were stone, with upper-story walls faced with shingles (fig. 125). In other instances, the entire house was covered by shingles, with the Roman arches—hallmark of the style—framed in wood and finished with shingles applied in radial patterns.

Not only was the Romanesque Revival style often interpreted freely in wood construction, but it was also rendered appropriately in stone, in a manner inspired by the great Boston architect, Henry Hobson Richardson. It is quite evident that the work of Richardson, which included buildings with both shingled and ashlar exterior surfaces, provided the inspiration for these.[5] In San Antonio, J. Riely Gordon designed a noteworthy house for B. F. Yoakum in beautiful Romanesque Revival

style—a mode in which this architect did some of his best work (fig. 126).

The prosperity of the times enabled many other Texans to commission architects to design pretentious houses, in which the fashions of the wealthy tastemakers of eastern cities were emulated. The imperial styles of the mansions in Chicago and New York City, as well as in other cultural centers, had profound impact on the design of houses in the Lone Star State. The tastes of the times certainly were influenced considerably by such prestigious eastern architects as Richard Morris Hunt and George B. Post. Hunt was well known for his high-style work, including the William K. Vanderbilt mansion (ca. 1882), and Post was known for the Cornelius Vanderbilt II mansion (1881); both Vanderbilt homes were in New York City.

Although none of the Texas mansions approached the magnitude of such works as Biltmore—another imposing Vanderbilt residence erected 1890–1895 near Asheville,

[5] For background on and illustrations of buildings by Richardson, see Henry-Russell Hitchcock, *The Architecture of H. H. Richardson and His Times.*

FIGURE 125. John Bookhout House, Dallas (1891). James E. Flanders, architect. *From* Art Work of Dallas, *1895,* Archives and Research Center for Texas and Dallas History, Dallas Public Library.

This handsome house with Romanesque forms and detail vocabulary was erected by an associate justice of the court of civil appeals. Located at the corner of Maston and Carouth streets, it had a stone base and a shingled upper section, a composition of form and materials providing repose and warmth. Throughout the exterior, the arch motif provided a unifying theme. In 1927 the building was razed.

FIGURE 126. Benjamin Franklin Yoakum House, San Antonio (ca. 1890). J. Riely Gordon, architect. *From* Art Work of San Antonio, *Daughters of the Republic of Texas Library, San Antonio.*

Designed for a prominent railroad official, this house was a fine example of Romanesque mode. Due to the expense of stone construction—the ideal medium—this style was not extensively used for houses in Texas. Nonetheless, several examples did appear. This structure was also distinguished by the several textures and patterns.

FIGURE 127. William Cameron House, Waco (1885). *Texas Collection, Baylor University, Waco.*

The Second Empire style—which has been much maligned as grotesque by mid-twentieth-century critics—provided a fashionable appearance for the house of William Cameron. Mansardic roofs, bay windows, porches, balustrades, and tower all were combined to produce a picturesque effect. Contrasting colors complemented the complex form composition. The story has it that Mr. Cameron built the house as a surprise gift to his wife.

North Carolina—the spirit of the Gilded Age was strongly expressed in the large Texas houses. Among the other styles intended to romantically exhibit personal success and cultural development through rich embellishment was the French Second Empire mode, which provided a plastic vocabulary of forms and details. Architectural features were copied from the buildings of France, an esteemed fountain of culture. In Texas the style had been imported for public buildings during the 1870's and remained popular for houses and governmental buildings throughout the 1880's. In the William Cameron, Sr., House, Waco, the Mansardic roofs, dormers, and cornice brackets of this mode all combined to provide a distinctive character (fig. 127). In Houston, a full panoply of Second Empire features in the C. S. House

dwelling signified the cultural consciousness as well as material prosperity of its builder (fig. 128).

Other styles of French inspiration were also thought to express the character and social level of the occupants. In Austin the J. H. Houghton House (1886–1887), the design of architect James Wahrenberger, exhibited fashionable stylistic features largely derived from the early French Renaissance and recalling the character of some of the mansions of the eastern millionaires (fig. 129). As was characteristic of many houses on a similar scale, the composition incorporated a cylindrical tower at one corner and a rectangular tower above the entrance.

Renaissance details, along with those from other historical sources, enhanced many other

FIGURE 128. C. S. House House, Houston (ca. 1885). *From* Art Work of Houston, *1894,* Houston Public Library.

As was often the case with large houses, this building occupied a site of about an acre—the north section of the block now bounded by Main, Calhoun, Travis, and Jefferson streets. Contributing to the character of the mansion were typical Second Empire features, including a Mansard roof with ogival profile over the main mass of the house and a Mansard roof with linear profile over the tower. Other typical noteworthy features included dormers, with both triangular and segmental pediments, iron crestings, bracketed cornices, quoinings, a bay window surmounted by a balustrade, window openings spanned with stilted arches with pronounced keystones, and deep porches.

By 1904, the building had been purchased by Dr. W. R. Eckhardt, and it is now gone.

houses. For example, Nicholas J. Clayton incorporated Renaissance details and Romanesque forms into the Morris Lasker House, Galveston (1889) (fig. 130). Because they occupied valuable downtown sites, many of these imposing houses are now gone, and their old sites are now asphalt-topped parking lots. Many of these homes exhibited the esteemed picturesqueness and elegance through a diversity of historical and geometrical forms. Among these was the Mrs. W. E. Lowry House, San Antonio (ca. 1890), a residence that displayed an irregular silhouette and a fantastic composition of forms in Moorish style but with Eastlake details (fig. 131).

Yet other interesting examples included the Thomas Jennings House in Fort Worth, into which was incorporated a variety of details including many of Classical origin (fig. 132), and the George M. Dilley House in Dallas, with its irregular geometrical composition and complex skyline, created by convex and concave curvatures of Moorish character (fig. 133). Although some examples of Moorish style remain in Texas, they are rare. The San Antonio National Bank, designed in Moorish fashion by Cyrus Eidlitz and completed in 1886, still stands, as does Corsicana's Temple Beth El, a wood-frame edifice with onion-dome-topped towers.

FIGURE 129. John H. Houghton House, Austin (1886–1887). James Wahrenberger, architect. *From* Art Work of Austin, *Austin–Travis County Collection, Austin Public Library.*

Built by Charles A. Shurr, this dwelling displayed interesting details and complex massing. High brick chimneys and intricate sheet-metal cornices produced a picturesque composition, which was greatly admired during the Gilded Age. Other noteworthy features included advancing and receding walls, porches, and a half-octagonal mass. Fine materials, including yellow pressed brick and ashlar limestone, contributed further to the success of the statement.

The building was demolished in 1973.

FIGURE 130. Morris Lasker House, Galveston (1889). Nicholas J. Clayton, architect. *Historic American Buildings Survey, Library of Congress, Washington, D.C.*

Displaying Classical French detailing, this fine house had walls of bricks finished with stucco. On the exterior it was enhanced with delicate ironwork and windows with intricate details. But the interiors were more elegant than the outside. In the rooms, with ceilings fifteen feet high, were oak and mahogany floors; door hardware was bronze. The building was razed in 1967.

FIGURE 131. Mrs. W. E. Lowry House, San Antonio (ca. 1890). J. Riely Gordon, architect. *From* Art Work of San Antonio, *Daughters of the Republic of Texas Library, San Antonio.*

To provide the requisite picturesqueness and elegance that were so much in vogue at the time this house was built, the architect employed complex forms and a variety of materials. The composition included such interesting features as ogival-profiled roofs and horseshoe arches, which created a Moorish character. This mood was complemented by brick, stone, iron, and wood, all woven into the expression. Finally, materials with contrasting colors provided additional variety.

FIGURE 132. Thomas Jennings House, Fort Worth (ca. 1895). *Courtesy, Fort Worth Public Library, Amon Carter Museum.*

Fulfilling the requirements of the owner for distinctive architectural character, this house incorporated an interesting juxtaposition of details. High brick chimneys and pitched roofs combined to provide an irregular skyline. Transomed windows on the left recalled the Romanesque, while the Palladian windows and dormer with a segmental pediment suggested the Renaissance. Typically for the times, stained glass appeared in the window transoms of the rooms accommodating formal uses. Other noteworthy features included the delicately scaled swags and dentils, which contrasted with broad wall surfaces and massive columns. Exterior materials of stone, brick, and shingles further contributed to the variety of details on the exterior.

FIGURE 133. George M. Dilley House, Dallas (ca. 1890). F. S. Allen, architect. *From* Art Work of Dallas, *1895, Archives and Research Center for Texas and Dallas History, Dallas Public Library.*

A variety of stylistic forms provided distinction for this large dwelling. Among the interesting features were the onion dome, horseshoe arches, and arabesque panels, reflecting Moorish origins of this architectural style. The house was basically symmetrical, except for the contrast between the octagonal and the cylindrical turrets. The scale was deceiving: it was much larger than it appears in the picture. The large windows in the turrets make the other parts of the building appear relatively small. The house was razed around 1924.

Another historical style providing the desired romantic picturesqueness was the Gothic Revival. In Galveston in 1885 Sampson Heidenheimer, a merchant, commissioned Nicholas J. Clayton to enlarge a house for him, adding a polygonal tower and other medieval details. The small, tabby-concrete house, which had been built at mid-century, was thereby transformed into what would be called "Heidenheimer's Castle" (fig. 134). Unfortunately, the building burned in the 1970's.

In addition to the above residential styles, which appeared in many large houses, yet other modes associated with European and eastern culture provided distinctive images for the affluent class. Near the turn of the century, the taste for classical formality began returning, and the love for asymmetrical irregularity

gave way to an appreciation of more formal composition. In Houston the house of Henry S. Fox, with its corner turrets recalling a French chateau, displayed a variety of details, including Classical columns, and presented a formal front facade (fig. 135). Conforming to trends in the East, Classical features and reposed composition also appeared in Fort Worth's Hyde Jennings House (fig. 136). The houses of J. I. Campbell and S. F. Carter, both of Houston, were yet other examples reflecting the transition in taste from Victorian picturesqueness to Classical formality (figs. 137, 138).

By using historical styles, then, Texas architects and their clients intended to express a cosmopolitan "modernity"; with architectural forms and with the use of elegant materials,

FIGURE 134. Sydnor-Heidenheimer House, Galveston (1850's; 1885). Nicholas J. Clayton, architect, 1885 Addition. *Ezra Stoller © ESTO.*

The original section of this house was built by Colonel John S. Sydnor, one-time mayor of Galveston. As in some other buildings in the region, walls were formed by tabby (a mixture of lime, sand, and sea shells), with oyster-shell aggregate.

Later, Sampson Heidenheimer, a successful merchant, purchased the property and enlarged the house. A central-hall-type plan was retained; from this the main living rooms and stair tower were accessible. The interior walls were plastered, and oak wainscoting was employed. According to a 1966 tour book, the four-story structure contained fifty-seven rooms and twenty-seven fireplaces.

On the exterior, the brick walls were stuccoed. The Medieval Revival details created a romantic statement, which certainly fulfilled the passion of the times for picturesqueness.

FIGURE 135. Henry S. Fox House, Houston (ca. 1900). J. A. Tempest, architect. *From* Art Work of Houston, *1904,* Houston Public Library.

Located on a half-block now occupied by high-rise commercial buildings, this charming residence reflected the graceful life-style of its occupants. A wide porch, symmetrically designed, announced the front door, while a porte cochere located at the side provided a point of arrival for carriages. At the back, along Travis Street, were servants' quarters and a carriage house.

FIGURE 136. Hyde Jennings House, Fort Worth (ca. 1898). *Courtesy, Fort Worth Public Library, Amon Carter Museum.*

Located at the corner of Lancaster and Summit streets, this large dwelling sported a design that revealed a decline in the interest in intricate compositions of picturesque elements in favor of more formal statements. Although such features as the porches, balconies, and chimneys still produced a charming effect, there were no turrets or towers. Nonetheless, roof crestings, different patterns of exterior wall finishes, and multiple colors provided a type of elegance that was still admired.

FIGURE 137. J. I. Campbell House, Houston (ca. 1900). *From* Art Work of Houston, *1904,* Houston Public Library.

The trend towards formal expression was further represented by this house. Although finialed turrets of different proportions created a picturesque composition, the building nonetheless was formally balanced about the front entrance. A porch with Classical details and balcony railings contributed further to the formality of expression.

owners of houses displayed their worldly status. During this era, with so much emphasis upon character, virtually any mode or combination of styles became acceptable, provided the form vocabulary allowed irregularity and accommodated the use of a variety of materials.

In the more formal architecture of these fashionable mansions, the complexity of the spaces generally complemented the exterior composition, just as it had done in Victorian houses. Broad flights of steps, wide verandas, and spacious entrances, all with elaborate details, provided interesting transitions leading up to the central hall. From this central space—using the formal Georgian and Greek Revival plans as points of departure—the

spaces for the parlors, chambers, and other rooms were plastically developed to provide forms that were picturesque on the exterior, arrangements that also provided good natural light and ventilation by allowing more openings into rooms. In the large houses a rambling stairway provided access to the second-floor dressing rooms and bedrooms and, on formal occasions, formed a setting for the graceful entrances of ladies dressed in crinoline. Since most of these large mansions were originally located conveniently near commercial districts, the sites of many eventually became parking lots or locations for office buildings and department stores.

Many of the Texans who built these opulent houses also helped finance facilities for public

FIGURE 138. Samuel F. Carter House, Houston (ca. 1900). *From* Art Work of Houston, *1904,* Houston Public Library.

A cylindrical turret and rectangular tower flanked the front entrance to this house. Italian Renaissance features were apparent in the tower with its balcony and in the urns atop the balcony railing posts. The severe form of the square entrance feature enclosing two columns reflected the influence of the École des Beaux Arts, the esteemed French school that provided the paradigm for the architecture curricula that were established in American schools during the latter part of the nineteenth century.

The site of the house is now occupied by Sakowitz Department Store.

entertainment and commissioned commercial buildings that were as ornate as their dwellings. Near the turn of the century, economic prosperity and the continuing interest in cultural advancement and entertainment resulted in the construction of quite a few chautauquas and opera houses. Virtually every county seat and well-established town had a place of assembly with a stage. The national chautauqua movement, which had originated in Chautauqua Lake, New York, reached Texas about 1889. In San Marcos that year the chautauqua program was established to include summer normal institutes for Sunday school, music, and teachers.[6] While almost all the chautau-

qua buildings are gone, in Waxahachie an octagonal auditorium erected in 1902 to accommodate religious programs, lecturers, poets, musicians, and comedians has been preserved and restored.

Also appearing on the business blocks of the well-established communities were opera houses. Financed by individuals or associations, these accommodated performances not only by traveling minstrels and opera companies but also by local groups. During the era of elegance, the color, pageantry, and content of these productions certainly contributed to the pleasure and cultural betterment of the communities in which they were viewed.

While some buildings were designed specifi-

[6] *Houston Daily Post,* May 15, 1889.

FIGURE 139. Fort Worth Opera House, Fort Worth (1881). J. J. Kane, architect. *Courtesy, Fort Worth Public Library, Amon Carter Museum.*

The formal composition apparent in the facade of this building was characteristic of opera houses. The dominant frontispiece with a balcony announced the grand entrance and provided a formal expression appropriate for the esteem given buildings serving cultural purposes. The remaining constituents of the facade were then carefully balanced about either side.

As was common, lease space was provided for stores on the ground level. The fronts of these spaces were composed of cast iron and glass, while the sections of facade above incorporated brick, stone, and galvanized iron.

Representative performances staged within included *Macbeth, H.M.S. Pinafore*, minstrel shows, and an "illustrated astronomical lecture with oxy-hydrogen lantern."

cally to house only operatic facilities, most served multiple functions. Commonly the ground-floor areas were rented to commercial concerns, while the upper stories were used for entertainment (fig. 139). Like bankers, the builders of opera houses preferred corner locations, which on one hand provided prominence and on the other allowed flexibility in the development of access to various functional areas. Typifying this, the Dallas Opera House, a three-story building with sandstone walls, had a grand entrance on Commerce Street and a balcony entrance on Austin, which allowed segregation of patrons (fig. 140). On the ground floor was commercial space; on the second floor were the stage and auditorium.

The basic designs for opera houses generally were consistent throughout the state, with variations occurring in size and opulence according to the sizes of the supportive populations. The fronts harmonized with the commercial buildings in the vicinity (fig. 141), and the interiors often were enhanced with chandeliers. Other decorative features were disposed according to rather standard schema.

FIGURE 140. Dallas Opera House, Dallas (1883). *From* Art Work of Dallas, *1895,* Archives and Research Center for Texas and Dallas History, Dallas Public Library.

Financed by twenty-two Dallas residents, this was a large building some 64 by 125 feet. With its bracketed cornice and its stilted lintels, it was a fine example of High Victorian Italianate style. It was built with sandstone walls capped by a sheet-metal cornice. Prior to the building's burning in 1901 many prominent stars performed there before Dallas crowds.

FIGURE 141. Grand Opera House, San Antonio (1886). *From* Art Work of San Antonio, Daughters of the Republic of Texas Library, San Antonio.

Located on a prominent site facing Alamo Plaza, near the Menger Hotel, this was a fine building with a typical facade. The front was balanced about the grand entrance, but a charming turret and an oriel window, along with a variety of patterns of openings, created an asymmetrical composition. A wide diversity of types of decorative features provided additional interest.

The typical performance area, of course, consisted of the stage, dressing rooms, and orchestra pit. Extending from this was the parquet, which provided seating on the lowest level. In the large theaters the dress circle provided a showplace for the fashionably dressed set. Above this, in the large theaters, there may have been one or more galleries for the middle classes.

Naturally, in the hot Texas climate builders gave considerable attention to ventilation of spaces, which rapidly accumulated heat from large assemblies of people. In Houston, for example, the Sweeney and Coombs Opera House (fig. 142) was situated on a site that allowed orientation of the front to the prevailing southeast breezes.

Opera houses also provided settings for art exhibitions and lectures. For example, the Fort Worth opera building in 1885 housed an art exhibition of world sights.[7]

Masonic lodges and the halls of other benevolent and social organizations, which were built in most Texas towns, had spatial arrangements much like those of the opera houses. Vividly indicating this similarity, the Masonic Temple in Palestine was converted easily into an opera house, which was razed in 1962. As in many opera houses, lease space was contained in the ground floor of lodge buildings, while meeting halls with high ceilings were contained in the upper areas—a traditional arrangement that had developed during antebellum days. The Masonic Hall in Fort Worth (1879) had for lease a lower story, with a ceiling height of fourteen feet, and a sixteen-foot-high upper story for a meeting hall. Later another Fort Worth Masonic building was erected with a second-story lodge room with a twenty-foot-high ceiling, which created a monumental space for the solemn Masonic work and at the same time allowed hot air to rise. In addition to providing revenue-producing space on the ground level, the multistory arrangement also provided the privacy re-quired by secret organizations—an important consideration in days before air conditioning, when windows had to remain open for ventilation during hot, humid evenings.[8]

Generally, these Masonic lodges were designed in commercial styles, similar to business structures in the areas in which they were located. However, occasional examples of Gothic styling appeared. Both the Masonic Temple in Palestine and the Masonic Hall in Galveston displayed Gothic details (fig. 143).

Another fine example of architecture built to accommodate a social organization was Harmony Hall, Galveston (fig. 144). Like other buildings erected by social organizations, it contained an assembly space on the second level—a spatial arrangement that facilitated good exterior composition. Through the ornamental design of this work, the prestige of the Harmony Society and its members was celebrated.

In prosperous towns and cities, increasing financial and commercial activity also created needs for large business buildings to replace the three- and four-bay, one- and two-story masonry buildings of the antebellum and Reconstruction periods. As in other building types, there was considerable motivation to demonstrate up-to-dateness; many viewed opulent commercial buildings as barometers of business and as enticements to capitalists to invest more money. Reflecting public attitudes, the *Galveston Daily News* reported that building improvements were indicative of substantial growth, but "it is not so much the number of buildings that are erected as the style and costliness of the same. . . ."[9]

In this optimistic atmosphere, architects worked with fashionable styles and progressive technology to provide character and improved functional qualities for large new buildings. Prosperous commercial-building owners demanded architectural statements

---

[7] *Fort Worth Daily Gazette,* March 31, 1887.

[8] *Fort Worth Daily Democrat,* June 11, 1879; *Fort Worth Daily Gazette,* November 3 and December 12, 1892, March 9, 1893.

[9] *Galveston Daily News,* October 3, 1875.

FIGURE 142. Sweeney and Coombs Opera House, Houston (1890). Eugene T. Heiner, architect. *From* Art Work of Houston, *1894, Houston Public Library*.

Erected on the site of Gray's Opera House, an earlier establishment, this was a large building about 100 by 150 feet. The ground floor reportedly had space for six stores or business places. The second floor contained the stage, parquette, and dress circle while the second and third levels contained galleries. On the front was one grand entrance.

The site of the opera house building is now a parking lot.

FIGURE 143. Masonic Lodge Building, Galveston (ca. 1880). Nicholas J. Clayton, architect. *From* Art Work in Galveston, *Texas Collection, Barker Texas History Center, University of Texas at Austin.*

This was among the finest Masonic temples in Texas. Cathedral-like details in Victorian Gothic style provided an appropriate expression for Masonry, which consisted of teachings based on Christian doctrines. The tower and fronts communicated an ecclesiastical mood. The whiteness of the building may have symbolized the purity associated with the symbolic white leather apron. However, polychromatic richness and contrast were provided by the roofing.

As was common with Masonic halls, this was a multifunctional edifice located on a corner. Entered through a strongly announced entrance to the right, the lodge hall was located on the second floor. The ground level space was leased to a furniture dealer at the time this photo was taken. The imposing structure is now gone.

FIGURE 144. Harmony Hall, Galveston (1882–1883). Nicholas J. Clayton, architect. *From* Art Work in Galveston, *Texas Collection, Barker Texas History Center, University of Texas at Austin.*

Harmony Hall was acclaimed for its beauty. Among the most ornate buildings in the state, it incorporated an interesting array of elements from the Renaissance Revival and geometric components, composed into an original statement.

Interior spaces were well organized: an entrance on Church Street provided access to a large dining hall and club rooms on the first floor and to a drama and music hall seating about nine hundred on the second. On one side of the entrance was a ladies' reception and dressing room; on the other a gentlemen's hat room and parlor. Accessible from a private entrance were a reading room, billiard room, and bar. The 1900 Galveston storm damaged the building; in 1928 it burned.

providing distinctive images. Illustrations of these structures often appeared with advertisements in newspapers and directories, thus creating a visual association with the businesses. A further expression of the importance of "image" was evident around the turn of the century, when banks imprinted perspective views of their buildings on checks and statements.

During the late nineteenth century, the impact architecture was believed to have upon the economic destiny of towns and the romantic attitudes that fostered the production of elaborately designed structures were demonstrated vividly in Fort Worth theatrical productions. There, the spirit of the times was expressed in parodies dramatizing commercial enterprise. *The Capitalist; Or the City of Fort Worth, the Texas Mikado,* with "Yankee-Doo" as a capitalist and "Pushmuch" as a real estate dealer, was produced to encourage investment in Texas. Other romantic indications of the relationship between architecture and commerce were apparent in *The Texas Spring Palace City, Fort Worth*, a parody on *H.M.S. Pinafore*, wherein two bankers called attention to the enterprising spirit behind the architectural accomplishments of the city.

As in residential work, the desired quality for commercial buildings was provided by a rich palette of materials and ornate details. While local foundries produced standard prefabricated iron components, they also produced custom designs. Recognizing the potential of a relatively new material, Galveston architect Nicholas J. Clayton designed ironwork that emphasized the inherent plasticity of the material. Considering the nature of iron as well as the purpose of the components, he employed custom-designed, locally manufactured columns on several commercial fronts. In these components the functions of beam and wall support were clearly shown by separate vertical structural members connected by an open web.[10]

Iron with delicate detailing was used on a number of commercial buildings in San Antonio and Fredericksburg. An example of this in San Antonio was the Maverick Building, a five-story work with balconies supported by thin columns and decorated with charming filigree (fig. 145). Masonry enclosing iron columns, combined with some ornamental metalwork, provided a wide range of means for elaborate designs providing images for the business contained within. This tendency was observed by Leopold Eidlitz, prominent architect and writer, near the end of the century. He noted, "Upon them [commercial buildings] are lavished in costly materials and decoration the forms of courts and palaces, in order to appeal to the attention of the community and to a remunerative patronage."[11]

Perhaps because prefabricated iron compo-

nents failed to provide sufficient variety, or perhaps because unprotected iron deformed severely when engulfed by intense heat and thus was not fireproof—or maybe it was a combination of both reasons—the popularity of exposed iron in the large Texas cities declined during the late 1880's. Thin metal columns with rectangular cross sections and sheet-metal cornices with elaborate patterns did continue to be employed thereafter in rural communities.

Elaborate decoration of street facades emphasized by imposing physical height provided the owners of commercial buildings with a means of expressing prominence in business. As in other building types, while styles were imported from the East Coast, their original paradigms had been in Europe. Although many fashions finally appeared, the street architecture of Renaissance Italy provided the greatest resources for complex details and elegant materials. Among the fine examples of Renaissance-inspired fronts reflecting affluence in Texas was a structure since razed: the Hancock Building (1880), Austin, a design with elaborate Classical features by F. E. Ruffini (fig. 146).

Although not so popular as the Classical, Gothic features did provide distinction for some commercial buildings. Among the fine examples of commercial Gothic in the capital is the Tips Building (1876). This work, with characteristic pointed-arched openings designed by Jasper N. Preston, was denatured when remodeled but is now being restored to its original character. In Houston, the Prince Building, now gone, likewise displayed delicate Gothic details, although other stylistic elements were incorporated into the design (fig. 147). Also in Houston the north corner of Main and Congress is still accented by a delightful High-Victorian Gothic commercial block (1883) with an animated surface and components reminiscent of the facade of the Provident Life and Trust Company Building, Philadelphia, designed by architect Frank Furness. Currently a place of business for exotic

[10]For illustrations, see Howard Barnstone, *The Galveston That Was*, pp. 90, 115; Willard B. Robinson, *Texas Public Buildings of the Nineteenth Century*, p. 123.

[11]Leopold Eidlitz, "The Vicissitudes of Architecture," *Architectural Record* 1 (April–June, 1892):474.

FIGURE 145. Maverick Building, San Antonio (ca. 1878). *From* Art Work of San Antonio, *Daughters of the Republic of Texas Library, San Antonio.*

This fine commercial building was distinguished by its wrought-iron work. Delicately scaled columns supported balconies that were enhanced by ironwork designs that varied on each story. All this made an imposing and unique statement. The building was demolished in 1921 to make way for the present office building designed by Lou Herrington.

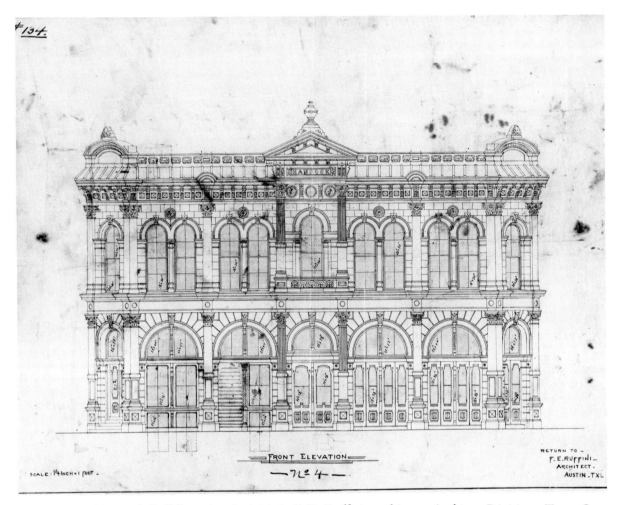

FIGURE 146. Hancock Building, Austin (1880). F. E. Ruffini, architect. *Archives Division, Texas State Library, Austin.*

Beautiful Renaissance Revival details distinguished the handsome facade. Although it was originally designed as a commercial building, nearly two decades later (1896) the building was converted into an opera house. Later it was remodeled into a movie theater, but then it was razed.

dancers, the Texas example, although somewhat denatured, is unique and ought to be preserved for posterity.

Business buildings with elaborate details expressed prosperity in a number of other cities of the state. In Galveston, using the Classical stylistic elements of the Italian Renaissance as a point of departure, Nicholas J. Clayton, who worked skillfully with intricate designs, created street architecture with· extraordinary richness, as exemplified by the W. L. Moody Building (fig. 148). While in the H. M. Trueheart & Company Building (1881–1882)—which has been restored—Clayton earlier had

employed elaborate composition and detailing, during the 1880's his work became richer, with more complex surface treatment, yet more strongly unified. The 1882 Greenleve, Block & Company Building, also by Clayton, originally a colossal, four-story merchant house with an elaborate cornice but now reduced to three stories, had an intricate exterior design with colored bricks, cut stonework, and fine cast iron.

By 1890, Clayton provided the sought-after richness in more restrained compositions, employing carefully arranged elements in the style of the Renaissance—consistent with na-

FIGURE 147. Prince Building, Houston (ca. 1890). *From* Album of Houston, Texas, *Houston Public Library.*

This handsomely proportioned building provided opulence through polychromatic materials and variety of stylistic details. Pilasters and stringcourses articulated the walls into a handsome, disciplined composition. Variety was provided by the juxtaposition of second-story stilted arches under third-story Gothic arches. A thin spire and a series of finials provided a delicate silhouette against the sky.

tional trends. A fine expression of this tendency was the Adoue & Lobit Bank Building (fig. 149). In compositions of this sort, Clayton, as well as others, adopted a style common for well-designed facades, using boldly projecting cornices to unify constituent parts and terminate the perspective of street-level views.

Elsewhere commercial buildings built by others exhibited similar opulence intended to glorify commerce, but they usually were less successful than the designs of Clayton. In Houston the Gibbs Building had complex detailing, although, as sometimes happened, the diversity of forms really needed a strong unifying element or theme (fig. 150). A more reposed palatial image was provided in the Bayou City by the Neo-Renaissance style developed for the Waddell Building (fig. 151). In

San Antonio, Joske Brothers Store (1888) was designed with Renaissance as well as nonconformist details (fig. 152).

Regardless of the style of the commercial buildings, designers developed common aesthetic qualities. Human scale and tactile warmth were provided by related proportions and by the decorative adornment of the buildings with both manufactured and natural materials. Stone, brick, and metal were exploited to enhance building exteriors; natural wood and stained glass were used extensively on interiors, all with care given to scale. The size of these features and their distribution was a matter of judgment: ornamental features too small for the form they decorated gave impressions of weakness; large and bold decoration gave impressions of coarseness. Moreover,

FIGURE 148. W. L. Moody Building, Galveston (1882). Nicholas J. Clayton, architect. *From* Art Work in Galveston, *Texas Collection, Barker Texas History Collection, University of Texas at Austin.*

On the broadside of the building, a five-part organization divided the facade into a well-proportioned and unified composition based on the Renaissance Revival style. A hierarchical system of proportions, with the visual dominance of the various units expressed in descending order from large to small, was skillfully developed. Surfaces were enhanced by a diversity of materials, colors, and geometric patterns. However, the precise forms of the details were secondary to the overall effect created by patterns of light and shadow.

The building still stands at 2202–2206 Strand, but considerable richness was lost with the removal of the cornice, the fourth story, and the loggia.

FIGURE 149. Adoue & Lobit Bank, Galveston (1890). Nicholas J. Clayton, architect. *From* Art Work in Galveston, *Texas Collection, Barker Texas History Center, University of Texas at Austin.*

Through opulent design, this fine commercial building exhibited Galveston's affluence. Architect Clayton exploited pilasters, triangular and segmental window pediments, boldly profiled stringcourses, and an intricately detailed entablature. It was a beautiful statement incorporating Renaissance Revival features. Although the structure still stands at 2101 Strand, the three stories have been expanded to four. The decorative details were stripped early in the century, leaving an insipid box. Known since 1976 as the Commerce Building (the Steele Building after 1919), it has been painted white.

FIGURE 150. Gibbs Building, Houston (ca. 1885). *From* Art Work of Houston, *1894,* Houston Public Library.

    Located at the northwest corner of Fannin Street and Franklin Avenue, the diverse combination of geometric forms created an imposing, if not handsome, appearance. As was often true of buildings with corner locations, a cylindrical form provided a focal point for the composition, while providing a visual transition from one facade to the other. Oriel windows terminated each elevation, while a cantilevered section surmounted by a feature enclosing the Lone Star was a prominent form on the south facade.

FIGURE 151. Waddell Building, Houston (ca. 1895). *Harris County Heritage Society, Houston.*

Traditional compositional principles with Neo-Renaissance stylistic elements dating from two eras gave this building distinction. The original section was three stories high with an oriel capped by a conical roof. The beginning or base of the composition was strongly expressed by heavy columns supporting a deep spandrel. Above this the second and third floors were treated as a middle, unified by the pilasters, while a cornice with simple lines terminated the composition.

During the early twentieth century three floors were added. Similar rhythms and elements helped tie the new and the old together. Although there was much diversity, the subtle vertical continuity provided by the columns, pilasters, and paired colonettes helped unify the work, and the overall effect was one of richness.

FIGURE 152. Joske Brothers Store, San Antonio (1888). Giles and Guindon, architects. *Institute of Texan Cultures*, *San Antonio*.

Polychromy and galvanized iron provided strong visual features on this commercial work. Alternating bands of light-colored stone and red brick created intense contrast. Finials surmounted the pilasters, which divided the walls into panels, further contributing to the complexity of the design. Other noteworthy features included the corner turret with ogival roof.

In 1938–1939, this building was incorporated by Joske's into an expansion of their new department store, but the historical sections are no longer evident.

Texas architects, at least the talented, recognized that sparseness of ornament increased the importance of form and proportion. Often in well-designed works, components with important structural values were enhanced with rich and complicated decoration. Finally, projections of details created patterns of light and shadow that emphasized proportions and pulled them together into a unified whole.

These same principles also applied to other types of commercial buildings, including banks and exchanges. On preferred corner locations, bankers commissioned buildings with elaborate embellishment and durable construction. As in other types of commercial

buildings many styles were employed; however, the most important aspect was not the style per se, but an up-to-date appearance in both exterior design and interior furnishings and equipment. In an 1890 address to the State Architects Association, architect James Wahrenberger expressed the perceived importance of design modernity when he commented, "It appears absurd that in this age of steam cars, electricity, etc., courthouses, post offices and other public buildings should be of such antique architectural style as to remind one of the dark ages of the inquisitions and the carrier pigeon." Another architect, A. N. Dawson, reflected this same attitude

FIGURE 153. Kampmann Building, San Antonio (ca. 1885). *Daughters of the Republic of Texas Library, San Antonio.*

Housing the Alamo National Bank, this commercial block displayed a wide variety of stylistic features, creating a Baroque appearance. On the ground story masonry was rusticated, and the bank entrance was flanked by two columns of carved stone. On the upper three stories, the openings were surmounted by pediments in several forms: flat, triangular, and broken. The whole was then crowned by a cornice with intricate patterns.

when he boasted that Fort Worth's "architects are up-to-date (so recognized all over Texas) and her buildings are modern in style and finish."[12]

Many buildings appeared in "modern" styles. When it was built, the Kampmann Building, San Antonio, was an elaborate display of up-to-date Renaissance features (fig. 153). Another showplace of modernity, the T. W. House Bank, Houston (1889), designed by Eugene T. Heiner, was three stories, with

a front of iron, brick, and terra-cotta, "with all embellishments in the way of modern ornamental architecture"[13] (fig. 154). The Evans Block, Fort Worth (1889), was in a style described as Venetian-Romanesque and was fitted, it was proudly announced, with three hydraulic elevators.

Other noteworthy finance facilities, now gone, included the National Exchange Bank Building (later renamed the Slaughter Building), Dallas, in Romanesque style with sand-

[12] *Dallas Morning News*, May 15, 1890; *Fort Worth Daily Gazette*, December 6, 1895.

[13] *Houston Daily Post*, June 1, 1889.

FIGURE 154. T. W. House Bank, Houston (1889). Eugene T. Heiner, architect. *From* Souvenir Anniversary Edition of the Houston Chronicle, *October, 1905, Houston Public Library.*

Local pride in this new building was expressed by the *Houston Daily Post* when it noted: "While Dallas and other cities are blowing about the erection of hotels and bank buildings, Houston is coming to the front in that direction. In the hotels line we already have the largest and most elegantly appointed hostelries in the state and now the banking house of T. W. House is going to erect a handsome three-story building. . . ."

FIGURE 155. National Exchange Bank (Slaughter Building), Dallas (ca. 1895, 1904). *Dallas Public Library*.

This was originally a five-story building with an entrance asymmetrically located. It was distinguished by rock-faced masonry and cut stonework.

In 1904 Colonel C. C. Slaughter, a wealthy West Texas cattle baron, purchased the structure and renamed it after himself. Subsequently he commissioned architects C. W. Bulger and Son to enlarge it. First it was expanded to the west (*left of photo*); then two more stories were added; finally, in 1909 the east wing was added. Incorporated into the additions were oriel windows and Sullivanesque ornamental features, both of which had originated in Chicago during the latter part of the nineteenth century. In 1940 the building was razed to make room for a new office building.

FIGURE 156. Banking Lobby, First National Bank, Fort Worth (ca. 1885). *Courtesy, First National Bank, Fort Worth, Amon Carter Museum.*

During the nineteenth century, as today, the interiors of bank buildings were finished with elegant contemporary materials. In this view, handsome woodwork, marble cabinet bases, and brass footrails gave the customer his first favorable impressions of the lobby. Consistent with the taste of the times, the ceiling was finished with sheet-metal panels with patterns stamped into them.

stone and granite walls (fig. 155). The interiors of these banking institutions were as elegant as the exteriors (fig. 156).

During the 1890's the Romanesque Revival style appearing in some of these banks also became popular for other commercial blocks. Erected by prominent Dallas entrepreneurs, two of the Sanger Brothers buildings were elegant examples of the round-arched mode incorporating principles of composition used by Henry Hobson Richardson (fig. 157). Unfor-

tunately, many of the most beautiful banks of this period have been replaced.

In addition to banks and other business blocks, buildings with specialized designs contributed significantly to the commercial character of Texas cities, although normally there was little attempt to indicate a specific function. While many of the early commercial blocks were elaborately decorated shells with open interiors or with minimal partitioning, many late-nineteenth-century buildings were

FIGURE 157. Sanger Brothers Complex, Dallas (1884, 1888, 1890). A. B. Bristol, architect. *Above, from the collections of the Dallas Historical Society; at right, Dallas Public Library.*

    The three buildings of the Sanger complex were designed with up-to-date technology and stylistic concepts. The first, a five-story building (*at right*), displayed Italianate details. With its stone base, Sullivanesque decoration, and Richardsonian composition, the six-story Romanesque work (*above*) was particularly handsome. Originally constructed as the Security Mortgage and Trust Building, it included skeletal framing techniques that had been developed in Chicago. Finally, in 1890, the third building was constructed for the Sanger brothers in Romanesque Revival style. In 1922 the Sangers purchased the Security Building.

After serving commercial purposes, the complex housed El Centro College. By 1977 these buildings were among the most important commercial buildings in the central business district of Dallas. Nonetheless, in spite of preservationists' determined legal efforts to save the structures, the Dallas County Community College District would not consider continuing use, and the buildings were battered to the ground in 1977.

designed to house special activities. This trend in commercial architecture resulted from industrialization, organization, and prosperity.

Among the commercial monuments with specialized functional provisions were newspaper plants, cotton exchanges, and board-of-trade buildings. Generally the buildings designed to serve programmed functions were acclaimed by contemporaries for progressiveness. For building the Galveston News Building (1883–1884), that publishing company was called "a pioneer in erecting an exclusive newspaper building." Providing a prestigious public image for the firm was an

ornamental and well-proportioned front, incorporating a beautiful composition of materials (fig. 158). Likewise, the Dallas News Building (1899), proclaimed "an ornament to the city," was built of stone and pressed brick and contained "every device for saving time and labor," a result of organization for efficiency.[14]

Other buildings housing specific functions included the cotton exchanges. Reflecting the energy of businessmen and the prosperity emanating from cotton, they were designed to

[14] *Galveston Daily News*, July 9, 1899.

FIGURE 158. Galveston News Building, Galveston (1883–1884). Nicholas J. Clayton, architect. *Galveston Historical Foundation.*

This was among the most beautiful commercial buildings erected during the era of elegance. Three stories high, it was fireproof and incorporated iron and Philadelphia red pressed brick, accented with white and pink marble in a facade of extraordinary richness and depth.

The interior spaces accommodated specific functions: on the ground floor were located the counting room, press, and printing machine with a capacity of eighteen thousand copies per hour; on the second floor were located editorial rooms; and on the third floor were the composing rooms.

Although the structure still stands at 2108 Mechanic Street, it has been completely denatured and is unrecognizable.

FIGURE 159. Galveston Cotton Exchange Building, Galveston (1877–1878). Gibbs and Moser, architects. *From* Art Work in Galveston, *Texas Collection, Barker Texas History Center, University of Texas at Austin.*

Located adjacent to the News Building, the Galveston Cotton Exchange Building attested to the romantic and exuberant spirit that permeated business activities during the last quarter of the nineteenth century.

The structure was three stories high (plus an attic) and faced with Philadelphia pressed brick and Austin limestone, and the exterior was decorated with symbolic features. Carved stone ornamentation depicted the cotton leaf, flower, and boll. A porch on Mechanic Street had spandrels decorated with horns of plenty. Atop the porch was a representation of a cotton bale and the motto *Cotton, the king.* On the corner pier was a carving symbolizing cotton in maritime commerce: a rudder, anchor, pulleys, ropes, and an entwining cotton plant. To represent vibrant activities within the building, bull's and bear's heads were carved on shields over the entrance. The building was razed in 1939 to give way to an Art Deco building, which still stands.

provide an elegant setting for trading activities. Among these, designed by Eugene T. Heiner in "modern" Renaissance style, was the Houston Cotton Exchange (1884), which fortunately still stands and has been restored on the exterior. Gone, however, is the Galveston Cotton Exchange (fig. 159), with its richly animated surface, which was built prior to the Houston Cotton Exchange.

The elaborately designed commercial fronts of the last decades of the nineteenth century not only optimistically expressed the competition and prowess of the business world; they also were intended to attract more capital and immigration to the state. During the late 1880's and early 1890's many boards of trade—the forerunners of the chambers of commerce—were organized in various communities with the specific purpose of promoting commerce. Basic to their raison d'etre was

FIGURE 160. Fort Worth Board of Trade Building, Fort Worth (1888–1889). Armstrong and Messer, architects. *From* The City of Fort Worth and the State of Texas, *courtesy John W. Hackney, Amon Carter Museum.*

This handsome Renaissance Revival building was finished with exterior materials of stone, pressed and molded bricks, and terra cotta. The four-foot-high base, in ashlar pattern, was blue Trinidad sandstone; above the water table, rich red sandstone from Colorado Springs, Colorado, was employed up to the level of the second floor. For the remainder of the facades, bricks and terra cotta were used. The heavy voussoirs, some of which reportedly weighed two tons each, the deep moldings, and the rich carvings astounded contemporaries.

The interior also was handsomely finished. Ground-level corridor floors were surfaced with mosaic tiles, and walls were wainscoted with panels of polished oak. Ceilings also were finished paneled woodwork. Other fine materials including cherry paneling, lead glass, and frescoed ceilings were used. To glorify the function of the building, there was an elegant boardroom finished with oak and oxidized silver hardware.

the desire to prove to eastern capitalists that Texas cities were safe and profitable places for investment. They also wished to show potential immigrants that the state had many amenities for permanent residents. In addition to encouraging new construction by others, the promoting organizations in some cases became sufficiently influential to secure buildings specifically serving their own purposes. In 1888–1889 the Penn Mutual Insurance Company built for the Fort Worth Board of Trade a handsome multistory office structure (fig. 160), which was acclaimed enthusiastically as "a monument to encourage capital to locate at Fort Worth."[15]

By the late 1880's, when these buildings appeared, architects had begun fireproofing multistory public structures. Following practices that had evolved in Chicago and New York City for high-rise buildings—which were much admired in Texas—designers enclosed exposed metal columns with masonry, thereby insulating against intense heat. This not only increased safety, it also provided a satisfactory solution to design. Thick masonry gave more visual support for heavy masonry fronts than the thin iron columns. Moreover, it allowed designers more latitude in developing the ornamental clothing for commercial buildings. This fireproofing, repose, and decoration generally were apparent in the commercial buildings of the last decade and a half of the nineteenth century. However, while the commercial hotels within the business districts were durably built, the resort hotels were not so safe.

While on the one hand the city hotels were designed with formal composition that harmonized with other street architecture, on the other hand the resort hostelries were designed with informal picturesqueness providing appropriate settings for leisure. Although they often covered more ground area than some other commercial buildings, downtown hotels shared the popular styles of the store facades.

The Capitol Hotel in Houston (1882), which was a new building on the site of the old capitol, and the Grand Central Hotel (1883) in El Paso were clothed respectively in Victorian Renaissance Revival and Second Empire details (figs. 161, 162). Likewise, the McLeod Hotel (1893) in Dallas was faced with Renaissance features (fig. 163). The Oriental Hotel (1893) in Dallas was in the then-fashionable Romanesque Revival style. All these hotels were designed with typical uniform rhythm or spacings.

A number of fashionable hotels, which, like the commercial buildings, were considered by many to be symbols of progress and wealth, contained interior spaces that were well appointed to celebrate the patronage of the travelers. Spacious lobbies with high ceilings, elevators, and rooms with marble-topped tables all contributed to a palatial character.

The resort hotels were conceived to appeal romantically to the new leisure class and were promoted by handsome pamphlets published by the railroads, which were interested in increasing passenger travel. Such hotels were located at various points within the Lone Star State to attract the patronage of those interested in health and recreation. Owners of these hostelries extolled the therapeutic benefits of certain mineral waters, as well as the healthful environments in which they were located. It was said that the waters from the ground in such towns as Mineral Wells and Waco would cure a wide variety of ailments. Wooton Wells, Robertson County, for example, sought the trade of "seekers of health and pleasure," and the pleasure resort of Dalby Springs, Bowie County, advertised waters curing "Dyspepsia, Dropsy, Enlargement of the Spleen and Liver, Scrofula, Gravel, Constipation and all diseases peculiar to females."[16]

In other sections of the state, where there were no mineral waters to be exploited, entrepreneurs attempted to capitalize upon the recreational potential of the terrain and en-

[15] *Fort Worth Daily Gazette*, March 25, 1888.

[16] *Dallas Morning News*, May 1, 1886.

FIGURE 161. Capitol Hotel, Houston (1882). *From* Art Work of Houston, *1894,* Houston Public Library.

Erected on the site of the first capitol of Texas was this fine Renaissance Revival hotel, with a frontage of 100 feet on Main Street and 150 on Texas Avenue. To attract the public, the interior contained steam elevators, gas, water, and other conveniences. After only three years the builder, A. Groesbeck, assigned interest in the building to William Rice of New York. Early in the twentieth century this building was razed to make room for the present Rice Hotel, a high-rise building that was begun in 1912.

FIGURE 162. Grand Central Hotel, El Paso (1883). *El Paso Public Library.*

Located on the site of the present Mills Building, this also was a fine example of an elegant hotel with Renaissance Revival details. The balconies with wrought-iron enclosures contributed to the homeyness of the atmosphere. Owned by Josiah Crosby and Anson Mills, the building burned in 1892.

FIGURE 163. McLeod Hotel, Dallas (1889). *From* Art Work of Dallas, *1895,* Archives and Research Center *for* Texas and Dallas History, *Dallas Public Library.*

This structure was among the finest hotels in Texas at the time it was completed. The windows and pilasters produced an interesting pattern. As if to dramatize the verticality of the facade, the configuration of the arches spanning the openings was changed on each story: at the main level they were semicircular; above they became progressively less rounded until, on the top story, they were flat. Other contrast was provided by the materials.

The name eventually was changed to the Grand Central, then to the Imperial. Finally in 1914 it burned.

FIGURE 164. Alta Vista Hotel, Corpus Christi (1890–1891). *Texas State Historical Association, Austin.*

Built by E. H. Ropes on a bluff that extended into the water, this hotel contained 125 rooms along spacious corridors. Verandas provided areas for promenades. On the third floor was a ballroom with elevated music stand.

Although the hotel building apparently was completed by 1891, due to a shortage of funding it was not furnished. When the Panic of 1893 struck, it was locked without ever having accommodated an overnight guest. It, along with nearby cottages, was located too far from the city to be profitable in future years. The structure was destroyed by fire in 1927.

vironment. Unlike that of the commercial hotels, the character of the resort facility was intended to communicate an informal association with travel and fun, rather than an organized formality identified with commerce. Thus the Arlington Heights Hotel (1892) in Fort Worth was in the style of an English inn, a mode conceived to project an image associated with leisure and travel. To communicate this same type of informality, the Alta Vista Hotel (Pavilion Hotel), Corpus Christi (1890), was designed with a generous number of balconies and porches (fig. 164). These same features were important aspects of the Tremont Hotel (1878) and the Beach Hotel (1883) in Galveston, the latter of which was among the most interesting in the nation (fig. 165). The Electric Pavilion (1882), another Galveston resort designed by Clayton, displayed similar character (fig. 166). Unfortunately, the charming appearances that made these resort hostelries so attractive proved to be their nemesis: the wooden frames of most have burned, and today none survive in Texas.

Other buildings likewise were constructed to produce profits from the new leisure class. Natatoriums and bathhouses provided a variety of baths, pools, and so forth, all for enjoyment as well as therapeutic benefit. To develop appropriate character for these natatorial establishments, architects incorporated features recalling similar pleasure palaces of antiquity. In Waco, for example, the Natatorium Hotel built in 1892 according to the designs of architect J. Riely Gordon was decorated with mosaic tiles, marble fountains, and jardinieres of tropical plants (fig. 167). The Fort Worth Natatorium, in a large four-story brick edifice, featured Russian, Turkish, and vapor baths in about forty bathrooms; also there was a swimming pool, sixty by one hundred feet.[17] In San Antonio the Hot Wells Hotel and Bathhouse,

[17] *Fort Worth Daily Gazette*, June 28, 1890.

FIGURE 165. Beach Hotel, Galveston (1883). Nicholas J. Clayton, architect. *From* Art Work in Galveston, *Texas Collection, Barker Texas History Center, University of Texas at Austin.*

Located on the beach, this was an extraordinary work designed to delight visitors. The recreational purpose was indicated by verandas in Stick style. The dominant octagonal center pavilion was complemented by half-octagonal end pavilions and an eight-sided bandstand.

The colors were vibrant: red and white bands on the roof and golden-green eaves. The ridges of the east and west pavilions were crowned with iron crestings painted bronze and gold.

The exciting design did not guarantee success, however. Although the hotel advertised rates from $2.50 to $3.50 per day (in 1889), it was not profitable. Finally, in spite of fire protection, including hoses located in the corridors and scheduled patrols by watchmen, the building was destroyed in a spectacular fire in 1898.

featuring hot sulphur-mineral water, thrived during the 1890's and early twentieth century. However, few of these once-popular facilities remain.

Additional structures for entertainment included roller skating rinks. One contemporary report from Greenville illustrated the popularity of these by calling the completion of a skating rink a cure for "the skating fever that has been raging . . . for months. . . ."[18]

Then, for the men who were not inclined toward physical activities, saloons provided "places of resort." Elaborate plate-glass mirrors and handsome woodwork of hardwoods

[18] *Fort Worth Daily Gazette,* March 23, 1885.

provided prestigious settings for social intercourse. Often adding to the richness were elaborately carved wooden columns and capitals supporting cornices above mirrors over the back bars.

While all these buildings enhanced the quality of community life for the residents, they also incidentally contributed to the attractiveness of the community to prospective immigrants. With pride, community organizations promoting the development of their cities and towns frequently cited buildings, events in the arts, and benevolent activities as evidence of cultural advancement. And then, as now, culture provided a strong enticement for capitalists and investors, since they were

FIGURE 166. Electric Pavilion, Galveston (1882). Nicholas J. Clayton, architect. *Galveston Historical Foundation.*

Erected by the Galveston City Railroad to stimulate travel to the beach, this was a large structure in Stick style. Patterns of woodwork, braces, and picturesque gables all were intended to delight the beach-goer. On the interior was a large recreational space spanned by arches. Alas, the building lasted only a short time: it burned in 1883.

sure that new residents, in turn, would be attracted.

Some buildings were planned with the specific purpose of encouraging immigration and attracting from abroad investment in new buildings and enterprises. To further promote the state, Texas planned expositions to publicize natural resources and other amenities. In 1889 work was begun on the Texas Spring Palace, Fort Worth, designed by Armstrong and Messer (fig. 168). Headlined as "A Great Event in the History of the Lone Star State," it was romantically proclaimed that the building and its contents would be a "grand karporama [display] of the material resources of the

state. . . ." According to other boastful claims, the enterprise would "be for Texas, all and much more than the great Paris exposition was to Paris. . . ." Hoping to profit from immediate passenger traffic as well as from long range immigration, the railroads advertised the Spring Palace in the East and offered excursion rates from "all points of the compass."[19] However, the imposing and colorful Spring Palace was destined for a short existence; in the spring of 1890 it burned to the ground.

[19] *Houston Daily Post,* April 5, 1889; *Dallas Morning News,* May 7, 1889.

FIGURE 167. Natatorium Hotel, Waco (1892). J. Riely Gordon, architect. *Texas Collection, Baylor University, Waco.*

    The water facilities of this establishment typified those of many natatoriums built in Texas, as well as throughout the west. A large pool was provided for the enjoyment of patrons. However, while this enterprise included a hotel, some did not. On the exterior, Romanesque Revival style provided the character that was considered so essential.

FIGURE 168. Texas Spring Palace, Fort Worth (1889–1890). Armstrong and Messer, architects. *Fort Worth Public Library.*

Containing about sixty thousand square feet, the Spring Palace was a wonderful and weird composition of turrets and towers, which represented agricultural products, and ogival arches. These were dominated by a large dome covered with decorations made of wheat. Within were exhibits of minerals, fruit and vegetables, and building materials, the last of which were assembled under the direction of architect W. C. Dodson. All were intended to advertise the culture and ambition of Texas.

Following the loss of the palace, promoters began raising funds for a pavilion at the World's Columbian Exposition in Chicago. Designers of the Texas exhibition hall incorporated features symbolizing the state's cultural heritage (fig. 169); such details as the Lone Star and likenesses of longhorn cattle provided character for the building, which contained exhibits intended to promote immigration and investment. On the interior, large, well-organized spaces also were elaborately decorated to provide a pleasant atmosphere for visitors (fig. 170).

Meanwhile, back home, architects from various parts of the nation were invited to submit plans for another local exposition building to promote Texas resources. In 1894 following the selection of plans, construction was begun in Waco on the Texas Cotton Palace. Demonstrating continuing interest in associating architecture with the state's cultural origins, this building was designed in Mission Revival style. However, it too was destined for a short existence; the palace burned after being open for only a few months. Nonetheless, although they may have been temporarily discouraged,

FIGURE 169. Texas Pavilion, World's Columbian Exposition, Chicago, Illinois (1893). Gordon and Laub, architects. *From* Sketches from the Portfolio of James Riely Gordon, *Dielmann Collection, Daughters of the Republic of Texas Library, San Antonio.*

With attitudes similar to those of other individuals in charge of other state pavilions at the World's Columbian Exposition, the directors of the Texas exhibition aspired to erect a building expressive of the culture of the Lone Star State. Architects Gordon and Laub were commissioned to design a building in Spanish Renaissance style of architecture. This mode, it was thought, would be commemorative of the Alamo, monument of Texas valor and patriotism.

A variety of regional ornamental features contributed to the character of the building. These were fabricated from staff (a mixture of plaster of paris and hemp).

FIGURE 170. Texas Pavilion, World's Columbian Exposition, Chicago. Interior View. *From* Sketches from the Portfolio of James Riely Gordon, *Dielmann Collection, Daughters of the Republic of Texas Library, San Antonio.*

The Texas Pavilion was made possible by donations of materials and money from across the state. If the proposal was in fact realized as planned, the interior of the reception room was finished with woods from Texas, to display the beauty of native materials. Other donations included a piano, carpet, and curtains. Statues of Sam Houston and Stephen Austin were contracted from Elisabet Ney, distinguished sculptor from Germany, who resided in Texas.

promoters were soon at work on a new, larger, and more permanent work—certainly a demonstration of the importance attributed to architecture in the promotion of the state's economy (fig. 171).

To provide opportunities for local and regional display and promotion of products, the State Fair and Exposition grounds were developed in Dallas, reminiscent, on a small scale, of the world's fairs. After a racetrack was laid out, architects were invited to compete for the commissions to design a judges' stand, grandstand, machinery hall, exposition hall, stables, and stock pens. The plans of architect W. H. Wilson were selected for the exposition hall, which no longer stands. It was a two-story building on a cruciform plan, capped with a dome over the crossing. Later many communities constructed exhibition and spectator buildings for local uses; these provided forums for the exchange of ideas as well as opportunities to present tangible evidence of mate-

FIGURE 171. Texas Cotton Palace, Waco (1909). Jacob Larmour, architect. *Texas Collection*, *Baylor University*, *Waco*.

Shortly after the destruction of the 1894 Cotton Palace, work again was begun on planning a new structure. Plans submitted by several local and out-of-state architectural firms were studied. However, work was delayed for over a decade. Like its predecessor, it was designed in Mission Revival style. Electric lights were used to outline the forms at night, thereby dramatizing them.

The Cotton Palace was closed in 1930 and stood vacant for several years. It had been demolished by the fall of 1940, when the cornerstone of the main building was mounted on a slab of granite and placed in Cameron Park.

rial and artistic advancement. Some remain; many others are gone.

Thus during the era of elegance romantic attitudes about the expression of character in architecture produced many opulent buildings. These structures reflected attainment and pride through a variety of historical styles, considered to be modern at the time. Above all, with all the variety of forms and details and the diversity in the use of various materials, these pretentious buildings were statements of individuality. Of course the means of obtaining this character are impossible today; economic limitations and the disappearance of many skills make these picturesque houses and rich commercial buildings irreplaceable. Nonetheless countless beautiful historic structures have been replaced by parking lots or by shiny new buildings; with careful planning many could have been saved. Unfortunately, not only these homes and places of business but also many institutional and governmental buildings erected to express dignity through beauty have also been lost.

6

Lost from the Era of Elegance: Institutional and Governmental Buildings

DURING the latter part of the nineteenth century, then, the culture of Texas improved rapidly. Wealth, of course provided the means to realize the physical facilities necessary for life-enhancing activities, not just for homes. Other forms of cultural improvement were apparent in the development of schools and the buildings designed to house them. Prior to the establishment of public schools during the last half of the nineteenth century, various private agencies had provided educational opportunities for those who could afford to pay. A number of segregated male and female institutes, boarding schools, and academies were founded by individuals. In addition, the Masonic Lodge opened schools in various parts of the state and assumed a major role in providing enlightenment to the young people. In 1871, following a number of previous attempts dating back to the era of the republic, free public schools finally were opened.

The level of instruction offered seems to have been reflected by the size and design of the school buildings. Primary schools generally were small buildings on a central-hall plan with little decoration, while high schools were large edifices with more complex interior arrangements. Secondary schools often displayed elaborate ornamentation on exteriors, suggesting the prestige of a higher level of instruction (fig. 172). Locations atop hills also

frequently reinforced visually the authority of the upper-level buildings.

The school facilities were designed as permanent edifices with apparently little expectation of future obsolescence. The incorporation of elaborate, palatial stylistic features indicates this intent to build for both present and future generations. Moreover, monumentality, symbolic of esteem for enlightenment, perhaps expressed a subjective confidence in the future of education and truth. Furthermore, the need to build structures that were as fireproof as possible required permanent masonry bearing walls. Nonetheless, during the twentieth century, increases in population and new approaches to educational processes required that virtually all these early buildings be replaced; most are gone.

Often selected through competitions, the architects of institutions throughout the state depicted stylistically the importance placed upon education and the pride associated with cultural improvement. East Dallas School was built with the dignity of Italianate character (fig. 173). Emphasizing the importance of the Fort Worth high school to the city, architect J. J. Kane boasted, "When strangers visit our fair, young city we can point to it [the building] with pride as an evidence of the liberality of our city in the cause of education." Plans for the building illustrated a limestone-walled

FIGURE 172. Public High School, Cleburne (1886). *Texas State Historical Association, Austin.*

In 1883 Cleburne constructed a new $20,000 public school according to the plans of A. N. Dawson of Fort Worth. Built by contractor M. F. Vosberg, the building was praised as a symbol of the culture and enlightenment of citizens of Cleburne and Johnson County. Unfortunately, it burned several years later. After inviting plans from interested architects, the city erected this modest building.

FIGURE 173. East Dallas School, Dallas (ca. 1886). Albert Ulrich, architect. *From Art Work of Dallas, 1895, Archives and Research Center for Texas and Dallas History, Dallas Public Library.*

Stylistic features of the fashionable Italianate mode provided character for this school. Brick walls with stone quoining, along with both Roman and segmental arches, were details that contributed to the architectural interest of the handsome building. The building was destroyed in 1948 to make room for the Baylor Dental Clinic.

FIGURE 174. Fort Worth High School, Fort Worth (1890). Haggart & Sanguinet, architects. *Courtesy Fort Worth Public Library, Amon Carter Museum.*

As was common for large school buildings, the architects for the Fort Worth High School were selected through a competition. Included among the contestants were J. J. Kane, A. N. Dawson, Armstrong and Messer, and J. B. Legg. The plans submitted by Kane were originally selected, but later the commission was awarded to Haggart & Sanguinet. They received $1,470.50 for their plans. Smith and Bardon were the contractors for the stone, brick, and woodwork.

The press expressed considerable pride in this academic building. One reporter for the *Fort Worth Daily Gazette* (January 9, 1890) lauded the building for its "most striking appearance . . . graceful proportions, elegance of detail, and superb modern interior arrangements."

edifice in Renaissance style. Another design, prepared the following year by the firm of Haggart and Sanguinet, was in Modern Renaissance style (fig. 174).[1] The public schools generally were designed in the modes that were fashionable at the time; hence the period of construction could be told by the decoration of the building. In Galveston the Ball High School (1884) was in Renaissance Revival design, with formal massing (fig. 175). The public school in Wichita Falls displayed a variety of freely composed stylistic features (fig. 176). In Houston, the Elysian Street School was designed in Richardsonian Romanesque style (fig. 177).

While exterior style and durability expressed public esteem for the high school buildings, the interior space compositions of many reflected consideration for the welfare of pupils and teachers. Indeed, concern about the interior environment at least occasionally formed the basis for selection of designers. In 1894 a Houston school committee selected from thirty plans submitted in a competition the designs prepared by Eugene T. Heiner, because they allowed good light and ventilation for the halls (fig. 178).[2]

[1] *Fort Worth Daily Gazette*, November 14, 1889.

[2] *Houston Daily Post*, January 10, 1894.

FIGURE 175. Ball High School, Galveston (1884). Nicholas J. Clayton, architect. *From* Art Work in Galveston, *Texas Collection, Barker Texas History Center, University of Texas at Austin.*

Classical features apparent in this school were fashionable in the United States at the time the building was begun. These seemed to reflect the rigid formal educational process conducted within, as well as the importance attributed to public enlightenment.

After this original section was completed, the Ball High School was enlarged several times. The dominant domed section provided a focal point that helped unify the parts. The architect was apparently proud of this design: he used a perspective of it to illustrate his advertisements in the *Galveston City Directory.* However, the building eventually was razed.

FIGURE 176. Public School, Wichita Falls (1890). *Texas State Historical Association, Austin.*

Massiveness and ornamentation attested to the importance of this building. Although educational edifices frequently were symmetrical compositions, picturesque irregularity—similar to that appearing in large residential buildings—was a significant aspect of this design.

FIGURE 177. Elysian Street School, Houston (ca. 1890). *From* Art Work of Houston, *1894, Houston Public Library.*

With walls of bricks, this was a fine example of a school incorporating Romanesque features. The strongly stated base, the Roman-arched openings with their archivolts, transomed windows, and patterned brickwork all contributed to the distinctive character.

FIGURE 178. Houston High School, Houston (1894). Eugene T. Heiner, architect. *From* Art Work of Houston, *1904*, Houston Public Library.

Incorporating a variety of stylistic elements, this monumental building was constructed with brick walls and stone trim. Housed within, in addition to classrooms, were a museum, library, and assembly hall.

At the same time public school buildings were becoming prominent additions to the built environment, new private schools also appeared as significant parts of some community scenes. Like the public edifices, private schools generally were formally planned and built in modern styles; parochial schools, however, generally reflected their religious basis through ecclesiastical styles. Among the finest expressions of religious purpose were the Ursuline academies in Galveston (fig. 179) and Dallas (fig. 180).

Considerably more pretentious, in most cases, than secondary schools were the buildings designed to serve the colleges and universities. The nineteenth-century development of public-supported institutions of higher learning naturally had been retarded by the Civil War and Reconstruction. However, after the conflict, colleges that had been established during antebellum days were expanded, and new institutions, both private and public, were opened. During this era of rapid expansion of educational systems, several existing institutions were moved to different cities, requiring new structures and leaving original buildings vacant. In 1878 Austin College moved from Huntsville to Sherman, and in the 1880's Waco attracted Baylor away from Independence. Another relocated institution was Add-Ran College, which moved first in 1895 from Thorp Spring to Waco, where it became Texas Christian University, then later to Fort Worth.

Near the end of the century several private college and university buildings were erected. Financed by churches, these at first housed the

FIGURE 179. Ursuline Academy, Galveston (1891–1894). Nicholas J. Clayton, architect. *From* Art Work in Galveston, *Texas Collection, Barker Texas History Center, University of Texas at Austin.*

The Galveston Ursuline Convent was established in 1847 by Bishop J. M. Odin and six nuns, and the first building was erected four years later. The success of the institution was well demonstrated by additions in 1861 and 1871 and by this building, which became the central unit.

High Victorian Gothic expressed the noble purpose of the institution. One of the most elaborately decorated buildings in the state, the Ursuline convent displayed a rich variety of materials and details. Masonry was exploited in different patterns, textures, and colors. Bold Gothic arches, delicate quatrefoil motifs, and sinewy pinnacles all contributed to lavishness of expression. Unfortunately, the building was destroyed in 1962 after it sustained damage from a hurricane. As attested by this structure, the architect worked well with the Gothic and Moorish vocabularies.

FIGURE 180. Ursuline Academy, Dallas (1882–1884, 1889, 1892). Nicholas J. Clayton (central section) and W. H. Harrell (two wings), architects. *From* Art of Dallas, 1895, *Archives and Research Center for Texas and Dallas History, Dallas Public Library.*

This was another fine example of romantic expression of purpose with the Gothic style. A delicate composition of pointed arches and other Medieval details suggested the religious basis of the institution. Under the direction of Ursuline Ladies, the course work of the school included music, classics, and foreign languages. The building, located on a block south of the intersection of Haskell and Bryan avenues, was razed in 1949.

FIGURE 181. St. Mary's College, Dallas (1886–1889). A. B. Bristol, architect. *Texas State Historical Association, Austin.*

Located near Ross and Garrett streets, this was a fine building, incorporating Victorian Gothic features that expressed the religious focus of the school. Founded by the Protestant Episcopal Church, the college began construction on this building in 1886, but shortage of funds delayed completion until 1889, when the institution was formally opened. Although other buildings were added, later financial difficulties forced the closing of the school in 1929, and the building was demolished in 1945.

FIGURE 182. Ann Waggoner Hall (1891), Polytechnic College of the Methodist Episcopal Church, South (Texas Wesleyan College), Fort Worth. Sanguinet and Dawson, architects. *Texas Wesleyan College, Fort Worth.*

The building program of Polytechnic College, a Methodist institution, was begun on a prominent hill in east Fort Worth. As was common, this building housed all the functions of the college, except the men's dormitory: spaces for classrooms, chapel, offices, and women's dormitory all were included. Among the courses taught were Bible, elocution, voice culture, mathematics, and languages.

In 1935, after Polytechnic had been joined by Texas Women's College, the name was changed to Texas Wesleyan College.

FIGURE 183. Main Building (1871–1874), Agricultural and Mechanical College of Texas (Texas A&M University), College Station. Jacob Larmour, architect. *Texas A&M University Archives, College Station.*

Under the provisions of federal legislation for the agricultural and mechanical colleges, the state was obligated to erect a college building and the U.S. government provided a land grant to endow costs of operation.

Construction of the first building for a land-grant school in Texas was accompanied by several difficulties. First, architect Carl de Grote was awarded the commission in 1871. However, shortly after construction commenced, the foundation work was condemned by architect Jacob Larmour, an Austin practitioner. Then Larmour was authorized to prepare new plans, and new contracts were let.

The bricks for this building were manufactured on the site.

entire academic program. Among those that no longer stand were the Baylor Female College, Belton, the cornerstone for which was laid in 1886, and St. Mary's College, Dallas (1886) (fig. 181). In Fort Worth the original Main at Polytechnic College of the Methodist Episcopal Church, South (1891), described as "English . . . with a touch of French," is no longer recognizable (fig. 182).[3]

For higher learning in Texas, the Civil War and Reconstruction had marked a turning point. During antebellum years changes were already underway in other sections of the country, but it was not until the period of recovery from the war that trends evolved to provide practical education supplementing some of the earlier liberal arts institutions.

The Civil War had given impetus to the development of colleges offering technical educa-

tion. In 1862 the Congress of the United States passed an act awarding large grants of land to each state to facilitate the development of schools providing "liberal and practical education of the industrial classes." After the war land-grant colleges were authorized in the southern states, and in 1871 the Texas Legislature created the Agricultural and Mechanical College of Texas "to bring about . . . a more modern and practical training."[4]

A pasture several miles from the Brazos River was selected for the site of the campus by a commission appointed by the governor and was donated to the state by the citizens of Bryan. Subsequently an architect was commissioned, and in 1876 a president and five professors opened the doors of a twin-towered edifice to about forty students (figs. 183, 184).

[3] *Fort Worth Daily Gazette,* January 3, 1886.

[4] H. P. N. Gammel, comp., *Laws of Texas 1822–1897,* 6:938–940.

FIGURE 184. Main Building, Agricultural and Mechanical College of Texas (Texas A&M University), College Station, View of drafting room. *Texas A&M University Archives, College Station.*

At the time the building was opened, the first floor held a horticulture room, a room for recitation, kitchen and dining room, and bedrooms. On the second floor were recitation rooms, library, museum, bedrooms, and parlor; on the third were additional classrooms; and on the fourth were an assembly space and the drafting room. This building burned in 1912.

FIGURE 185. Gathright Hall (1876), Agricultural and Mechanical College of Texas (Texas A&M University), College Station. *Texas A&M University Archives, College Station.*

Designed with a Mansardic roof similar to that of the Main building, this structure served as a mess hall and dormitory. In addition, it had the distinction of housing the president of the college for a period.

FIGURE 186. Mess Hall (ca. 1897), Agricultural and Mechanical College of Texas (Texas A&M University), College Station. *Texas A&M University Archives, College Station.*

As enrollments increased, additions to the campus continued. Rather than adhering to one style for all buildings, administrators of established institutions generally favored comforming to the fashions of the times. Thus this building, erected near the turn of the century, displayed picturesque turrets and pavilions, yet it was balanced and symmetrical in composition. The two turrets formed a formal entrance.

This, then, was the first state-supported institution of higher learning. Like other colleges and universities of the time, A&M expanded rapidly. In 1876 Gathright Hall was the second building completed (fig. 185). In 1887 a dormitory was added; in 1889 the Assembly Hall was completed; and in 1892 Ross Hall, another dormitory, was built. Shortly thereafter, a hospital, assembly hall, creamery, laundry, ice plant, natatorium, and new mess hall all appeared (fig. 186). Other significant structures dating from the 1890's included a testing laboratory for determining the strengths of building materials.[5]

The University of Texas formally admitted its first students in 1883 into a partially completed temple of knowledge whose style was intended to indicate the high values placed upon education in the state. Eagerly anticipating the opening, the *San Antonio Daily Ex-*

press announced, "It will be an occasion of the greatest moment in the history of the state. . . ." In his opening address, Ashbel Smith, president of the Board of Regents, proclaimed that the main building had a "character for solidity and excellence that will defy the corroding hand of time for ages" (fig. 187). However, during the 1930's the building was destroyed to make room for a new Administration Building and the General Library.[6]

In other types of state buildings, too, styles communicated the importance and dignity of the institutions housed within. The North Texas Insane Asylum (Terrell State Hospital), Terrell, a building with a "stately appearance," was designed, according to a contemporary report, to be "devoid of all superfluous and

[5] Henry C. Dethloff, *A Pictorial History of Texas A&M University, 1876–1976*, p. 26; *Fort Worth Gazette*, March 20, 1895. The mess hall was featured in *American Architect* 58 (1897):27.

[6] *San Antonio Daily Express*, September 15, 1883; Ashbel Smith, "Opening Address," *San Antonio Daily Express*, September 16, 1883. For a general history of the University of Texas at Austin, see William James Battle, "A Concise History of the University of Texas," *Southwestern Historical Quarterly* 54 (1951):391–411.

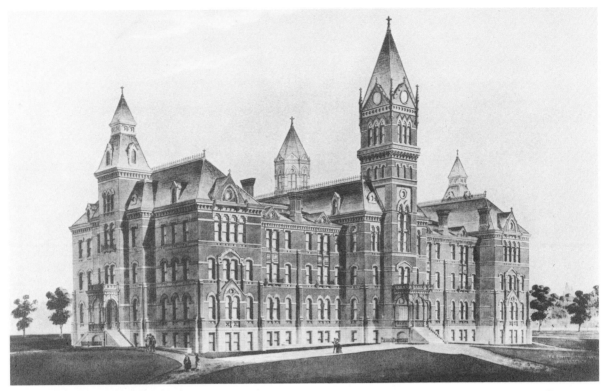

FIGURE 187. Main Building (1883–1899), University of Texas, Austin. F. E. Ruffini, architect. *Barker Texas History Center, University of Texas at Austin.*

Selected from a group of eight plans submitted by "scientific architects" residing in several parts of the state, Ruffini's design called for durable and attractive materials. The basement walls were stone, the superstructure bricks, and the facing pressed bricks. Cut stone used for accent provided the polychromy essential to the Victorian Gothic style. Porticoes were supported with columns of cast iron, and, on the interior, hall floors were laid with marble tiles. The composition was completed by a galvanized-iron cornice and inclined roofs covered with slate. When finally finished, the four-story building was 280 feet long and was dominated by a central tower 140 feet in height.

useless ornamentation, but at the same time substantial and imposing in its general appearance, and in keeping with the dignity of the state."[7] Nothing remains of this original work. The design of Southwest Texas Lunatic Asylum, San Antonio, reflected this same character—even though mental illness was looked upon with shame by most people (fig. 188).

While the architectural styles of these state

institutions had as their prime purpose the expression of beauty, esteem, and modernity, styles in ecclesiastical edifices had additional motivations. The Medieval era provided the space and form necessary to symbolize divinity in many Texas ecclesiastical buildings, particularly those of the Catholic, Episcopalian, and Lutheran denominations. For these groups with close liturgical ties to the Middle Ages, edifying details identified with the great ages of Christianity provided a sentimental backdrop for worship. Details derived from European churches and cathedrals provided the symbolic decorative backdrop appropriate to a complicated liturgy.

Although the cross and pointed arch were

[7] *Houston Post*, October 3, 1883. Perhaps the layout of the buildings in Terrell was representative. The first floor of the main building was occupied by offices, parlors, and the attendants' dining room; nearby was a kitchen. On the second and third floors were apartments for the attendants. Patients were housed in eight wards, each of which was complete in itself, with dining room, washroom, bathroom, and sleeping apartments. The walls of the wards were decorated with paintings of scenery.

FIGURE 188. Southwest Texas Lunatic Asylum (San Antonio State Hospital), San Antonio (1892). *From* Art Work of San Antonio, *Daughters of the Republic of Texas Library, San Antonio.*

During the nineteenth century several state hospitals were built. The first state facility for the care of the mentally ill was opened in Austin in 1861. Located about five miles south of San Antonio, this asylum was the third state facility established for the care of the mentally ill. It was opened in 1892. During the ensuing year 142 patients were received. All the historic buildings were razed in 1977.

basic, within the symbolism of the Gothic Revival language there were numerous combinations of other ornamental features, thus allowing considerable variety of design. Complexity of detail was subject primarily to the beliefs and wealth of the congregation and the talents and experience of the architect.

The spaces and forms of the late-nineteenth-century Catholic churches and cathedrals were designed according to European and colonial customs. Within, the sanctuary was the most prominent space, forming a focal point for worshipers and processions passing through doorways into the narthex, then under a balcony into the nave. In large naved churches, the emphasis upon sacred symbols was dramatized further by the rhythm of the windows and occasionally by columns, placed in the nave to create side aisles, which also provided a strong progession leading to the sacred areas.

Fortunately, large, well-designed and well-built Catholic churches continued to satisfy physical and liturgical needs in the twentieth century, and the most significant examples are still standing. Nonetheless, some important buildings—for example, Saint Patrick's Cathedral, Corpus Christi (1882)—are gone (fig. 189).

Lutheran churches also employed traditional spatial organization and styles. A number of edifices on cruciform or basilican plans were erected in the state, but many of these have been razed. Historically, Lutheran churches, of course, were most prominent in areas settled by Germans and Swedes. For example, churches had been built in Fredericksburg in 1857, Round Top in 1858, and Berlin in 1861; later these were replaced by more substantial buildings.[8]

Like the Catholic and Lutheran parishes, Episcopalians built distinctively. Communities with small congregations built charming churches with frame or masonry walls and simple exteriors, but with interiors enhanced

[8] Rudolph Leopold Biesele, *The History of the German Settlements in Texas, 1831–1861*, p. 64.

FIGURE 189. Saint Patrick's Cathedral, Corpus Christi (1882). Charles Carroll, architect and builder. *La Retama Library, Corpus Christi.*

This was an interesting frame structure with a variety of Gothic details interpreted in wood. It served as a cathedral from 1912 until 1940. In 1951 the building was dismantled, and parts were used in the construction of a new church, Our Lady Star of the Sea at North Beach.

The plan and interior were noteworthy. One transept of the cruciform plan was used as a chapel, the other as a sacristy. When sisters were cloistered there, a colonnade extended between the side chapel and the altar. Separated from side aisles by ranges of arches, the nave was spanned by a wooden barrel vault. Ceilings and wall surfaces were lavishly decorated.

FIGURE 190. Church of the Good Shepherd, Corpus Christi (ca. 1896). *Texas State Historical Association, Austin.*

    This was a fine example of the Carpenter Gothic style. The board-and-batten siding was commonly used on frame buildings and accented the verticality of the building. The steeple was severely damaged in a 1919 hurricane. Then the church was moved, and a brick front was added. Still later it was incorporated into All Saints' Church, but eventually it was demolished in 1964.

by exquisite woodwork. On the exteriors steeply pitched roofs, pointed-arched openings, and buttressed walls communicated the ecclesiastical functions of these buildings, many of which are still in use. Charming Carpenter Gothic style appeared in a good many churches, exemplified by the Church of the Good Shepherd, Corpus Christi (fig. 190).

    While these traditional forms of wood construction continued in use past the turn of the century for small Episcopal churches, large edifices were designed in high styles and built with masonry (figs. 191, 192). Many of these structures incorporated English Gothic features, such as buttresses with stages, windows with pronounced hoods, and lofty towers with pinnacles, suggesting a communion between heaven and earth.

While the liturgical churches could express their dedication to deity through symbolic decorative features associated with the ancient era of devout dedication to Christianity, the symbolic use of particular historical styles was less important for the evangelical groups. To be sure, Evangelical Protestantism had developed out of strong protest against authority of the church, elaborate ritual, and opulent architecture. Abroad and in New England, the architectural consequences of this reaction at first was the elimination of decorative features.

    The simplicity of the Protestant rites also was advantageous to those establishing new churches in sparsely settled areas. During the westward expansion, Baptist and Methodist ministers preached from porches, in houses, in courtrooms, or in Masonic Lodge halls,

FIGURE 191. Saint Matthew's Cathedral, Dallas (1894–1895). Sanguinet and Messer, architects. *From* Art Work of Dallas, *1910, Archives and Research Center for Texas and Dallas History, Dallas Public Library.*

Located at the corner of South Ervay and Canton streets, this was a fine Episcopal church built of grey sandstone. At first the windows were of cathedral glass in simple diaper patterns, but later these were replaced by stained glass.

In an 1891 competition, Bertram G. Goodhue, a prominent American church architect, had been selected to do the work. Several years later, however, he was replaced. Although many parishioners urged its preservation, the building was demolished in 1937, and the parish moved to the chapel at St. Mary's College.

FIGURE 192. Saint Matthew's Cathedral, Dallas. View of nave and chancel. *From* Art Work of Dallas, *1910, Archives and Research Center for Texas and Dallas History, Dallas Public Library.*

Characteristic beauty was experienced by worshipers in this fine cathedral. With traditional spatial relationships and hierarchical symbolism, the details were beautifully designed and excellently executed. According to contemporary accounts, woodwork was oak or southern pine, stained dark.

The interior spaces were developed according to tradition satisfying liturgical requirements of the Episcopal church. The altar, symbolic of the sacramental throne of Christ, was the focal point; of secondary importance in the hierarchy of the chancel were the pulpit and lectern. Also prominent was the bishop's throne, symbol of episcopal authority.

without elaborate trappings, thus becoming accustomed to straightforward settings. However, with the development of affluence, decoration was sanctioned. The frame of mind that admired elaborate decoration was expressed by Bowler, an author on church architecture, when he wrote that the house of God "should at least compare well with our dwellings in everything promotive of the finer feelings of the soul. Never should we be content in allowing the worship of God to be conducted in a mere barn-like edifice. . . ."[9]

Since formality of the worship services was less important to Protestants than to Catholics, the designs of Presbyterian, Methodist, and Baptist churches appropriately could be more picturesque or "modern" in composition. Buildings were often asymmetric, and corner entrances situated below towers, rather than axially positioned doors, were developed, thus providing access from two streets. The First Baptist Church, Houston, an edifice in High Victorian Gothic, epitomized this picturesqueness (fig. 193).

Although the Gothic Revival prevailed, especially in Catholic churches, other styles did appear as well, particularly in Protestant churches. Influenced by the 1870's ecclesiastical work of H. H. Richardson, architects throughout the country and in Texas designed large edifices in Romanesque Revival style— virtually every large community has (or had) a church in Romanesque style erected during the last decade of the nineteenth century or the first decade of the twentieth. One of the first examples of Romanesque design was the First Presbyterian Church (1872), Galveston, by Jones and Baldwin of Memphis, Tennessee, which still stands. Nearly two decades later, Nicholas J. Clayton, who had been sent to Galveston to supervise the construction of this church, designed Sacred Heart Catholic Church in Galveston in a robust Romanesque style (fig. 194). This picturesque Catholic church has now been lost.[10]

[9] George Bowler, *Chapel and Church Architecture*, p. 8.

A fine example of Romanesque Revival appeared in the First Congregational Church, Dallas, another edifice with asymmetrical composition and a dominant corner tower (fig. 195). A more elaborate example of Romanesque style expressed through polychromatic masonry was the First Presbyterian Church (1889–1890) in Fort Worth, which was finally destroyed after being used as a tire warehouse for several years. On a larger scale, the First Presbyterian Church in Houston also displayed Romanesque features (fig. 196). Inside this edifice, as in many others across the state, the spaces were freely organized to accommodate the religious services (fig. 197).

Interiors were developed to facilitate the emphasis of Protestantism upon the interpretation of the Bible through individual experience. Since the sacraments, focusing upon the altar, were rejected, the sacred areas were deemphasized. Then the pulpit, rather than the altar, was placed at the center to become the focal point, reflecting the emphasis placed upon preaching Christ's gospel (fig. 198). In place of an altar, a table representing the Last Supper was situated in front of the pulpit and served for the communion—the altar, some said, had pagan origins in sacrificial ceremonies.

In addition to these essential modifications in the evangelical churches, the spaces for assembly were changed. Since the lay person was a "listener" rather than an "actor" as in the liturgical churches, and since the minister was an "actor" rather than a "prompter" as in the liturgical churches, the assembly spaces and pulpit areas were developed to provide good light, sight lines, and clear acoustics. These differences led to the use of half-circular or quarter-circular auditorium shapes and comfortable seating. Representative was the First

[10] Among the well-known churches by Richardson were Trinity, Boston (1873–1877), and Brattle Square Church, Boston (1870–1872). See Henry-Russell Hitchcock, *The Architecture of H. H. Richardson and His Times*, pp. 111–117, 136–145. The architectural journals of the 1890's published many projects of ecclesiastical buildings done in Romanesque style.

FIGURE 193. First Baptist Church, Houston (ca. 1890). *From* Art Work of Houston, *1894,* Houston Public Library.

Victorian Gothic details distinguished this edifice. Bricks of contrasting color, pointed arches, and buttresses provided architectural interest. The large star was also noteworthy.

During the nineteenth century many churches existed near city centers. However, with the growth of the populations, parishioners moved to new outlying neighborhoods and established new churches. Due to declines in memberships and increases in land values, it became impossible to maintain the downtown buildings, and countless examples were razed in the rapidly expanding cities.

FIGURE 194. Sacred Heart Church, Galveston (1884). Nicholas J. Clayton, architect. *Courtesy Rosenberg Library, Galveston.*

This was a wonderful example of Richardsonian Romanesque design. Built on a traditional cruciform plan, it was a delightfully picturesque work with an elaborate composition of towers, tourelles, Roman arches, and decorative patterns of bricks. In addition to the color of the brickwork, bands of polychromy produced by different colors of slate roofing added richness.

The edifice was destroyed by the 1900 storm. Several years later it was replaced by a building in Moorish character, which still stands.

FIGURE 195. First Congregational Church, Dallas (ca. 1890). *From* Art Work of Dallas, *1895, Archives and Research Center for Texas and Dallas History, Dallas Public Library.*

Located at the corner of North Harwood and Bryan, this was another fine example of asymmetric composition. The offset tower, with its spire, and the arrangement of steeply pitched, intersecting gable roofs were characteristic of numerous Baptist, Methodist, and Congregational churches.

FIGURE 196. First Presbyterian Church, Houston (ca. 1900). *From* Art Work of Houston, *1904*, Houston Public Library.

Near the turn of the century, many churches were built in Romanesque Revival style by Presbyterian groups. In this imposing stone edifice, the lofty corner tower beckoned worshipers to its doors at the base. The theme of the Roman arch, in various proportions, prevailed throughout, creating a visual relationship between the various forms. The tourelles, with their pinnacles flanking the tower spires, are other noteworthy Romanesque features.

FIGURE 197. First Presbyterian Church, Houston. Interior View. *From* Art Work of Houston, *1904, Houston Public Library.*

This appears to have been one of the finest Protestant interiors of the turn of the century. Semicircular seating focused upon the space containing the pulpit. Overhead, high decorative vaults springing from slender columns provided a distinctive ceiling. Chandeliers and stained-glass windows further enriched the interior. The magnificent space, when alive with play of sunlight colored by the stained glass, with the majestic music of the organ, and with resounding voices in hymns, must have created moving experiences for worshipers.

FIGURE 198. First Methodist Episcopal Church, Dallas (ca. 1890). Interior view. *From* Art Work of Dallas, *1895, Archives and Research Center for Texas and Dallas History, Dallas Public Library.*

Typically for Methodist churches, the pulpit was the focal point of the interior. Although circular arrangements of seating were quite common in the Protestant churches, in this auditorium seating was placed on a linear layout.

FIGURE 199. First Baptist Church, Fort Worth (1887–1889). Bullard and Bullard, architects; A. N. Dawson, supervising architect. *From postcard in possession of Mrs. Laura H. Portwood, courtesy Fort Worth Public Library, Amon Carter Museum.*

Formerly located at the corner of Second and Jones streets and designed by architects from Springfield, Illinois, the church was built with Granbury limestone walls and a roof of slate in Gothic Revival style. The imposing structure had a tower 150 feet high and a ridge 80 feet high.

FIGURE 200. First Methodist Church, Lubbock (ca. 1900). *First Methodist Church, Lubbock.*
    Frame churches on a scale similar to this were built throughout the West. Economical to construct, these ordinarily were built without the assistance of architects. Details were simple but effective. A belfry provided a suitable symbol, while shingle patterns and a bit of gingerbread enhanced the building.

Baptist Church, Fort Worth (fig. 199), which was built in 1887–1889 but is now gone.

While the large church edifices ordinarily were designed by architects, the small buildings were designed by members of the congregations or builders who apparently used plan books. Consequently, small frame churches with similar designs but some variations in detailing appeared in diverse locations throughout the west. Many of these incorporated simple Gothic Revival details and gingerbread (fig. 200).

Such styles as Gothic and Romanesque, of course, were not meaningful expressions for Jewish temples. The verticality of the Gothic was inappropriate for a faith that emphasized life on earth rather than the life to come. Instead, Moorish stylistic elements were considered appropriate in view of ethnic origins in

the Middle East and were used for the Temple Beth El in Corsicana and the Temple Moses Montefiore (1900) in Marshall (fig. 201). The former, with its twin towers surmounted by onion domes, is still in use; the latter was razed during urban renewal in 1971. In Galveston there was the Congregation B'nai Israel Synagogue, an opulently detailed building, which has been denatured (fig. 202).

These ecclesiastical edifices of Texas, along with certain other public buildings, were highly esteemed by the morals-conscious society of the nineteenth century. As prominent built landmarks in communities, they were often cited by local presses as indicators of improving social conditions. However, if the character of religious buildings represented dedication to deity and social order through positive influences, conversely, at the other ex-

FIGURE 201. Temple Moses Montefiore, Marshall (1900). J. Riely Gordon and Cornelius G. Lancaster, architects. *Courtesy Mrs. Louis Kariel, Jr., Marshall.*

With walls of brick trimmed with stone, this was a representative Texas Jewish temple of the nineteenth century. Moorish horseshoe arches, alternating brick and stone voussoirs, and a metal-roofed hemispherical dome all contributed to the oriental character. An annex, made in the 1930's, was financed by sales of hot tamales—an unusual project for Jewish women.

FIGURE 202. Congregation B'nai Israel Synagogue, Galveston (1870). Fred Stewart, architect. *From* Art Work in Galveston, *Barker Texas History Center, University of Texas at Austin.*

A blending of Victorian Gothic features with Moorish details gave this fine synagogue distinction. Pointed arches, quatrefoil arches, and horseshoe arches provided interesting variety for the openings; archivolts on both Gothic and Moorish lines accented these. Lavishness was added by polychromatic masonry, buttresses, and pinnacles.

Over the years the original charm of the elegant work has diminished with the removal of details and modernization of fabric. The building was stuccoed in 1889. In 1953 it was sold and became a Masonic Temple. It stands, in denatured form, on Twenty-second Street, between Avenues H and I.

treme, the quality of detention facilities represented attempts to secure peace and security through restraint and punishment.[11]

Jails were often cited as improvements en-

couraging immigration. To reassure local residents that their communities were safe from lawless elements, it was important not only that the late-nineteenth-century jails be secure, but also that the physical structure itself communicate impressions of strength. Many individuals retained vivid impressions of depredations wrought by criminals—particularly during the years immediately following the Civil War, when there was inadequate law enforcement. Many others realized the expense and difficulty of detaining those accused of crimes without proper facilities. To those with strong convictions concerning due process of

[11]Even during the republic, churches were considered important manifestations of social order: "A church is more than a work of art; it is a symbol . . . of religion. . . . Churches are the outward consecration of our cities, of our villages. . ." (*Telegraph and Texas Register* [Houston], September 18, 1839). Nearly half a century later, a reporter wrote, "Truly do churches, as do schools and streets and sidewalks attract and hold the home seeker and investor" (*Fort Worth Daily Gazette*, March 17, 1887). Another reporter observed, "It is surely much cheaper to build churches than jails" (*Fort Worth Daily Gazette*, June 12, 1884).

law, substantial jails were important in order to secure criminals from mob justice.[12]

In the years immediately following the Civil War there was perhaps no greater urgency for architecture than the need for jails. The demoralization created by the war had resulted in an increase in lawlessness, as was evident at the state penitentiary, where the population nearly trebled in one year. Moreover the local jails were in an unsafe and deplorable condition. Consequently, virtually every county built a new jail during the last quarter of the nineteenth century.[13]

As in antebellum years, a wide variety of building techniques was used to build jails; the selection of a particular type of construction was influenced by the wealth and level of development of the communities. As late as the 1880's in the newly established western towns, primitive methods continued to be used. For Throckmorton County, specifications called for a "Lock-up or Calaboose . . . to be 14′ sq. and built out of 2 × 6 lumber laid flatways and spiked together. . . ." Obviously, this was economical, but certainly not secure. In Bandera, 8 × 8 timbers planted into the ground vertically, with small windows secured by iron bars, were used for the walls.[14]

While most of the counties at one time had flimsy jails similar to this, these buildings soon were replaced with substantial brick or stone blocks with small openings filled with bars (fig. 203). Nonetheless the sense of security emanating from the simple forms and the masonry-wall construction of early jails in some cases may have been more psychological than physical—prisoners could dislodge stones or bricks or tunnel under walls. Although the masonry shells assembled with soft lime mortar were sometimes improved by reinforcing them with metal, it was not until the facility with freestanding iron cages was developed that jails in reality became strong.

The forms of the jails generally were dictated by their interior functions. On small jails the simple masonry cube was employed; on larger facilities L-shaped, T-shaped, or cruciform-type plans reflected the zoning of cells and the segregation of living quarters (fig. 204). Out of consideration for the comfort of the prisoners, in many jails towers rose from the centers, providing ventilation shafts for hot air rising from the cell blocks. With the large windows made possible by freestanding cell blocks and large openings in the floors, these provided efficient natural ventilation.

As it did for churches, the Medieval period provided sources for design features for buildings like jails, for which strength of enclosure was an important attribute. Romanesque works and castles from the Medieval period provided configurations of details on many detention facilities. Heavy stone walls, crenellated parapets, and turrets with embrasures, all of which had been functionally developed to increase the strength of ancient military architecture, provided nineteenth-century architects with appropriate features for buildings where security was essential. These associations may have been reinforced by popular literature of the period—for example, *Ivanhoe*—where Medieval settings were developed romantically.[15]

Medieval stylistic elements often were abstracted, and geometrical elements occasionally were integrated into the design of jails. Crenellations, for example, in most cases were not on the large scale that had permitted arch-

[12] For background information on crime in Texas, see Walter P. Webb and H. B. Carroll, *The Handbook of Texas*, 2:411–414.

[13] Webb and Carroll, *Handbook of Texas*, 2:412; *Standard* (Clarksville), February 1, 1873. In 1876 the state legislature passed an act requiring counties to provide "safe and suitable jails . . . properly ventilated, and not overly crowded with prisoners" (*Vernon's Texas Civil Statutes*, Art. 5115, enacted 1876).

[14] Office of the County Clerk, Commissioners Court Minutes, Throckmorton County, vol. 3 (July 8, 1890); Office of the County Clerk, Commissioners Court Minutes, Bandera County, vol. 2 (June 12, 1885), p. 115.

[15] For military schools also architects found the castellated architecture of the Medieval period to be a natural expression of their function—similar to the buildings of the United States Military Academy at West Point, New York. Thus the Texas Military Institute (1870) had a building with military character, albeit the design was much attenuated in detail.

FIGURE 203. Mitchell County Jail, Colorado City (ca. 1883). *Colorado City Museum, Colorado City.*

This jail was similar to many built in the western counties near the end of the nineteenth century. It had a straight forward design with relatively little ornamentation. The large-scaled masonry units were intended to communicate strength.

ers of antiquity to seek protection behind the merlons while shooting their arrows through the crenels. Exhibiting the symbolic application of small-scale elements was the Tom Green County Jail (1884) in San Angelo, designed by West Texas architect Oscar Ruffini (fig. 205).

In some instances the Medieval military details were exploited into fantastic romantic expressions, with elaborate compositions of towers, turrets, and battlements; yet interior functions were still accommodated efficiently. The projected Duval County Jail, San Diego, by J. Riely Gordon would have been an interesting composition with a high central tower. The Comanche County Jail, Comanche

(1903), was similar, but remodeling has removed many features (fig. 206). However, with a design similar to these, the Brown County Jail, Brownwood (1902), still survives with most of its original fabric. In all these there was variety of design, yet common proportions and the predominance of the theme of military architecture created a strong harmony and unity in the architectural statement—consistent with ideas on aesthetics prevalent during the Victorian period.

The ancient architecture of lords and knights was not, however, the only style used for detention facilities. By virtue of its massiveness, the Romanesque Revival was deemed suitable as an expression of strength, which at

FIGURE 204. Anderson County Jail, Palestine (ca. 1885). *From* Catalogue: The Pauly Jail Building and Manufacturing Company, *1889.*

Many architects had little practical experience in jail design. The Pauly Jail Building and Manufacturing Company employed its own architects to provide complete professional services to towns and counties throughout the country. Although many professional designers apparently objected, the Pauly company considered detention a specialty in which it had outstanding proficiency. Many Texas counties built jails using the services of Pauly's architectural representatives; many others built jails after the plans of local architects but with equipment supplied by Pauly. This Palestine jail was among the works for which both professional services and equipment were supplied by the Pauly company.

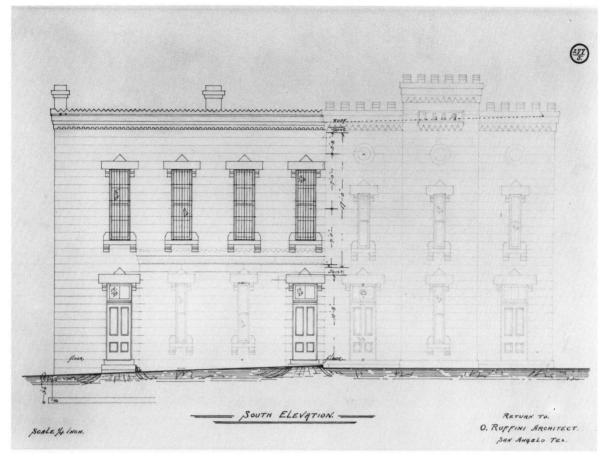

FIGURE 205. Tom Green County Jail, San Angelo (1884), Oscar Ruffini, architect. *Archives Division, Texas State Library, Austin.*

As indicated by this architectural drawing, simple but interesting decoration appeared on this jail. In the original section on the right, symbolic crenellations terminated the walls. Pronounced window lintels and sills provided additional interest. On the addition on the left, the decoration of the parapet was geometrical, but the treatment of the openings repeated the details of the original.

In spite of efforts to save the structure, Tom Green county commissioners authorized demolition in the mid-1970's.

the same time allowed picturesque compositions. Second Empire styling also appeared in some jails, probably in response to the urge to be fashionable (fig. 207).

Although these jails were once thought to be design manifestations of reform in detention facilities, today virtually none meet current reform standards unless they have been remodeled. Just as public attitudes in their times created pressures to replace the obsolete antebellum and Reconstruction jails, today new

codes require that late-nineteenth-century jails be replaced by more modern facilities. Many have been destroyed; others will soon go. However, a significant number of the late-nineteenth- and early-twentieth-century buildings—for example, the Milam County Jail, Cameron (1895), designed by the Pauly Jail Building and Manufacturing Company— are now museums.

Jails, though an important sign of both material and cultural progress, did not become as

FIGURE 206. Comanche County Jail, Comanche (1903). Martin and Moodie, builders. *Southwest Collection, Texas Tech University, Lubbock.*

The calaboose built for Comanche County was the most romantic statement made with architecture for Texas jails. A variety of features in this Romanesque Revival design are reminiscent of ancient military architecture. The tower, along with the turrets, is terminated at the sky with merlons and crenels. Elsewhere, corbeled features (projections from the building) create impressions of machicolations—apertures in cantilevered floors developed to allow defenders of castles to pour boiling fluids or missiles upon assailants. Included also were loopholes, tall but narrow slits through which ancient archers could shoot arrows at a wide range of trajectories. The Comanche County building was completed for a sum of $27,000 and still stands, but the tower and other features have been removed.

prominent in the built environment of the county seats as the courthouses. Except the state capitol, no nineteenth-century buildings were esteemed more highly by the general public than the temples of justice.

As mentioned earlier, the social role of the Texas courthouse contributed to its importance, hence to the motivations of Texans to build imposing structures. A courthouse, with its public spaces and amenities, attracted people to conduct personal business, as well as to engage in social intercourse. For example, in

addition to their official function, courtrooms often were used for socials and dances, concerts and parties. Religious groups often used them for services until churches could be built.[16] However, most county commissioners courts eventually passed resolutions restricting uses to official functions. Even then, trials

[16] As early as 1838, the Travis County Courthouse was used for Sunday school (*Telegraph and Texas Register* [Austin], December 15, 1838). In 1876 use of space in the Tarrant County Courthouse was approved for "public entertainment, concerts, parties, etc." (*Fort Worth Democrat*, March 15, 1873).

FIGURE 207. Harris County Jail, Houston (ca. 1890). Eugene T. Heiner, architect. *From* Art of Houston, *1894,* Houston Public Library.

Planned by a well-known designer of jails, stylistically this was one of the most elaborate nineteenth-century jails in the state. The Mansard roof was crowned with crestings and covered with slate. The elaborate cornice with segmental pediments and the brick walls trimmed with cut stone were other significant features.

themselves seem to have attracted large audiences—people perhaps seeking entertainment—which required large courtrooms. The several functions of the courthouses attracted various forms of commercial enterprise, which contributed to the economic improvement of communities as well as to the permanence of the county seat.

County commissioners in virtually every county authorized the construction of a new courthouse during the 1880's or 1890's; some, whether from necessity or whim, built new edifices in both decades. Times were prosperous, enabling commissioners to levy taxes sufficient to finance large buildings. Then, in 1881, the state legislature authorized the counties to sell bonds to pay for new structures. While in such far-western towns as Lubbock these new structures were wood framed (fig. 208), in other counties the new courthouses—which replaced temporary, antebellum, or Reconstruction buildings, some of which were also quite substantial—were designed to last indefinitely. Little or no thought was given to future obsolescence.[17]

During the era of elegance the organization

[17] An act authorizing the county commissioners courts of the several counties of this state to issue bonds for the erection of a courthouse and to levy a tax to pay for the same, was approved February 11, 1881, according to a bond filed in the Erath County Courthouse, Stephenville. On March 27, 1885, this was amended to include jail bonds.

FIGURE 208. Lubbock County Courthouse, Lubbock (1891). Gill, Moad & Gill, architects. *Southwest Collection, Texas Tech University, Lubbock.*

While the older counties of the state were erecting durable, expensive courthouses, the newly formed West Texas counties constructed relatively economical structures. Before the arrival of the railroads, masonry was unavailable, and even wood was expensive to haul by wagon.

The City of Lubbock was not founded until 1887, and the county was not organized until 1891, the year this structure was built. In 1899 the city's population was only 293.

The events in the development of county governmental housing in Lubbock were typical. Commissioners at first convened in a house; then an office was leased. Finally it was ordered that a frame courthouse be built. That building was used until the early twentieth century, when a new masonry edifice replaced it on the public square.

of the interiors of courthouses continued to be informed by tradition and setting but reflected the increasing size and complexity of local government. On the ground level, a plan with office areas divided into four quadrants by two symmetrically placed corridors continued antebellum practice (fig. 108). While providing for good cross ventilation, this also allowed the general development of entrances facing commercial properties on all four sides, as observed earlier, a tradition reflecting the importance of settings in the centers of public squares. However, there were some variations on this, for example in the Hood County

Courthouse, Granbury (1889–1891), and the Lampasas County Courthouse, Lampasas (1883), where there were no north entrances.

The public esteem for law and justice created a preference for courthouses with imposing character. Texas architects worked to create designs that were capacious, imposing, and artistic. Architecture that appeared plain, gloomy, and monotonous received few encomiums. A wide variety of historical styles was employed in developing courthouse designs—modes fashionable in other parts of the United States, original compositions, and styles that satisfied county pride.

FIGURE 209. Harris County Courthouse, Houston (1883–1884). E. J. Duhamel, architect. *From* Art Work of Houston, *1894, Houston Public Library.*

Reportedly the heights of this courthouse's interior spaces were proportioned according to the horizontal dimensions. The four fronts were alike, with entrances opening into corridors extending through the building.

The building must have been well ventilated. In the center, where the corridors intersected, was an open stairway, which provided communication to a second-floor lobby, from which the courtrooms could be entered. To provide good air circulation, the ceiling of this lobby opened into the tower; on the inside of this was a balcony, on the outside a gallery.

The building was demolished in the early part of the twentieth century to make room for the present courthouse.

Admiration for picturesqueness and elegance probably motivated commissioners to approve the Victorian Gothic style for the Harris County Courthouse built in 1883–1884 (fig. 209). However, perhaps because of its lack of historical association with governmental buildings of the past, this mode was used only rarely in Texas civic architecture. Far more favored during the eighties were the styles incorporating Classical features from Renaissance architecture.

The Italianate, characterized by broad cornices, brackets, and gable roofs provided character for many courthouses during the 1880's. In this style, J. E. Flanders designed the Stephens County Courthouse, Breckenridge

FIGURE 210. Stephens County Courthouse, Breckenridge (1883). J. E. Flanders, architect. *Courtesy Jan Hart, Swenson Memorial Museum of Stephens County, Breckenridge.*

Built on a cruciform plan, this temple of justice was located on the corner of the public square. It incorporated Italianate details along with geometric decorative features. A statue to the goddess of justice provided a reminder of the purpose of the building. It was used until the present Classical edifice was erected in 1926.

FIGURE 211. Bell County Courthouse, Belton (1884–1885). J. N. Preston & Son, architects. *Texas State Historical Association, Austin.*

Local pride as well as contemporary aesthetic values were expressed in the newspapers upon the completion of this fine building. According to the *Fort Worth Daily Gazette* of May 19, 1885, "Among the many new court-houses that have been built in the state during the past few years, as well as now in the course of construction, it seems to be universally agreed that the Bell-county court-house . . . surpasses them all in beauty of design and elegance of finish."

The three-story building incorporated fine masonry and sheet-metal work. Walls were cut stone; portico columns and capitals were carved stone. Cornices, balustrades, pedestals, urns, and shell ornaments were spun zinc and galvanized iron; the roof was tin with a pattern resembling slate.

The building has been extensively remodeled. The tower and the sheet-metal cornices are gone, thus changing the character. The interior has been modernized.

FIGURE 212. Bastrop County Courthouse, Bastrop (1883–1884). J. N. Preston, architect. *Texas State Historical Association, Austin.*

Formed with bricks and sheet metal, fine Renaissance Revival details characterized this courthouse. At each corner of the pavilions were tall brick pedestals formed in patterns of brickwork to represent stone quoining and pilasters with simple capitals. Balconies supported by delicate iron columns emphasized the entrances. A variety of arches—flat, segmental, and semicircular—contributed additional interest.

The building has been rather drastically denatured by the removal of the tower, the elimination of the cornice, changes of brick details, and the application of a coat of plaster.

(1883), of which only an entrance feature remains on the square (fig. 210), and the Shackelford County Courthouse, Albany (1883), which still stands. Commissioners also favored this mode for the Llano County Courthouse, Llano (1884), a brick building now gone, designed by Alfred Giles in a form that was virtually identical to the old Gillespie County Courthouse, Fredericksburg (1881–1882), which is now used as a library.

Closely related to the Italianate in appearance were buildings in the Renaissance Revival style. The first revival of the Renaissance mode that spread across the United States beginning in about 1840 also became fashionable for Texas courthouses during the

1880's, although by this time designers freely innovated on the ornamental features. The Classical details and traditional three-part composition—beginning, middle, and end—of this mode imparted monumental character. In the Bell County Courthouse, Belton (1884–1885), designed by J. N. Preston & Son, porticoes with colossal columns in traditional composition provided an exceptional, stately appearance (fig. 211). This same style and similar composition characterized the Bastrop County Courthouse (1883–1884) in Bastrop (fig. 212). The popularity of Renaissance Revival for Texas courthouses continued into the 1890's, when the imposing Comanche County Courthouse, Comanche, was built in a refined

FIGURE 213. Comanche County Courthouse, Comanche (1891–1892). Larmour and Watson, architects. *Comanche Public Library, Comanche.*

The architectural developments leading to the construction of this fine building were typical of those in many counties. First a double log cabin, then located in Cora, housed county government. Then the seat of government was moved to Comanche, and a second building was erected in 1859, but it burned during the Civil War. It was nearly a decade before another courthouse appeared, with Classical details and brick walls. This served until 1889 when it, too, was destroyed by flames.

The work on the fourth courthouse, with its walls of sandstone from a local quarry, was greeted with typical enthusiasm. However, the building was destroyed in 1939 to make room for the fifth Comanche County Courthouse, which still serves. A courthouse similar to the 1890's edifice, designed by the same architects and built in 1890–1892, stands today in Cameron, Milam County.

FIGURE 214. Runnels County Courthouse, Ballinger (1888–1889). Eugene T. Heiner, architect. *Courtesy O. L. Parish, Jr., Ballinger.*

In plan and style this fine courthouse was similar to several other West Texas courthouses dating from the eighties. On the ground floor a corridor, which provided good cross ventilation, extended between the offices. Above, accessible from two stairways, was the centrally located district courtroom; this space was flanked on the east and west by offices. The courtroom was ventilated through the stairways located on the east and west as well as windows in the north and south walls. Positioned in the center of a two-block square that had been set aside by the Santa Fe Railway Company before lots were sold, the structure incorporated local stone accented with sheet-metal work.

Although this structure still stands, twentieth-century remodelings have resulted in the removal of important historic details and the addition of new rooms. In 1941 wings were added on the east and west.

version of the mode, according to the plans of J. Larmour and A. O. Watson (fig. 213).

Eugene T. Heiner also used the Renaissance Revival as a point of departure for several courthouses. Among these is the Columbus County Courthouse, Columbus (1889), another building that has been remodeled but that today retains much of its original character. The Runnels County Courthouse, Ballinger (1888–1889), a structure that also has been much modified, had Italianate details but was covered with Mansard roofs (fig. 214). Perhaps the ultimate development of this combination in Texas was in the Falls County Courthouse, Marlin (ca. 1888), where a build-

ing with High Victorian Italianate features was crowned with Mansard roofs (fig. 215).[18] The Uvalde County Courthouse, Uvalde (1890), by B. F. Trester, Jr., was composed in a similar manner but with simple details (fig. 216).

The Mansard roofs that had become popular in Texas during the 1870's also crowned many courthouses during the 1880's. These forms were used by Alfred Giles on the Bexar County Courthouse, a building that was used less than a decade (fig. 217).

[18] For a description of the High Victorian Italianate style see Marcus Whiffen, *American Architecture since 1780: A Guide to the Styles*, pp. 97–100.

FIGURE 215. Falls County Courthouse, Marlin (ca. 1888). Eugene T. Heiner, architect. *Texas State Historical Association, Austin.*

Crowned by a complex of Mansard roofs, this county building displayed richly detailed walls in high style. The center pavilions, which announced the entrances, were surmounted by triangular pediments and enhanced by semicircular and stilted arches with geometrical ornamental features. The corner pavilions, which housed office spaces, contained openings spanned by pediments with designs that were varied on each story. Flat arches with archivolts returning part way down the sides were employed on the ground level.

The masonry work also was distinguished by variety. Quoining with stones of different textures appeared at the ground-level corners and the upper-level corners of the pavilions. Pilasters with geometrical ornament were incorporated into the upper section. The dominant center mass, which accommodated the spacious courtroom, had wide windows framed by a variety of decorative features.

F. E. Ruffini and his brother Oscar also apparently preferred the Second Empire style for many of their courthouses. Like several other architects, the Ruffinis developed basic courthouse plans that were used in several design competitions. During times when most courthouse architects were selected by commissioners through competitions, it was expedient to develop a standard scheme and modify it to fit specific budgets and requirements; thus the counties of Blanco, Sonora, and Concho have, still standing, similar courthouses designed by the Ruffinis during the 1880's. The Mills County Courthouse, Goldthwaite (1889), was similar to these but was replaced in the twentieth century (fig. 218). In these, the fronts were designed as a series of planes receding from the center.

During the last twoscore years of the nineteenth century, friendly competition among counties placed a strong emphasis on the development of architectural character. Using traditional basic plans, architects employed a combination of styles to provide the exterior distinction so much admired. These compound modes often provided uniqueness that

FIGURE 216. Uvalde County Courthouse, Uvalde (1890). B. F. Trester, Jr., architect. *Archives Division, Texas State Library, Austin.*

Designed along traditional lines, this courthouse displayed fanciful details. Among these were decorative window heads on both the first and second stories. On the latter, stained glass transoms were indicated. Other features designed to produce interest included the roof cresting of sheet metal, brick chimneys with decorative brickwork, and the tower, which incorporated a variety of ornamental features. This building was razed to make room for the present courthouse, which was completed in 1927.

FIGURE 217. Bexar County Courthouse, San Antonio (1882–1883). Alfred Giles, architect. *Daughters of the Republic of Texas Library, San Antonio.*

Through a design competition, the plans of Alfred Giles were selected for a new courthouse for Bexar County. Similar to a number of other public buildings erected during this period, the temple was Second Empire in style. Dominant Mansard roofs crowned the three-story structure. Other noteworthy features included the cast-iron cresting, balconies, and bull's-eye windows. This building, which incorporated parts of an earlier structure, was demolished after the county commissioners constructed a new courthouse, using the plans of Gordon and Laub—a fine Romanesque Revival edifice, which is still in use.

FIGURE 218. Mills County Courthouse, Goldthwaite (1889). F. E. Ruffini, architect. *Archives Division, Texas State Library, Austin.*

Built of native stone, this courthouse was a fine example of Second Empire style. The receding wall planes and the Mansard roof with its wrought-iron cresting were characteristic.

As was common in the stone-walled courthouses, several types of masonry were employed. Quarry-faced ashlar was used for the walls and cut stonework for the watertable door sills, window caps, string-courses, and door pilasters.

FIGURE 219. Aransas County Courthouse, Rockport (ca. 1890). J. Riely Gordon, architect. *Texas State Historical Association, Austin.*

Although the building that was finally realized was much less elaborate in design than that originally proposed by Gordon, the Aransas courthouse nonetheless was distinctive. Moorish stylistic features were composed into three- and five-part facade compositions. Horseshoe arches, along with ogival roofs, provided the character that was much admired. As a result of its architectural interest, the building was pictured in *Leslie's Illustrated*, October 18, 1890.

In 1871, Rockport was the seat of justice for Refugio County, but later that year, when Aransas County was created, it became the county seat of that county.

satisfied county pride. In the Aransas County Courthouse, J. Riely Gordon employed combined Moorish forms and Romanesque features and rendered them with polychromy to provide distinction (fig. 219). In the Goliad County Courthouse, Goliad, Alfred Giles employed Italianate and Mansardic features, as well as tower forms flanking two of the entrances. The towers were reminiscent of those on the United States Government Building at the World's Columbian Exposition (fig. 220). Italianate and Second Empire components

were combined to provide distinguished character for the El Paso County Courthouse, also designed by Giles (fig. 221). In the Val Verde County Courthouse, Del Rio, Second Empire and Romanesque Revival styles were combined.

The Mansardic-Italianate compound, combined with various geometrical elements, was freely exploited by W. C. Dodson in several courthouses erected during the 1880's. Corner pavilions with Mansardic roofs provided relief, and center pavilions with triangular pedi-

FIGURE 220. Goliad County Courthouse, Goliad (1894). Alfred Giles, architect. *Texas State Historical Association, Austin.*

The third courthouse in the county's history, this edifice, with its walls of limestone and brick, incorporated fine masonry work. The five-part facades featured corner pavilions and central pavilions, which announced the entrances. Rising above all was the dominant tower.

The quarry-faced, light-gray masonry was accented by red sandstone stringcourses. Cut stone was employed for the pilasters, thus providing strong contrast of textures. Additional interest was provided by the arches—Roman, segmental, and flat—with voussoirs providing subtle contrasts in color.

The character of the building suffered from a storm in 1942. The tower was damaged and subsequently was removed. Later a wing was added on the south.

COURT HOUSE.

FIGURE 221. El Paso County Courthouse, El Paso (1884–1886). Alfred Giles, architect. *Texas State Historical Association, Austin.*

Into this large courthouse was incorporated a variety of stylistic elements and colors. Italianate pediments and Mansardic-roofed pavilions, along with a high center tower, all contributed to the interest of the architecture. Slate roofing in contrasting colors contributed further to the complexity of the decoration.

Contractors at the commencement of the work were Britton and Long of Houston. However, following a court case involving the architect and the contractors over alleged changes in the plans and specifications, J. H. Britton dissolved partnership with J. T. Long; the former finished the work. Shortly thereafter, presumably with the permission of the architect, similar plans were used for the Presidio County Courthouse (1886), Marfa, which still stands.

This El Paso County Courthouse was replaced by a monumental Neoclassical building by Trost and Trost.

ments or gables with Italianate bracketed cornices emphasized the entrances. Around the points of access geometrical ornamentation of cut stone contrasted with the roughfaced stonework of walls. Within this formula a wide range of expression was possible, depending upon the budget of the county, as indicated by contrasting the Anderson County Courthouse with the county seat of Fannin County (figs. 222, 223), which was similar to the present Hill County Courthouse in Hillsboro.[19]

Reflecting national trends of the late 1880's and early 1890's, the Romanesque Revival appeared in many counties. At the time, it provided an up-to-date image, which satisfied several levels of taste. On one hand the picturesqueness of the mode satisfied public tastes for the irregular, yet, on the other, the modular compositions of arches satisfied the appreciation for order that was characteristic of monumental architecture. Then masonry construction with a variety of color provided the

[19] For an illustration of the Hill County Courthouse see

Willard B. Robinson, *Texas Public Buildings of the Nineteenth Century*, p. 231.

FIGURE 222. Anderson County Courthouse, Palestine (1884–1885). W. C. Dodson, architect. *Courtesy Camera Corral, Palestine.*

This courthouse was similar to many designed by W. C. Dodson for Texas. It was characterized by a soaring tower and four-pavilioned massing. This same scheme appeared in such other courthouses as those for Johnson County (1882–1883) in Cleburne, which is gone, and Hood County (1889–1891) in Granbury, which still stands. The Palestine building burned in 1913, after which the present courthouse was constructed in Classical style.

FIGURE 223. Fannin County Courthouse, Bonham (1887–1888). W. C. Dodson, architect. *Courtesy Mrs. Joe Welch, Bonham.*

    This was among the most handsome and elaborately detailed courthouses designed by W. C. Dodson. The dominant portico, supported by paired columns, strongly announced the entrance and created a grandiose point of arrival. Throughout, cut stone and galvanized-iron ornamental features were employed to enhance the temple.

    The plan was square. On the ground floor were offices and the meeting room for the commissioners court. Above were additional offices and the district courtroom, a two-story high space.

FIGURE 224. Brazoria County Courthouse, Brazoria (1894–1895). J. Riely Gordon, architect. *From Sketches from the Portfolio of James Riely Gordon, Dielmann Collection, Daughters of the Republic of Texas Library, San Antonio.*

This four-story work boasted granite columns and walls of red pressed brick with red sandstone trim. The Greek-cross plan, with entrances at the reentrant angles and an open shaft opening into the tower, afforded excellent ventilation.

Only two years after this edifice was completed and some five years after the town of Angleton was established, the cornerstone was laid for a new courthouse with Classical details in the new community, which was located near the geographical center of the county. Gordon's building then remained vacant for a number of years. Finally, after a tornado seriously damaged the building, it was leveled to the ground.

polychromy and durability that were much admired.

Among those who developed a strong facility for composing with the vocabulary of the Romanesque was J. Riely Gordon. With imagination, Gordon ameliorated the hot climate with skillful courthouse planning and developed the Romanesque style into an appropriate expression for county government. Preferring to unify the tower aesthetically and structurally with the courthouse mass, he positioned interior spaces to allow continuous support walls, rather than relying upon timber trusses to support a tower framework clad in sheet metal over the district courtroom. In the Brazoria County Courthouse, Brazoria (1894–1895), which is gone, the masonry tower was centrally located (fig. 224).

On the interiors tower-bearing walls were perforated with arched openings at every floor level, and a stairway was placed within, thereby creating a tall air shaft; rising hot air was ventilated to the exterior above the roofs. In deference to the need for direct access to the stairways and to the corridors surrounding them, a ground floor plan in the form of a

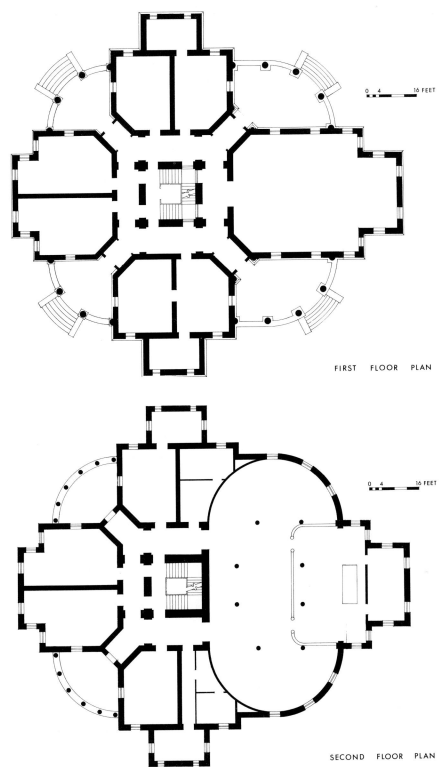

FIRST FLOOR PLAN

SECOND FLOOR PLAN

FIGURE 225. Brazoria County Courthouse, Brazoria (1894–1895). J. Riely Gordon, architect. *Drawings by author.*

The plans of the Brazoria County Courthouse were similar to those employed by Gordon for several other Texas temples of justice. On the first floor, the county courtroom was located in the right arm of the cruciform shape. Apparently the tax assessor was officed on the left, county judge and county clerk in the offices at the top and bottom. On the second floor were the large oval courtroom, district clerk's office, and offices for the county and district attorneys. On the third floor were a courtroom gallery and spaces for the grand jury and petit jury.

FIGURE 226. Lamar County Courthouse, Paris (1895–1896). Messer, Sanguinet & Messer, architects. *Texas State Historical Association, Austin.*

Early in 1894 county officials condemned their Mansardic-roofed courthouse and ordered it taken down. About a year later the cornerstone for this fine edifice was laid. Constructed by Martin, Byrnes, & Johnston, the temple displayed fine Romanesque Revival details. The exterior walls were built with Texas granite.

In 1916, after a fire, this building, too, was ordered dismantled. Then the present courthouse, designed in Classical style by the architectural firm of Barry & Smith, was constructed.

FIGURE 227. Brazos County Courthouse, Bryan (ca. 1892). Eugene T. Heiner, architect. *Bryan Public Library, Bryan.*

This was an interesting composite building in Romanesque Revival style that also incorporated Second Empire forms. The structure had an oblong plan; two facades were seven-part compositions—unusual in Texas—and two were three-part. French Mansard roofs with crestings surmounted the mass, while a tower with these features rose from the center. However, small triangular pediments accented these.

The design of the polychromatic masonry was remarkable. Contrasting stonework was employed to emphasize the stringcourses, archivolts, and pilaster bases and capitals. Finally contrasting color also was used at the entrances for the arch voussoirs.

Greek cross evolved, with entrances at the reentrant angles (fig. 225).[20]

Other architects in the state designed courthouses in the fashionable Richardsonian Romanesque style—a variation reflecting the personal innovations of the prominent Boston architect. Among these were the architects who designed a courthouse in this mode in Paris for Lamar County (fig. 226). The Brazos County Courthouse in Bryan was another fine Romanesque edifice that is now gone (fig. 227).

Like the county governmental buildings, the federal courthouses and post offices appearing in many Texas cities were focal points of their environment. They were designed to express the dignity of government yet to embody the

[20] However, there are numerous precedents for the placement of towers above the cruciform plan type; for example, the Abbey Church of Lessay, Normandy, France, a Romanesque building.

distinctive character that was so much admired during the latter part of the nineteenth century. As with the earlier antebellum federal building in Galveston, the designs were created in the office of the supervising architect of the treasury, in Washington, D.C.[21] However, construction was supervised by prominent local architects.

During the era of elegance relatively large sums of federal money were spent on architecture in Texas to provide the facilities necessary for the state's rapidly increasing population and expanding economy. Of course, then as now, congressmen certainly were eager to see fine new federal works in the districts they represented; their political futures often were affected by their success in obtaining passage of bills financing buildings. While Galveston's antebellum Custom House, Post Office, and Courthouse was the only federal governmental structure in Texas until near the end of the century, during the 1880's and 1890's new structures appeared in most of the major cities.[22]

These federal buildings were planned as multipurpose edifices housing post offices, federal offices, and federal courtrooms, although the mail and court functions generally were separated clearly in a hierarchical manner. The post office was placed on the ground floor, while the court functions were situated on the upper levels. Locations at street intersections allowed separate public entrances on the two avenues, although the access to the courtrooms, often emphasized by a tower, was usually the focal point of the exterior composition.

The romantic inclinations of the times, as well as changing eastern tastes, were epitomized by the federal buildings dating from the

era of elegance, few of which stand today. While in Austin the first Texas federal building to be constructed since before the Civil War was in a reposed Italian Renaissance Revival style,[23] in Houston designers seem to have been interested in romantically developing regionalism. This interest in distinctive character was recorded by one reporter when he wrote that the federal buildings were commonly "designed . . . with embellishments for securing certain architectural effects." Perhaps because someone associated a style developed in a hot climate abroad with the Gulf Coast heat, the Moorish style was chosen to provide distinction for the Houston federal building (fig. 228). However, although some of the press acclaimed it "a handsome structure," others criticized it because it was "so strongly oriental that its design . . . was not appropriate for a public building in America."[24]

The buildings completed in the eighties and nineties were designed in a more restrained compound style (fig. 229). In Galveston, concepts of regional expression produced a building with a Mediterranean flavor, but with less flamboyance than the one in Houston. Romanesque arches, Palladian motifs, Classical cornices, and Spanish roof tiles all were combined to produce an effect considered to be appropriate for the physiography of Galveston. Also designed in compound style was the Waco governmental building, which in 1886 incorporated both Grecian and Gothic orders.[25]

Perhaps regionalism also influenced designers in developing the style for the San Antonio Post Office and Courthouse (fig. 230). In a masculine Romanesque statement, the importance of the military aspect of the local heritage was expressed.

The "modern" Romanesque details, composed into different forms, also appeared in

---

[21] Originally, the office was in charge of designing buildings necessary for the collection of customs and internal revenue taxes for the Treasury Department. However, the responsibilities of the office were expanded during the second half of the nineteenth century to include post offices, federal courthouses, and land offices.

[22] Donald J. Lehman, *Lucky Landmark*, p. 76.

[23] See Roxanne Kuter Williamson, pp. 84–86. The building stands at Colorado Avenue and Sixth Street.

[24] Percy Clark, "New Federal Buildings," *Harper's Weekly* 32 (May 19, 1888):368; *Houston Daily Post*, August 25, 1889.

[25] *Fort Worth Daily Gazette*, April 18, 1886.

FIGURE 228. Houston Federal Post Office and Courthouse (1888–1889). Will A. Freret, Supervising Architect of the Treasury. *From* Art Work of Houston, *1894,* Houston Public Library.

This building was erected by Kelly Brothers, contractors from New Orleans. It was some 75 by 140 feet in plan and cost over $60,000.

As was typical of the federal buildings of the period, it had a double front. The main public access was on Franklin Street; employees entered from Fannin Street. The post office occupied the ground floor, and the courtroom and offices were situated on the second.

The three-story structure was finished with a brilliant polychromatic exterior. Base walls were stone, with terra-cotta trim; above, the walls were laid with alternating courses of light and dark red bricks.

Horseshoe arches also contributed to the richness of the surface.

FIGURE 229. Galveston Customhouse, Post Office and Courthouse (1886–1892). Mifflin E. Bell and Will A. Freret, Supervising Architects of the Treasury. *From* Art Work in Galveston, *Barker Texas History Center, University of Texas at Austin.*

To provide space for governmental activity of rapidly increasing size this magnificent structure was built at the corner of Church Street and Rosenberg Avenue.

Although plans were developed for the building by Mifflin E. Bell and construction was commenced in 1886, legislation authorizing a larger building stopped work. Construction resumed the following year on plans modified by Will A. Freret. The early construction was superintended by Nicholas J. Clayton.

During the great Galveston storm of 1900, the building served as a refuge for many residents. In 1935 it was razed to make room for a new post office and courthouse.

FIGURE 230. San Antonio Post Office and Federal Building (1888–1889). *From* Art Work of San Antonio, *Daughters of the Republic of Texas Library, San Antonio.*

Rigid cubical and cylindrical forms with Romanesque details provided a distinctive image for federal government in the Alamo City. A high tower accented by a tourelle formed a focal point of the massing. A corbel table at the parapet provided an effect similar to that of the openings (machicolations) developed for Medieval castle defense.

J. Riely Gordon originally was appointed supervising architect to oversee construction. However, misunderstandings developed among the contractor, the office of supervising architect of the treasury, and Gordon, and the San Antonio architect was deposed.

other regions of the state. In Jefferson and Fort Worth, the orderly and fashionable Richardsonian Romanesque style was employed on the federal post offices and courthouses. Although the Jefferson structure, a brick building, is now used as a museum, the one in Fort Worth, a stone edifice, has been gone for many years (fig. 231).[26]

[26] For an illustration of the Jefferson building, see Robinson, *Texas Public Buildings*, p. 258.

Other important public buildings dating from this era include the state capitol. While the history of this extant building is outside the scope of this work and has been told elsewhere, the story of the temporary capitol is not so well known. This structure, which served for an interim period, is another important building that also has been destroyed.

Recognizing that the antebellum capitol was too small and too inferior in design to be appropriate for state government, people began

FIGURE 231. Fort Worth Federal Post Office and Courthouse (1892–1896). Willoughby J. Edbrooke, Supervising Architect of the Treasury. *From* The Book of Fort Worth, *Amon Carter Museum, Fort Worth.*

Under the supervision of J. J. Kane, local architect, this fine building was constructed with walls of Pecos sandstone. The details of the building, handsomely contrived, reflected the influence of Henry Hobson Richardson. Turrets, arches with prominent archivolts, and heavy voussoirs all provided the variety of design that was so much admired at the time.

The ornamental stone carving was done by John La Due, a young Frenchman. This work apparently was accomplished by first hiring sculptors or modellers to prepare models from full-size working drawings made in Washington, D.C. Then carvers worked from these three-dimensional forms.

agitating for a new building as the eighties approached. In 1880 a capitol building commission, appointed by the governor, advertised a competition to select plans. After the commission chose the plans of Elijah Myers, a contract was awarded, under which three million acres of state land (which became the famous XIT Ranch) were exchanged for a new building. In spite of numerous difficulties, construction proceeded, and the capitol was dedicated in 1888.[27]

Meanwhile it had been necessary to develop temporary quarters for state government, since, in the first place, the new capitol was to occupy the site of the old. Furthermore, in 1881 the old Greek Revival work burned. For a temporary building, the plans of F. E. Ruffini, local architect, were selected. Lo-

[27] Texas Capitol Building Commission, *Final Report of the*

Capitol Building Commissioners Upon the Completion of the New Capitol; Daily Statesman (Austin), May 17, 1888. See also Frederick W. Rathjen, "The Texas State House: A Study of the Texas Capitol Based on Reports of the Capitol Building Commissioners," *Southwestern Historical Quarterly* 60 (1957):433–462.

FIGURE 232. Temporary Capitol, Austin (1883). F. E. Ruffini, architect. *From* Art Work of Austin, *Austin–Travis County Collection, Austin Public Library.*

While this building was under construction, the house of representatives convened in Millet's Opera House, and the senate assembled in the Armory Hall. Built of cut stone, the edifice was well designed according to function. On the first floor was the executive department; on the second, the legislative; and on the third, the judicial. The building burned in 1899, about a decade after the present capitol was completed.

cated across Congress Avenue from the Travis County Courthouse, near the new capitol site, the fine temporary capitol was dedicated on January 1, 1883 (fig. 232).[28]

As a result of several circumstances, the esteem for the picturesqueness of the era of elegance to which the temporary building belonged declined rapidly during the late nine-

[28] *Fort Worth Daily Gazette*, January 2, 1883; *Standard* (Clarksville), January 12, 1883.

ties. The heavy Classicism of the World's Columbian Exposition made a profound impact on American taste. Then too, the depression of 1893 certainly marked a turning point; as often has happened, emergence from difficult times was accompanied by changes in attitudes. Moreover, the American desire for change led to rejection by a new generation of the picturesque styles of previous years. Then, throughout the country, the influence of various academic programs emphasizing rigid

Classicism became prominent. Consequently during the early part of the twentieth century new aesthetic values produced architecture with a different character.

As was the case with other architecture of the nineteenth century, some of the most significant institutional and governmental edifices have been lost. Although good examples of Gothic Revival churches and Richardsonian Romanesque courthouses remain, countless beautiful examples have been destroyed. Moorish buildings are an endangered species. Likewise a number of excellent university buildings have been wrecked. Some were condemned for structural inadequacies, others were simply in the way of progress. In many instances it appears that decisions to remove some fine historic buildings were made without giving adequate attention to preserving and reusing them. Interestingly, Victorian builders appear to have expressed little concern for their antebellum heritage; by the same token, mid-twentieth-century architects and critics viewed the era of elegance with contempt, while greatly admiring the Greek Revival and folk architecture.

7

The Twentieth Century

As the twentieth century dawned, Texas enjoyed economic conditions favoring the development of art and material culture. Although a discouraging panic in the early 1890's retarded construction—and, at the same time, marked a turning point with respect to taste in art—the completion of the Lucas Gusher bringing in black gold at Spindletop (1901) marked the beginning of a period of prosperity. Subsequently during the 1920's a petroleum boom in the Panhandle and other parts of the state contributed further to the wealth of the era. Meanwhile ranching in West Texas, cotton farming in Central Texas, and agriculture in South Texas all added to the prosperous times (many ranchers also became wealthy from dual ventures in cattle and either oil or industry).

During the first decades of the century, industry and business, much of which was petroleum related, expanded by leaps and bounds. In addition, railroads continued to develop, expand, and increase their profits. The large bank deposits from all this made possible the erection of many substantial buildings, the construction of roads, the development of seaports, and the building of dams and lakes for city water supplies. Cultural growth was apparent in the establishment of art museums and in the organization of sym-

phony orchestras, as well as in the design of buildings in eclectic styles.

At the turn of the century the population was continuing to increase rapidly. Countless annexations were made to cities across the state, providing housing sites for both the upper and middle classes. Typical, in Houston, were Shady Side (1916) and Broadacres (1923), the latter of which was designed by architect William Ward Watkin. In Dallas, the Swiss Avenue area—now a historic district— was built between 1905 and 1925, and South Boulevard, a Jewish neighborhood, grew up during the 1910's and 1920's.[1]

The city beautiful movement, which had evolved after the World's Columbian Exposition in Chicago, made a noteworthy impact on many Texas cities. Parks and plazas were developed, streets were widened, and in many towns boulevards, such as Camp Bowie in Fort Worth, were laid out, with brick-paved vehicle lanes separated by green bands of grass. Moreover, landscaped esplanades enhanced the fronts of some important public buildings. Two examples that still exist were the two-block square located in front of the Crockett

[1] William L. McDonald, *Dallas Rediscovered: A Photographic Chronicle of Urban Expansion, 1870–1925*, pp. 126–161; Howard Barnstone, *The Architecture of John F. Staub: Houston and the South*, pp. 6–8.

County Courthouse, Ozona (1907), and Ferris Plaza, conceived by the planner George E. Kessler, which runs in front of the Union Depot in Dallas (1914–1916).[2] While many of these green areas remain, others have been taken out to provide more spaces for automobiles.

The prosperous times of the early part of the century made possible the construction of many pretentious houses on sites prominently located within the communities and cities. Along broad streets and wide boulevards appeared residences of successful industrialists, capitalists, and ranchers. Reflecting changes in the times, many of the houses were Classical and stately in character rather than Romantic and picturesque, as they had been during the previous era of elegance.

During the early decades of the twentieth century, design features derived from both ancient Greek and Roman architecture again provided formal appearances, much as they had during the 1880's and 1890's. Working on a larger scale than the earlier Victorian architects, many designers during this period employed two-storied porticoes supported by columns on a colossal order and encompassing a balcony. Still reflecting considerations for the hot climate, one-story porches providing outdoor living spaces appeared at the sides and backs of these large houses. Also common were cylindrical porch forms, which flanked the large entrance feature. Then, balustrades, modillions, fretworks, dormers, and captain's walks all complemented the Classical theme. Virtually every community had one or more of these large and stately houses; in the cities, most are gone, in the small towns, many remain. Among the fine examples of the formal residence design were the T. L. Hackney House, Houston (fig. 233), and the house of J. Ashford Hughes, Dallas, both now gone (fig. 234).

However, in many communities where houses were built during the prosperous twenties and thirties, styles with American rather than European origins characterized the dwellings of the middle and upper classes. The Prairie style, pioneered by Frank Lloyd Wright, reached Texas, and many architects designed houses, as well as other structures, with the horizontal emphasis and geometrical decoration characteristic of the mode. In many residential buildings, broad, overhanging roofs capped the brick walls of symmetrically composed buildings.

In addition bungalows appeared, reflecting architectural innovations from the West Coast. In communities—particularly those in West Texas—that grew rapidly during the oil boom of the 1920's and 1930's, many frame and brick houses were built with complex compositions of boldly projecting gables and porches—hallmarks of the mode. In some cases, for example in Wichita Falls, entire neighborhoods were filled with these. Although many examples remain, countless other fine houses in this style are gone.

While the forms of the Prairie and Bungalow styles respectively reflected the flat prairies of the Midwest and the wood tradition of the Far West, revivals expressing ethnic associations also appeared. The Mission style appeared in residences and virtually every other building type. With a stylistic vocabulary that was displayed to countless visitors in the California Pavilion at the World's Columbian Exposition, this mode appeared in the Golden State during the 1890's and subsequently became fashionable in all the southwestern states. Employing details from the missions of the Southwest—most prominently arches, tiled roofs, curvilinear-profiled parapets, and plain stuccoed walls—architects created a wide variety of expressions.

The Spanish Colonial architecture of Mexico, Texas, and Arizona, as well as the Renaissance buildings of Spain also provided sources of twentieth-century style. Perhaps the design of the Roman Catholic Church of Saint Francis on the Brazos, which still stands in Waco, illustrates the impact of the Spanish Renaissance Revival; built in 1931, it is a faithful re-

[2] McDonald, *Dallas Rediscovered*, pp. 204–205, 209.

FIGURE 233. Thomas L. Hackney House, Houston (ca. 1900). *From* Art Work of Houston, *1904,* Houston Public Library.

Built by a successful lumber manufacturer, this house displayed features that were characteristic of the times in wealthy communities. Columns with Ionic capitals, certainly made from plaster, supported Classical entablatures. Although the detail on these entablatures varied, heavy modillions and fret over the portico enhanced the work. Other noteworthy features included a dormer with a scroll pediment rising above the portico, a captain's walk, and oval windows. To complement the large scale of the form, the masonry was rusticated.

FIGURE 234. J. Ashford Hughes House, Dallas (ca. 1900). *From* Art Work of Dallas, *1910,* Archives and Research Center for Texas and Dallas History, Dallas Public Library.

Classical design provided formal distinction for this large house. Formal composition and the use of monumental features created a strong statement. After Hughes moved out of the house, it served a religious function but then was demolished in 1960 to make way for a new expressway.

FIGURE 235. YMCA Building, El Paso (1907). Henry Trost, architect. *El Paso Public Library.*

This handsome building reflected the influence of Chicago architect Louis Sullivan. This influence was particularly noteworthy in the design of the podium of the building, in the arches encompassing two floors, and in the expression of the top story as the terminal feature of the composition. The "organic" ornamentation of the entrance arch, the window spandrels, and the cornice also is reminiscent of Sullivan's designs.

Sullivan's work was well known by Trost. He had worked for the Chicago architect during the 1880's, when Sullivan was doing some of his best work. In 1958 the YMCA vacated the building, which was one of the most important designed by Trost, and in 1961 it was demolished.

production of the church in Mission San José in San Antonio.

The Spanish Renaissance Revival likewise characterized some Texas houses, as well as other building types. Following the style's appearance in the Texas Pavilion in the Columbian Exposition, where it was intended to portray the heritage of the Lone Star State, it provided the potential for formal composition with elements that related romantically to the region. This mode, with configurations of details imported from Spain, was used in various towns and cities during the early decades of the century.

During the early part of the century Young Men's Christian Associations were organized in the large Texas cities.[3] New buildings were constructed to provide the necessary facilities. However, these first buildings, some of which were fine designs, are now gone (fig. 235).

It was during the early decades of the twentieth century, too, that the golden era of railroading developed, resulting in a rash of station building. Reflecting the financial success of the companies, large—in several instances, monumental—terminals were erected in Texas. While many cities had union terminals that were used by most if not all railroads serving their people, in several instances the individual

[3] In Dallas, for example, fund raising was underway on December 1, 1905. See the *Dallas Morning News,* December 5, 1905.

railways constructed large terminals that, through opulence, symbolized the economic importance of the communities they served. In addition to providing passenger service, the stations contained offices and public amenities. Among these stations were the Texas and Pacific terminal, Fort Worth (fig. 236), destroyed by fire in 1904, and the Union Depot in Waco (fig. 237), destroyed by a tornado in 1953.[4]

Such stations as the Dallas Union Terminal (1916), by architect Jarvis Hunt of Chicago, and the Union Terminal of Houston (1909–1911), by Wetmore and Warren of New York City—both of which still stand—were large-scaled universal statements in Beaux-Arts style. However, in many cases the railroad companies preferred to express an identity with their region in styles that would be memorable for arriving passengers—certainly this was desirable for public relations in days when pride in regionalism was developing. Typical of this effort was a large union terminal in Wichita Falls, built in Mission Revival style (fig. 238). A more elaborate and even more vivid expression of locale in Mission Revival style was the San Antonio station built by the Katy Railroad (fig. 239).

Interested in obtaining the best possible designs, railroad officials commissioned prominent architects from the East to design passenger depots. Among these, in addition to Hunt, was Daniel H. Burnham, architect of the monumental Union Depot in Washington, D.C., who was selected as architect for the El Paso Union Passenger Depot (1905–1906). This fine work in straightforward Renaissance Revival design, which stands but which has been much remodeled, was dominated by a campanile with a broach spire.

The favorable economy springing from railroading, oil, and other enterprises spawned the construction of many new commercial buildings. In order to dispatch their work efficiently, businessmen needed central locations. This naturally increased the values of building sites for commercial space and office buildings. High-rise buildings were essential if investors in architecture were to receive optimum returns from the rental of spaces.

The technology and aesthetics of the commercial style had evolved in the East. Elisha Graves Otis had invented the elevator in the 1850's, and its safety had been rapidly perfected; the importance of this development has already been noted. Monolithic concrete construction or steel skeletal framing with masonry and terra-cotta fireproofing became standard as Texas builders borrowed techniques that had originated with the Chicago School. Of course skeletal framing allowed fast construction, thus enabling investors to begin realizing profits from rentals at the earliest date. Concrete construction was stable, but in the early years of the use of concrete there was uncertainty over the most efficient methods of reinforcement—a fact that was reflected by the large number of patents issued for various systems.[5]

Investors soon found that elegant designs for building entrances and elevator lobbies, as well as good natural lighting and ventilation were sound investments, attracting prestigious clientele. The Praetorian Building, Dallas (1907), a fifteen-story, fireproof steel work by architects C. W. Bulger and his son Clarence, was a pioneer Texas skyscraper that still stands, but in much-altered condition.

Many low-rise buildings and skyscrapers alike displayed Georgian, Greek, or Roman ornamental details rendered in stone or terra cotta, according to traditional principles. In El Paso the St. Regis Hotel (1904) was a fine example of a low-rise building incorporating this kind of Georgian detail (fig. 240). In Dallas the Southwestern Life Building exemplified the

[4] For a survey of railroad stations in Texas see Keith L. Bryant, Jr., "Railway Stations of Texas: A Disappearing Architectural Heritage," *Southwestern Historical Quarterly* 79 (1976):417–440.

[5] Many patented systems for reinforced concrete were advertised periodically in *American Architect and Building News*.

FIGURE 236. Texas and Pacific Union Passenger Station, Fort Worth. R. S. Wathen, architect. *Courtesy Fort Worth Public Library, Amon Carter Museum.*

    This was designed by the chief engineer for the railroad and was a facility intended to accommodate large volumes of passengers. Similar to many other large stations built throughout the West near the turn of the century, it was in Romanesque Revival style—a mode that remained popular for public buildings in Texas past the turn of the century. Distinguishing features included polychromatic masonry of brick trimmed with red Pecos sandstone. Among the other noteworthy features were rhythms of arches, gables, and loopholes, all combined to unify the composition. Additionally, the tower provided a focal point for the neighborhood. The building burned in 1904, was rebuilt, then destroyed in 1937.

FIGURE 237. Union Depot, Waco (ca. 1900). *Texas Collection, Baylor University, Waco.*

Handsomely designed, this building displayed features that were characteristic of many large stations in the South. The building stretched along the tracks and was surrounded by long loggias. A lofty tower with polychromatic masonry provided a landmark that announced the depot.

FIGURE 238. Union Station Railway Terminal, Wichita Falls (1910). Lang and Witchell, architects. *Wichita Falls Museum of Art and History.*

This terminal was built to serve the Missouri, Kansas and Texas, Fort Worth and Denver, and Wichita Falls and Southern railways. As was common, passenger facilities were at one end, mail and baggage at the other. On the inside, which was attractively decorated, were a general waiting room and separate waiting spaces for the ladies and the "colored." A dining room, entered through the tower doorway, also was provided for the convenience of travelers. Offices were on a second floor above the dining room.

The design was a fine example of Mission Revival style. With low-pitched, red-tiled roof and balconies, which were typical of the mode, the tower formed a prominent landmark. Other significant features included the decorative terra-cotta work in the parapets. This fine edifice was razed in recent years to lower the taxes on the site.

FIGURE 239. Katy Station, San Antonio (1917). Frederick J. Sterner, architect. *From* San Antonio, City of Destiny and Your Destination, *Daughters of the Republic of Texas Library, San Antonio.*

Designed by a New York architect and built by the Missouri Kansas and Texas Railway Company, this station had a Mission Revival style that projected an appropriate image for one of the gateways to the Alamo City. The entrance, with its elaborate detailing patterned after the Churrigueresque features of Mission San José church, contrasted with plain walls and towers. Curvilinear-profiled parapets and clay roof tiles were other noteworthy features.

However the most remarkable features were on the interior. The large, high-ceilinged waiting room was decorated with tile, marble, and bronze. It was spanned with wooden beams with carved decorations finished in dark natural colors. Flooring of mosaic tiles also contributed to the Spanish atmosphere. In June, 1968, the building was bulldozed.

FIGURE 240. St. Regis Hotel, El Paso (1904). Trost and Trost, architects. *Texas State Historical Association, Austin.*

Built in Georgian Revival style, this elegant hotel was located near San Jacinto Plaza. After serving as a showplace in El Paso for many years, the building was destroyed in 1977 by a mysterious fire. Prior to the fire the State National Bank of El Paso had begun demolition of the structure. The site is now a parking lot.

high-rise office buildings displaying floral decoration rendered in terra cotta (fig. 241). The Mills Building, El Paso (1910–1911), conformed to the same formula of composition, but the ornamental features were somewhat more simple, providing a distinctive statement (fig. 242). The first two are gone; the Mills Building is much remodeled.

Classicism based upon Renaissance sources had been given impetus by the World's Columbian Exposition in Chicago, an event wherein the architecture was to be an "object lesson." In the West at least, further impetus for Classicism seems to have been provided by the Louisiana Purchase Exposition of 1904 in St. Louis. Although built on a smaller budget than at the Chicago show, monumental courts and buildings with imposing Classical designs provided stately images. Designed by Charles H. Page of Austin, the Texas Building reflected the Classical theme (fig. 243).[6]

In Texas, public buildings of various functional types displayed formal designs. Large columns and massive entablatures, modeled after the Classical paradigms of Europe and often arranged in original compositions, provided distinctive appearances for many prestigious commercial buildings. Using a common vocabulary, various architects designed structures with formal character that provided images for many banks, particularly.

In Texas, of course, the interest in architectural image had developed during the nineteenth century; it continued into the twentieth and is yet apparent today. Various institutions have continually used photographs and drawings of their buildings as advertisements. Historically, as today, bankers demanded distinction according to the aesthetic values of the period, which required durability and beauty. To provide the desired image, in the early part of this century monumental Classicism once

again permeated designs, suggesting that the enterprise contained within was a cornerstone of local or regional economy. Thus the Fort Worth National Bank (ca. 1910) was a monumental edifice with High Renaissance Revival stylistic features, from a second Renaissance Revival (fig. 244). The opulence and monumentality of the interiors complemented the lavishness of the exterior.

The Classicism preferred by bankers and city officials also prevailed in buildings with highly valued public functions and cultural purposes. Among the elaborate examples, now gone, was the Central Fire Station in Houston (fig. 245). Throughout the state Classical colonnades and cornices distinguished art museums and libraries, some of the latter of which were partially financed by the Andrew Carnegie Foundation. Among the fine Neoclassical monuments dedicated to cultural enlightenment was the Carnegie Library in Houston (fig. 246). In Bryan the massive, Classical-style Carnegie Library still stands. In Fort Worth, the Carnegie Library was a fine Neo-Renaissance edifice (fig. 247).

The assembly and performance buildings that replaced the nineteenth-century opera houses also were formal designs. In Houston, for example, the Houston City Auditorium displayed Renaissance details, although the massing was functional (fig. 248).

The Classicism that characterized other buildings with high cultural purposes also appeared in some school buildings. However, due to economic limitations, ornamentation generally was more limited than on other public buildings. Like those of the nineteenth century, the structures housing high schools were the most elaborate designs of the public educational facilities below the college level—physically as well as stylistically.

The high school was developed into a highly organized institution, with various courses of instruction, requiring large floor square footages and complex spaces; yet planning was formal, requiring considerable study to develop balanced, disciplined arrangements.

[6]U.S. Congress, House, *Report of the Committee on Awards of the World's Columbian Commission*, 57th Cong., 1st sess., 1901, House Doc. No. 57, p. 19; W. W. Seley Collection, Texas Collection, Baylor University; Franz K. Winkler, "The Architecture of the Louisiana Purchase Exposition," *Architectural Record* 15 (1904):337–360.

FIGURE 241. Southwestern Life Building, Dallas (1911–1913). Lang & Witchell, architects. *From the collections of the Dallas Historical Society.*

This sixteen-story office building was among the fine high-rise works erected during the early decades of the twentieth century. It had a skeleton framework, the vertical lines of which were expressed by the wide pilasters enclosing the columns. Between these, verticality was emphasized by thin dividers. As was typical, each facade was a "closed" composition: that is, a complete composition enframed by the heavy corner piers, the base, and the cornice.

This building was wrecked in 1972 to make room for a parking lot.

FIGURE 242. Mills Building, El Paso (1910–1911). Trost and Trost, architects. *Texas State Historical Association, Austin.*

Owned by Brigadier General Anson Mills, the Mills Building incorporated up-to-date design features. Reinforced concrete was employed for the structure—this material was widely in use throughout the state by this time. On the exterior, while retaining traditional compositional principles, the design was relatively straightforward: piers and mullions expressing the verticality of the design and a broad cornice terminating the composition. All this reflected the influence of Louis Sullivan.

While the building still stands, remodeling has destroyed its original quality. The exterior has been painted dark brown, and bronze reflective plate glass has been installed.

FIGURE 243. Texas Building, Louisiana Purchase Exposition, St. Louis (1904). Charles H. Page, architect. *Shannon-Haynes Family Papers, Texas Collection, Baylor University, Waco.*

 Designed on the plan of a star and financed by private contributions, this structure was acclaimed by a circular as the "most beautiful and unique piece of construction on the grounds." The lone star motif, of course, was a patriotic symbol. The colossal columns, entablatures, balconies, and dome, along with the triumphal entrance motif and a statue of liberty, were all noteworthy features. This same plan was employed for the Star of the Republic Museum, Washington-on-the-Brazos.

On the exterior, symmetrical compositions of masses, openings, and Classical features created a disciplined expression. Among the noteworthy academic institutions was the Corpus Christi High School of 1911 (razed 1961–1962), a work for which the opulent Renaissance detailing at first prompted the epithet, the "new brick palace."[7] The same formal planning that was characteristic of school plants with Classical features also characterized academic architecture with Romantic features.

 The use of other styles was perhaps based on intellectual associations between current function and historic style. Some modes were used because they expressed contemporary purpose through reflecions of past cultures. Due to associations with the English Medieval universities, the Gothic Revival provided identity of educational purpose; the Spanish Colonial Revival, like some other styles, provided an as-

[7]Unidentified newspaper clipping in "Corpus Christi High School," Historical Files, La Retama Public Library, Corpus Christi.

FIGURE 244. Fort Worth National Bank (ca. 1910). *Courtesy Mrs. Laura H. Portwood, Fort Worth, Amon Carter Museum.*

Elaborate Renaissance decoration enhanced this fine bank building. Ionic columns of colossal order supporting an entablature with a broken pediment prominently announced the entrance. Deep rustication of the base and the top story contributed further to the lavishness of the exterior.

FIGURE 245. Central Fire Station, Houston (1903). *From* Art Work of Houston, *1904,* Houston Public Library.

This was an elaborate statement in Renaissance Revival style. Rusticated pilasters, balconies, balustrades, and pediments were combined to create an intricate composition. The domed cylindrical corner form contributed to a Baroque character. All this, of course, expressed the considerable importance attributed to the public facilities designed for protection against fires.

FIGURE 246. Carnegie Library, Houston (ca. 1900). *From* Art Work of Houston, *1904,* Houston Public Library.

This library was a monumental temple incorporating ancient Roman architectural forms. Massive pediments faced the streets on two sides. The entrance was situated under a dome supported by Corinthian columns. Balustrades, pedimented windows, and statuary all added to the formality of the statement. A Woolworth department store now occupies the site.

FIGURE 247. Carnegie Library, Fort Worth (1901). Herbert Greens, architect. *Courtesy Fort Worth Public Library, Amon Carter Museum.*

This was among the handsome libraries erected in the state during the early part of the century. Attractive proportions and composition characterized the work. Also noteworthy were the pilasters separating the Roman arches and the large corner pilasters with recessed courses of bricks, which created a satisfactory scale for the monumental work.

sociation with cultural origins in the Southwest. The stylistic features of both styles were considered beautiful. The Fort Worth High School, dating from the early part of the century, displayed Gothic detailings, but that building is now gone.

The original buildings at Texas Technological College (Texas Tech University) are outstanding examples of Spanish Renaissance style, a mode that was selected to express the historic cultural origins of the Southwest. That style was also thought appropriate because "The great table lands of West Texas . . . have likeness in color and character to the table lands of central Spain. . . ."[8]

[8] Paul W. Horn, "Presidents' Papers," B139.2B, Wyatt C. Hedrick File, Southwest Collection, Texas Tech University, Lubbock.

Whereas Romantic features characterized a number of educational edifices during the early decades of the twentieth century, the Gothic vocabulary was most extensively exploited in ecclesiastical buildings. Countless churches through the state were designed on basilican and cruciform plans and displayed pointed arches, tracery, rose windows, and towers. As in previous eras, the sects with the closest liturgical ties to the Catholicism of the Medieval period most favored the Gothic. While many Protestant congregations, too, demanded this style, others preferred the Romanesque Revival. Yet others employed the monumental variations of Classical design. Commanding pedimented porticoes with columns in Roman orders and high flights of steps announced the entrances to many Baptist,

FIGURE 248. Houston City Auditorium, Houston (ca. 1910). *From George Beach*, Views of Houston, *1916, courtesy Houston Public Library*.

Bricks and stones were the materials used to form an interesting array of Classical features on this monumental composition. Architectural masses indicated the nature of the interior spaces. The auditorium and the accesses to it were marked by Florentine arches; vertical circulation was indicated by projecting masses. Secondary spaces were contained within the lower forms.

Among the other details were rustication of surfaces and the use of Greek fret in the stringcourse separating the two levels of openings.

FIGURE 249. El Paso City Hall, El Paso (ca. 1915). *Courtesy El Paso Public Library*.

The original city hall for El Paso had been constructed in 1882. Containing both police and fire departments, it had been used until 1899, when it was replaced by a new building. Some fifteen years later this imposing edifice was constructed upon a cruciform-type plan. It was demolished in 1960.

FIGURE 250. Nolan County Courthouse, Sweetwater (1915–1917). C. H. Page and Brother, architects. *Southwest Collection, Texas Tech University, Lubbock.*

Work toward this new courthouse, which replaced nineteenth-century works, commenced with an architectural competition. The firm of C. H. Page and Brother, Austin, was successful, and in 1915 contractor B. P. Berry and Company began work; however, construction was not completed until 1917, by the Shaw Construction Company, which had taken over the original contract.

Fine Classical details were developed in terra cotta, providing strong contrast with the red brick walls. Columns in Ionic order supported an entablature with prominent modillions. On the interior, marble wainscoting and coffered ceilings with plaster egg-and-dart moldings were noteworthy.

Presbyterian, and Methodist churches. As before the turn of the century, plans continued to be developed to provide comfort, satisfactory acoustics, and clear sight lines.

Yet other manifestations of Classical spirit were apparent in those city halls and county courthouses that replaced some picturesque Victorian ones. Particularly in the counties that experienced increases in wealth as a result of the oil booms, large new courthouses with monumental forms were erected. In the El Paso City Hall (ca. 1915) monumental pediments, dome, and portico in Classical style provided dignity of expression (fig. 249).

Other significant changes in courthouse design occurred in the use of materials. Generally, bricks replaced stones for walls, and terra cotta replaced galvanized iron for cornices; the

flutings on columns, too, often were terra cotta. On the interiors marble slabs replaced wood wainscots, and ceramic tiles or terrazzo replaced encaustic tile or pine flooring. All told, the aesthetic effect of the twentieth-century courthouse was colder yet more authoritative than the character of the nineteenth-century examples. Among the fine buildings incorporating these developments was the Nolan County Courthouse, Sweetwater (1915–1917), a handsome structure erected in the middle of the public square (fig. 250). The building was demolished only a few years prior to this writing. The Lubbock County Courthouse, Lubbock (1915–1916), was yet another handsome building that has been demolished (fig. 251).

In most other temples of justice during the

FIGURE 251. Lubbock County Courthouse, Lubbock (1915–1916). Rose and Peterson, architects. *Lubbock County Commissioners Court.*

Erected on the public square, which was placed a half-module off the street grid, this building was the focal point of the approach on Texas Avenue. It was designed by a Kansas City, Kansas, architectural firm.

The materials used were durable and attractive. Reinforced concrete was employed for the structural components. On the exteriors, cut stone and bricks were used. Corridor floors were terrazzo, and wainscots were marble. Window frames and sashes were metal.

This courthouse was demolished in the 1960's, after a decision was made to extend Texas Avenue through the block on which it was located.

early decades of the century, the interior organization remained essentially the same as in nineteenth-century courthouses that had been designed by such architects as F. E. Ruffini, W. C. Dodson, and Eugene T. Heiner. In the ground stories corridors located on the two axes divided the area into offices and provided for excellent cross ventilation; the second floor contained offices and large courtrooms with high ceilings. The interior space arrangements in most cases were a perpetuation of nineteenth-century traditions. In Stanton, the Martin County Courthouse (1908) was built on a cross-type plan (fig. 252); it was demolished in the 1970's. Corridors and high ceilings

provided for efficient natural ventilation; rotundas and openings through floors not only facilitated ventilation, but also provided impressive interior spaces as focal points.

While many public buildings were in Neoclassical or Renaissance Revival styles, some were designed in the style of pompous Beaux-Arts Classicism which combined ancient Greek and Roman forms as well as Renaissance forms. Monumental stairways, paired columns of colossal order, heavy sculpture, and complex treatment of wall planes all were characteristic. Among the fine examples was the McLennan County Courthouse in Waco, which still dominates its surroundings. Other

FIGURE 252. Martin County Courthouse, Stanton (1908). *Texas State Historical Association, Austin.*

This structure replaced an 1885 courthouse that had been declared unsafe. Another fine example of a courthouse in Classical style, it was built around a central stair shaft, which was entered at the reentrant angles. Accessible from this space were the offices on the ground level and the courtroom on the second floor. The building was remodeled in the early 1950's but was demolished in the 1970's.

examples included the Galveston County Courthouse, which is gone.[9] The Beaux-Arts style appeared in a number of small banks as well as several Texas courthouses.

All these developments of the first three decades of the twentieth century were interrupted by the depression of 1929. During this era, of course, construction again was retarded. Some architects were employed by the government during the mid-thirties to do survey work under the program of the Historic American Buildings Survey; some were employed on restoration or reconstruction of such buildings as Fort Belknap under the Works Progress Administration. Also under this program several nineteenth-century county courthouses were wrecked, and new works erected on the site of the old. To decorate the interior of some of the public buildings a number of artists were employed to create murals—usually with regional content.[10]

At the turning point of the second third of the century, a formal approach to design continued to prevail, but Classical components

[9] For an illustration of the Galveston County Courthouse, see Willard B. Robinson, *Texas Public Buildings of the Nineteenth Century,* p. 256–257.

[10] C. W. Short and R. Stanley-Brown, *Public Buildings: A Survey of Architecture of Projects Constructed by Federal and Other Governmental Bodies between the Years 1933 and 1939 with the Assistance of the Public Works Administration.*

were transformed into geometrical masses. More pushing and pulling and upward and downward lifts of masses occurred. At the same time ornamentation that previously had been based on historical precedent was changed into hard-edged linear abstractions.

Developments made possible by rapidly expanding technology, communications, and transportation were accompanied by other evolutions in architectural style. During the 1930's quick movement provided by automobiles and locomotives found counterparts in new design concepts. Rapid repetition of geometrical decorative elements created the impressions of strength and vitality in the style known as Art Deco. Reeding, rhythmic triangular forms, and Wurlitzer motifs all were employed. At the same time, interior-exterior relationships were developed, with similar decorative themes used on both inside and outside, providing further unity. The most important Art Deco buildings displaying these features remain. Among these, the Cotton Exchange (1939) in Galveston, the Gulf Building (ca. 1935) by Alfred C. Finn in Houston, the Dallas Power and Light Building (1930) by Lang and Witchell, and the Travis County Courthouse (1930–1936) by Page Brothers in Austin are all in use.

The true significance of new buildings, particularly those less than fifty years old, is hazardous to evaluate. Moreover, the most important statements are still standing. Nonetheless, it is essential that attempts at evaluation be made so that conscious decisions can be taken about which deserve to be preserved as part of Texas' ongoing architectural heritage. In this respect, it is timely to note contemporary developments concerning preservation. While the story of innumerable important historic structures now gone from Texas is over, the history of some continues, with the support of interested parties. The appreciation of the presence of the tangible past has led to a virtual preservation revolution.

During the mid-twentieth century the preservation of our remaining architectural heritage has been encouraged by a number of organizations and agencies. The San Antonio Conservation Society has purchased properties, funded restoration, and sponsored programs promoting historic preservation; this group has been influential not only in Texas but also in other states. In addition, several other heritage societies in the state have been instrumental in saving buildings for posterity. The Galveston Historical Foundation, with the use of revolving funds, has restored commercial buildings along the Strand, as well as Ashton Villa—now a museum—and has provided leadership in preservation activities.

Texas legislation has provided for other conservation activities. In 1953 the Texas Historical Survey Committee was authorized to provide leadership in the field of historic preservation. In 1973 this agency became the Texas Historical Commission, and its responsibilities were expanded to include the administration of the National Register Program and the preparation of a statewide preservation plan. In addition, services are provided to local agencies and individuals interested in restoration. The Texas Historical Foundation also sponsors programs relating to preservation.[11]

To some extent Texas law has supported other efforts toward preservation. Historic districts have been established by law in San Antonio and Dallas. In 1971 the Act Relating to the Preservation of Historic Courthouses was passed, requiring that county officials notify the Historical Commission before authorizing work that might damage the architectural-historical integrity of their courthouse. It empowered the commission to delay any work for 180 days, during which time options could be explored. Nonetheless, several courthouses have been wrecked since the law was passed.

More comprehensive protection is provided

[11] *Vernon's Texas Civil Statutes*, Art. 6145; *Historic Preservation in Texas*, 1:73, 76, 79. For a survey of the legal aspects of preservation in Texas, see Susan Abigail Schatzel, "Public Historic Preservation in Texas," *Texas Law Review* (1971):267–321.

by the National Register programs, formerly run by the National Park Services, Office of Archeology and Historic Preservation, now by the Heritage, Conservation and Recreational Services. Buildings that are included on the National Register of Historic Places—a listing of structures or objects of national, regional, or local significance—cannot be demolished with the support of federal funds, although they may be wrecked by local moneys. In addition, the Tax Reform Act of 1976 provides additional incentive to preserve by allowing such advantages and discouragements as accelerated depreciation and prohibition of the deduction of demolition costs.[12] Nonetheless,

many National Register buildings are now gone.

In retrospect, it is unfortunate that some types of buildings are now lost and unfortunate that many irreplaceable, beautiful works are gone. However, there yet remains a rich heritage, not only from the eighteenth and nineteenth centuries, but also from the twentieth. With care, representations of the diverse aspects of this heritage may be preserved, and posterity may retain some examples of every aspect of the architectural legacy that is being created today.

[12] *The National Register of Historic Places.* Washington, D.C.: Office of Archeology and Historic Preservation, U.S. De-

partment of the Interior [occasional publication]; "Preservation and the Tax Reform Act of 1976," *Preservation News,* supplement (1977). Information is available from the State Historic Preservation Officer, Texas Historical Commission, Box 12276, Capitol Station, Austin, Texas 78711.

Architectural Glossary

adobe: building material composed of a mixture of mud and either straw or grass; ordinarily formed into blocks and dried in the sun.

arabesque: a decorative panel displaying patterns of geometrical or naturalistic forms.

arcade: a range of arches and their supports.

arch: a structural member made of a series of wedge-shaped masonry units following one or more curvatures to span an opening in a wall.

architrave: the part of an entablature supported by columns or pilasters; the lowest of the three horizontal divisions of an entablature.

Art Deco: a twentieth-century architectural style characterized by crisp forms, stylized sculpture, and geometrical ornamentation.

ashlar: stone masonry made up of blocks with rectangular faces.

atrio: see atrium.

atrium: an entrance court.

baluster: a small vertical support, or short column, for a handrail.

balustrade: a railing supported by a series of balusters or short posts.

banqueta: in Spanish colonial and Mexican architecture, a seat or step along a wall.

barge board: the board appearing at the gable edge of a roof, often with decorative patterns.

Baroque: a style developed during the late Renaissance, characterized by elaborate decoration.

barrel vault: a long, masonry structural unit spanning a space and composed of numerous small stones or bricks placed to form a circular cross section.

basilica: originally an ancient Roman building type, rectangular in plan, with an apse and a nave, used for public purposes. Early Christians adopted it for their churches.

bastion: a triangular projecting feature composed of two flanks, which enabled defense of the enclosure from which it protruded.

bay: a space between columns, piers, or walls.

bay window: a window with angled sides that projects from a wall, beginning at the ground.

beam: a straight, load-supporting structural member.

Beaux-Arts ("fine arts"): École des Beaux-Arts, France, a school which, during the nineteenth and early twentieth century, based its teachings upon formality and a study of the past.

belfry: a small bell tower.

blockhouse: a work with walls of hewn logs, designed for defense.

box construction: a building technique wherein thin boards are employed to enclose rooms in a manner similar to that used to build wooden boxes.

bracket: a support for an overhang or other projecting feature.

breezeway: see dogtrot.

broach spire: a tapered structure with an octagonal plan, rising from a tower.

bunkhouse: a house serving as a dormitory for cowboys.

buttress: a pier projecting from a wall.

cabin: a small dwelling, constructed with log walls.

campanario: a bell tower

campanile: a bell tower.

canal: in Spanish colonial and Mexican architecture, a drain trough that conducted water from the roof.

capital: the top component of a column. It rests upon the shaft.

casa grande: in Spanish colonial and Mexican architecture, the principal house on a ranch.

cat: narrow bundles of straw, grass, or moss mixed with wet clay, used to form chimneys.

center-matched boards: siding wherein edges abut to produce a flush surface.

chancel: the sacred space of a church at the end of a nave, from which the clergy conduct services.

Churrigueresque: named for the Churriguera family of Spanish sculptors, a style of architecture characterized by lavishness in the use of both geometrical and representational features. See also Ultra-Baroque.

cistern: a storage tank for water, usually underground.

clapboard: a narrow board, tapered in cross section, used on exterior walls.

Classical: based upon ancient Greek or Roman art.

cloister: a covered passage, along the side of a building, open to an adjacent court.

colonnade: a series of columns.

compound style: an architectural mode wherein features from two or more historical sources are combined to make up the decorative vocabulary.

console: a bracket used to support a cornice or other projecting feature.

convent: a building used to house those dedicated to religious life.

convento: see convent.

cornerstone: a chief stone, usually hollow, ordinarily located in the base of the northeast corner of a building and inscribed with information about construction.

cornice: the upper member of an entablature.

court: an exterior space enclosed in whole or part by a building.

crenel: the opening in a battlemented wall through which defenders discharged missiles against besiegers in Medieval days.

cresting: a decorative member placed upon the ridge of a roof.

crib: an enclosure formed by logs notched together at the corners.

crosset: a side projection, or "ear," appearing at the top of a door or window casing.

dentil: a small rectangular block, used in a series to form a decorative band under a cornice.

dogtrot: the open space between two log rooms, under the same roof that extends over those rooms.

dome: a hemispherical roof.

dormer: a form, with a gable and window, projecting from a pitched roof.

double log cabin: a building with two rooms separated by a breezeway, all under a continuous roof; also called a dogtrot cabin.

drum: a hollow cylindrical form upon which a dome or cupola is supported.

dugout: a building placed mostly or wholly below ground.

Eastlake style: named for English tastemaker Charles L. Eastlake, this style is distinguished by ornamental lathe work, including elaborate spindle work and often complex wood details.

encaustic tile: a building material with vitreous colored surface.

entablature: in Classical architecture, the group of components surmounting a wall, group of columns, or pilasters.

fachwerk: German half-timber wall construction.

false front: that street facade on a commercial building that rises above the roof lines.

fanlight: a semicircular or semi-elliptical window with radiating division bars.

feather graining: a technique of painting surfaces with feathers.

finial: a decorative feature placed at the apex of a roof, parapet, or tower.

fluting: a series of channels or grooves.

fort: a place strengthened for defense.

fortification: a work of defense.

French doors: double doors.

fret: a decorative band with linear patterns.

friary: a monastery.

frieze: a horizontal part of an entablature located below the cornice and above the architrave.

gable: the triangular section of a wall under the edges of a pitched roof.

gallery: a roofed space adjacent to a building.

Georgian style: a Classical English style prominent from about 1702 through 1830.

gingerbread: ornamentation, often intricate, and in curvilinear form, cut with a jigsaw.

Gothic Revival style: a mode of design in which architectural features were patterned after European work of the thirteenth, fourteenth, and fifteenth centuries. It was popular in some version in America throughout the nineteenth century and for churches and college campuses throughout the first three decades of the twentieth.

Greek Revival style: a nineteenth-century mode of design in which features were patterned after ancient Greek architecture.

half-dugout: a dwelling that was built partially underground.

half-timber: a form of wall construction employing hewn framing members, ordinarily secured with mortise and tenon joints.

High Victorian Gothic: a mode of architecture employing features patterned after Medieval European work and incorporating materials of various colors. It was popular in America in the 1870's and 1880's.

High Victorian Italianate: a style incorporating features from the Italian Renaissance era of architecture. It is characterized by openings spanned by stilted arches, lintels with hoods returning part way down the sides, and lintels and jambs with curved fillets between them. It was popular in America during the 1870's and 1880's.

hipped roof: a roof made of inclined planes sloping up from all four sides.

horno: an oven with a bee hive form, made of adobe, located outdoors.

hood: a molding located above a door or window.

Ionic order: a mode of architecture wherein the volute, a spiral scroll, forms a prominent feature of the capital.

Italianate style: a mode of architecture with a decorative vocabulary derived from Renaissance Italy.

jacal: a primitive type of shelter constructed from logs, branches, reeds, or mud, roofed with shingles or thatch.

lantern: a structure with windows in its sides placed at the apex of a dome or tower.

lean-to: a secondary structure roofed by a plane with a single slope, supported by an adjacent building.

lintel: a beam spanning a space or a wall opening.

log cabin: a shelter with walls of horizontal logs notched together at the corners but with relatively crude construction.

log house: a structure similar to a log cabin, but incorporating more refined construction.

loophole: an opening in a wall through which small

arms were fired.

macadam: a compacted layer of gravel.

Mansard: a roof with each side made of two sloping planes, one of which is steep, the other low pitched.

Marktplatz: in German communities, the town market place.

masterbuilder: an individual who provided complete architectural services of design and construction.

mission: a complex of buildings providing housing for clergy and Indians as well as their activities.

Mission Revival style: a mode of architecture, popular during the first four decades of the twentieth century, wherein features were patterned after forms and details of the California missions of the eighteenth and nineteenth centuries.

modillion: a decorative bracket used in series as a part of a cornice.

molding: a continuous member forming a transition between two surfaces.

mortise and tenon: a joint consisting of a cutout in one member and a tongue in another.

muntin: a small divider in a window sash.

natatorium: a building containing one or more swimming pools.

nave: the space where worshipers are seated in a church.

Neoclassical: during the second half of the eighteenth and the first half of the nineteenth centuries, a revival of Classical architectural forms, particularly from ancient Rome and Greece.

nogging: brick, stone, or mud placed to fill the openings in a heavy timber framework.

oriel window: a projecting window supported above the ground by brackets.

palisade: an enclosure formed by posts planted into the ground with spaces between them.

palisado: Spanish colonial and Mexican type of construction wherein walls were formed with vertical posts planted side by side into the ground.

Palladian: patterned after the work of Andrea Palladio, an Italian Renaissance architect.

parapet: a wall rising above the roof.

pediment: a feature, usually triangular but sometimes segmental in form, located above a colonnade, wall, or wall opening.

pendentive: a structural form employed to support a dome.

piano nobile: the main story of a building, located on the second-floor level.

picket wall: a wall formed with posts planted into the ground.

picturesque: irregular, sometimes complex, composition of architectural forms.

pilaster: a pier projecting from a wall, ordinarily structural.

pinnacle: a terminal decorative feature rising above a spire, lantern, and so forth.

plaza: an open space in a town reserved for community activities.

plaza de mercado: market place.

pointed arch: an arch with either straight or curved sides that form a salient at the crown.

polygon of fortification: a geometric form on which works for defense were laid out.

portales: porches.

portico: entrance porch.

Prairie style: a mode developed on the Midwestern prairies at the turn of the century, wherein architects avoided the use of eclectic features. Horizontal lines, wide roof overhangs, and geometric patterns were characteristic.

presidio: in Spanish colonial architecture, a fort.

pueblo: a village; communal Indian dwelling.

puncheon: a log hewn with one side flat.

punchwork: repetitive decorative patterns made with a steel punch or a chisel.

purlin: a secondary structural member spanning beams or trusses.

quatrefoil: a four-lobed figure.

Queen Anne style: a mode developed in England during the early eighteenth century; also one which was revived during the latter part of the nineteenth century.

rafter: a structural member supporting a roof deck.

raised cottage: a dwelling wherein the main floor level is supported well above the ground on piers.

ranch headquarters: the principal group of buildings on a ranch.

rancho: a Spanish or Mexican ranch headquarters.

reja: grillwork for a window.

Renaissance style: a European mode beginning in the fifteenth century with a decorative and structural vocabulary derived from ancient Roman times.

reredos: a wall forming a backdrop for an altar.

retablo: see reredos.

Richardsonian Romanesque style: a mode of architecture based upon ancient Romanesque work but with innovations developed by the Boston architect Henry Hobson Richardson.

Roman arch: a round arch, thus semicircular.

Romanesque Revival style: a nineteenth-century mode of architecture in which European work of the eleventh through the thirteenth centuries provided the models. The hallmark of the style is the Roman arch.

Romantic style: an architectural fashion with symbolic meaning.

rostrum: a raised platform for a pulpit.

round arch: see Roman arch.

rusticated: stonework with beveled or rebated edges that emphasize the joints.

sacristy: a space in a church where vestments are stored. It is also used by the clergy for robing.

Second Empire style: a nineteenth-century mode of design named for the French Second Empire of Napoleon III. A hallmark of the style is the Mansard roof.

segmental arch: an arch with a form that is circular but with a curvature that is less than a semicircle.

shake: a hand-split shingle.

shellcrete: a type of concrete in which a mixture of sand, seashells, water, and either lime or cement are formed into walls or other components.

Shingle style: an architectural mode wherein the wall surfaces of buildings were covered with shingles. Queen Anne forms of the style are common.

side lights: panes of glass installed at the sides of doors.

Stick style: a type of architecture distinguished by exterior wall patterns formed with boards creating both diagonal and rectangular panels that suggest a hidden structural framework.

stilted arch: an arch with a short vertical section at each end.

stockade: an enclosure formed by planting posts into the ground, side by side.

style: a manner of ornamentation, construction, and planning; a vocabulary of architectural components.

Sullivanesque: named for the Chicago architect Louis H. Sullivan, buildings or decorations in this mode are well composed and visually strong, with ornamentation composed of naturalistic-geometric patterns.

suspension bridge: a bridge with a roadbed supported by cables suspended from vertical supports.

swag: a low-relief ornamental configuration representing plant forms suspended between two points.

terra cotta: clay building material that is fired.

terrazzo: flooring material with marble chips embedded in cement, the surface of which is ground smooth after setting.

thatch: roof covering of grass, straw, or tule.

tipichil: a mixture of lime, sand, and gravel.

torreón: a turret.

town square: a block in a community reserved for public use.

trace: the plan outline of a fortification.

transom: a hinged window above a door.

treenail: a wooden peg used to pin joints.

triple-hung window: a window with three sashes that slide vertically.

tronera: a loophole.

truss: a structural component made of relatively thin members arranged in triangular patterns so that each member is in either compression or tension.

turret: a cylindrical tower.

Tuscan order: a Classical order characterized by simplicity.

Ultra-Baroque: Mexican Churrigueresque style of architecture that originated in Spain in the work of the Churriguera brothers in Barcelona, Spain, and then was imported into Mexico. It was characterized by elaborate surface decoration.

vara: a Spanish unit of measure equal to $33\frac{1}{3}$ inches.

vereins kirche: German community church.

verge board: see barge board.

Victorian: a period of art characterized by picturesque compositions coinciding with the reign of Queen Victoria.

viga: a beam.

villa: a village.

weatherboard: see clapboard.

Bibliography

Unpublished Sources

"Act of the Visit of the Royal Commissioner of 1767 to the Town of Laredo." General Land Office, Austin.

Allen, Winnie. "The History of Nacogdoches, 1691–1830." Master's thesis, University of Texas, Austin, 1925.

Anderson, Garland Sadler, Jr. "The Courthouse Square: Six Case Studies in Texas, Evolution, Analysis, and Projections." Master's thesis, University of Texas, Austin, 1968.

Bunting, David Edison. "A Documentary History of Sam Houston Normal Institute." Master's thesis, University of Texas, 1933.

Clayton Collection. Rosenberg Library, Galveston.

Connally, Ernest Allen. "The Ecclesiastical and Military Architecture of the Spanish Province of Texas." Ph.D. dissertation, Harvard University, 1955.

Federal Post Offices and Courthouses Collection. Public Buildings Service, National Archives, Washington, D.C.

Fisher, Charles W., Jr. "A New Look at Liberty's Seven Courthouses, 1831–1972." Manuscript in possession of Fisher, Liberty, Texas.

Fritz, William. "Album of Houston, Texas." Photographic album, ca. 1910, in possession of Houston Public Library, Houston.

Gentry, Mary Jane. "Thurber: The Life and Death of a Texas Town." Master's thesis, University of Texas, 1946.

Giles, Alfred. "View Book, 1898–1929." Manuscript in possession of Palmer Giles, Comfort, Texas.

Goeldner, Paul. "Temples of Justice: Nineteenth-Century Courthouses in the Midwest and Texas." Ph.D. dissertation, Columbia University, 1969.

Gonzales, Jovita. "Social Life in Cameron, Starr, and Zapata Counties." Master's thesis, University of Texas, 1930.

Hanna, Edith M. "The Indigenous Architecture of Fredericksburg, Texas." Master's thesis, North Texas State University, Denton, 1942.

Historic American Buildings Survey Collection of Measured Drawings and Photographs. Library of Congress, Washington, D.C.

Juarez, José Roberto, Jr. "An Architectural Description of Dolores Ranch." Manuscript report. Lubbock: Ranching Heritage Center, Texas Tech University, 1976.

Lamb, Dinah Leigh. "Selected Historic Domestic Architecture of San Antonio, Texas, Influenced by the Spanish-Mexican Culture." Master's thesis, East Texas State University, 1969.

Melchior, Rudolph, Papers. Historical Files, Institute of Texan Cultures, San Antonio.

Ratchford, Fannie. Photographic Collection. Archives, Texas State Library, Austin, Texas.

Reese, James Verdo. "A History of Hill County to 1873." Master's thesis, University of Texas, 1961.

Ruffini Collection. Archives, Texas State Library, Austin, Texas.

Smith, W. L. "The Development of Sam Houston State Teachers College." Master's thesis, Southern Methodist University, 1928.

Wilhelm, Hubert. "Organized German Settlement and Its Effect on the Frontier of South Central Texas." Ph.D. dissertation, Louisiana State University, 1968.

Public Documents

Findlay, George P., and D. E. Simmons, comps. *Index to Gammel's Laws of Texas, 1822–1905.* Austin: Gammel Book Company, 1906.

Gammel, H. P. N., comp. *The Laws of Texas, 1822–1897.* 10 vols. Austin: Gammel Book Company, 1898.

Laws and Decrees of the State of Coahuila and Texas, in Spanish and English. To Which is Added the Constitution of Said State: also The Colonization Law of the State of Tamaulipas, and Naturalization Law of the General Congress. Translated by J. P. Kimball. Houston: Telegraph Power Press, 1839.

Office of the County Clerk. County Commissioners Court Minutes: Archer, Armstrong, Bandera, Bastrop, Bell, Bexar, Blanco, Bosque, Bowie, Brazoria, Brewster, Brown, Caldwell, Clay, Comal, Comanche, Concho, Crockett, Denton, Dimmit, Donley, Edwards, Ellis, Erath, Fannin, Fayette, Floyd, Gonzales, Hamilton, Hill, Hopkins, Johnson, Kendall, Lamar, Lee, Leon, Lubbock, McCulloch, Mason, Milam, Nacogdoches, Red River, San Saba, Shackelford, Smith, Stephens, Sutton, Van Zandt, Washington, Wharton, Wise.

———. Deed Records: San Augustine, Washington.

Plans of Public Buildings in Course of Construction for the United States of America Under the Direction of the Secretary of the Treasury, Including Specifications Thereof. 5 vols. Washington, D.C.: U.S. Government Printing Office, 1855–1856.

Recopilación de leyes de los reynos de las Indies. Madrid: Cosejo de la Hispanidad, 1943.

U.S. Congress, House. *Report of the Committee on Awards of the World's Columbian Commission.* 57th Cong., 1st sess., 1901, House Doc. 57.

———. *Report of the Secretary of War.* 32nd Cong., 1st sess., 1851, House Exec. Doc. No. 2.

U.S. Congress, Senate. *Exploration of the Red River of Louisiana, in the Year 1852,* 32nd Cong., 2d sess., 1853, Senate Exec. Doc. 54.

———. *Report of the Secretary of War.* 36th Cong., 1st sess., 1859, Senate Exec. Doc. No. 2.

U.S. War Department, Quartermaster General's Office. *Outline Description of Southwestern Military Posts and Stations, 1871.* Washington, D.C.: U.S. Government Printing Office, 1872.

U.S. War Department, Surgeon General's Office. *Circular No. 2.* July 27, 1871. Washington, D.C.: U.S. Government Printing Office.

———. *Circular No. 3: Approved Plan for a Regulation Post Hospital with Twenty-Four Beds.* November 23, 1870. Washington, D.C.: U.S. Government Printing Office.

———. *Circular No. 4: Plan for a Post Hospital of Twenty-Four Beds.* Washington, D.C.: U.S. Government Printing Office.

———. *Circular No. 4: A Report on Barracks and Hospital with Descriptions of Military Posts.* Washington, D.C.: U.S. Government Printing Office, 1870.

Vernon's Annotated Civil Statutes. Kansas City, Mo., 1962.

Texas Newspapers

Austin Record, June, 1869–December, 1887.

Daily Bulletin (Austin), November 27, 1841–January 18, 1842.

Dallas Herald, January 4, 1860–December, 1885.

Dallas Morning News, October, 1885–December, 1929.

Fort Worth Daily Democrat (daily), July 4, 1876–February 4, 1880; (weekly) February 4, 1880–July 4, 1880; (daily) July 4, 1880–December 10, 1881.

Fort Worth Democrat (weekly), 1871–1882.

Fort Worth Democrat-Advance, December 11, 1881–August, 1882.

Fort Worth Gazette, August, 1882–April, 1896.

Galveston Daily News, February 21, 1865–February 17, 1887.

Houston Daily Post, February 23, 1881–December 30, 1906.

Matagorda Bulletin, August 9, 1837–May 9, 1839.

Northern Standard (Clarksville), see *Standard.*

Red Lander (San Augustine), September, 1841–September 13, 1851.

San Antonio Express, July 16, 1867–March 31, 1887. The title varies frequently (*San Antonio*

Daily Express).

Standard (Clarksville), April 2, 1853–December 6, 1888. This paper appeared under the name *Northern Standard*, August 20, 1842–October 16, 1853.

Telegraph and Texas Register (Columbia), March, 1837–April, 1837.

Telegraph and Texas Register (Harrisburg), April 14, 1836.

Telegraph and Texas Register (Houston), May 2, 1837–January 21, 1853; March 8, 1843–January 21, 1853.

Telegraph and Texas Register (San Felipe de Austin), October 10, 1835–March 24, 1836.

Texas Gazette and Commercial Advertiser (Brazoria), July 23, 1832.

Texas Republican (Brazoria), July 5, 1834–March 9, 1836.

Texas Republican (Marshall), May 26, 1844–June 4, 1869.

Contemporary Architecture

American Architect and Architecture. 1876–1900.

American Architect and Building News. 1876–1917.

"Architecture in the United States." *American Journal of Science and Arts* 17 (1829): 99–110, 249–273; 18 (1830): 11–25, 212–236.

Art Work in Galveston. Chicago: W. H. Parish Publishing Co., 1894.

Art Work of Austin. Chicago: W. H. Parish Publishing Co., 1894.

Art Work of Dallas. Chicago: W. H. Parish Publishing Co., 1895.

Art Work of Dallas, Texas. Published in Twelve Parts. Chicago: Gravure Illustration Co., 1910.

Art Work of Houston. Chicago: W. H. Parish Publishing Co., 1894.

Art Work of Houston, Texas. Published in Twelve Parts. Chicago, 1904.

Art Work of San Antonio. Published in Twelve Parts. Chicago: W. H. Parish Publishing Co., 1894.

Barber, Geo[rge] F. *The Cottage Souvenir Revised and Enlarged, Containing Over Two Hundred Original Designs and Plans of Artistic Dwellings.* Knoxville, Tenn.: S. B. Newman & Co., 1892.

———. *Modern Artistic Cottages, Or the Cottage Souvenir, Designed to Meet the Wants of Mechanics and Home Builders.* De Kalb, Ill.: privately printed, [ca. 1885–1890].

Beecher, Catherine E., and Harriet Beecher Stowe. *The American Woman's Home: or, Principles of Domestic Science; being a guide to the formation and maintenance of economical, healthful, beautiful, and Christian homes.* New York: J. B. Ford and Co., 1869.

Benjamin, Asher. *The Practice of Architecture.* Boston: Benjamin B. Mossey, 1836.

Bicknell, A. J. *Detail, Cottage and Constructive Architecture Containing 75 Large Lithographic Plates. Published Under the Direction of A. J. Bicknell, Showing a Great Variety of Designs, Cornices, Brackets, Windows, Window Caps, Doors, Piazzas, Porches, Bay and Dormer Windows. Observatories, Towers, Chimney Tops, Balconies, Canopies, Scrolls, Gable and Sawed Ornaments, Fences, Stairs, Newels, Architraves, Mantels, Plaster Finish, etc. etc. Including 45 Perspectives, Elevations and Plans of Modern Designs for Cottages with Details and 18 Elevations of Summer Houses, Villas, Sea-Side-Cottages and Country Houses Together with 14 Designs for Street and Store Fronts, with Inside Finish for Stores and Banks: Also Framing for Dwellings, Barns, Exhibition Buildings, Roofs, Bridges etc. etc. Making in all a Practical Book for Architects, Builders, Carpenters, and all who Contemplate Building or Remodeling Wood, Stone or Brick Buildings.* New York: A. J. Bicknell and Co., 1873.

Bowler, George. *Chapel and Church Architecture, with Designs for Parsonages.* Boston: J. P. Jewett, 1856.

Clark, Percy. "New Federal Buildings." *Harper's Weekly*, May 19, 1888, pp. 365–368.

Comstock, William T. *Modern Architectural Designs and Details Containing Eighty Finely Lithographed Plates, Showing New and Original Designs in the Queen Anne, Eastlake, Elizabethan, and Other Modernized Styles, Giving Perspective Views, Floor and Framing Plans, Elevations, Sections, and a Great Variety of Miscellaneous Exterior and Interior Details of Dwellings of Moderate Cost. Also, a Number of Designs of Low Priced Cottages in the Various Popular Styles, Adapted to the Re-*

quirements of Seaside and Summer Resorts, and Suburban and Country Places. Also, Several Designs for Modern Store and Office Fronts, Counters, Shelvings, Etc., Etc., Comprising Original Drawings by a Number of Prominent Architects of Different Localities, Prepared Expressly for This Work. New York: privately printed, 1881.

Downing, Andrew Jackson. The Architecture of Country Houses; Including Designs for Cottages, Farm-Houses, and Villas, with Remarks on Interiors, Furniture, and the Best Modes of Warming and Ventilating. New York: D. Appleton and Co., 1856.

———. Cottage Residences; or a Series of Designs for Rural Cottage Villas, and Their Gardens and Grounds Adapted to North America. New York: Wiley and Halsted, 1856.

Eastlake, Charles L. Hints on Household Taste in Furniture, Upholstery, and Other Details. Edited by C. C. Perkins. 1st Am. ed. from rev. London ed. Boston: J. R. Osgood, 1872.

Eastman, Seth. A Seth Eastman Sketchbook, 1848–1849. Austin: University of Texas Press, 1961.

Eidlitz, Leopold. "The Vicissitudes of Architecture." Architectural Record 1 (April–June, 1892): 471–484.

Field, M. City Architecture: Designs for Dwelling Houses, Stores, Hotels, etc. New York: G. P. Putnam and Co., 1853.

Gideon, Samuel E. Historic and Picturesque Austin. Austin: Steck Co., 1936.

Gordon, James Riely. Sketches from the Portfolio of James Riely Gordon, Architect. St. Louis: A. B. Benesch Publishing Company, 1896.

Hart, J[oseph] Coleman. Designs for Parish Churches in the Three Styles of English Church Architecture; with an Analysis of Each Style, a Review of Nomenclature of the Periods of English Gothic Architecture, and Some Remarks Introductory to Church Building, Exemplified in a Series of Over One Hundred Illustrations. New York: Dana and Co., 1857.

Hoffman, David. "A Building Specification for Andrew Female College." Newsletter of the Society of Architectural Historians, Texas Chapter 6 (December, 1977):10–12.

Jobson, F. J. Chapel & School Architecture, as Appropriate to the Buildings of Nonconformists, Particularily to Those of the Wesleyan Methodists; with Practical Directions for the Erection of Chapels and Schools Houses. London: Hamilton, Adams, and Co., 1850.

Lefever, Minard. The Beauties of Modern Architecture. New York: D. Appleton & Co., 1835.

Lethaby, William Richard. Architecture, Mysticism and Myth. 1891. Reprint. New York: George Braziller, 1975.

"Methodist Church Architecture." National Magazine, Devoted to Literature, Art, and Religion 7 (December, 1855–January, 1856): 497–512, 8 (February–March, 1856): 220–225.

"The 1905 Catalogue of Iron Store Fronts, Designed and Manufactured by Geo. L. Mesker & Co., Architectural Iron Works, Evansville, Indiana." APT Bulletin 9 (1977):3–40.

Patterson, W. M. A Manual of Architecture: for Churches, Parsonages and Schoolhouses. Containing Designs, Elevations, Plans, Specifications, Form of Contract, Rules for Estimating Cost of Buildings, with Suggestions on Acoustics, Ventilation, Heating, Lighting, Painting, etc. Nashville: Methodist Episcopal Church South, 1875.

Plans of Buildings, Moldings, Architraves, Base, Brackets, Stairs, Newels, Ballusters, Rails, Cornice, Mantels, Window Frames, Sash, Doors, Columns, etc. for the Use of Carpenters and Builders; Adapted to the Style of Building in the United States. Cincinnati: Hinkle, Guild and Co., 1862.

A Plea for the Use of the Fine Arts in the Decoration of Churches. New York: J. F. Trow, 1857.

Ruskin, John. The Seven Lamps of Architecture. 5th ed. London: Allen, 1894.

Some Work from the Office of Sanguinet and Staats Successors to Messer, Sanguinet and Messer, Architects, Fort Worth, Texas. N.p., 1896.

Sparks, Charles H. Description of the Patent Rotary Steel Jail. Chicago, n.d.

Stuart, James, and Nicholas Revett. Antiquities of Athens, Measured and Delineated. 4 vols. London: J. Haberkorn, 1762–1816; new edition, 1825–1830.

Upjohn, Richard. Upjohn's Rural Architecture. New York: G. P. Putnam, 1852.

Vaux, Calvert. Villas and Cottages: A Series of Designs Prepared for Execution in the United States. New York: Harper and Brothers Publishers, 1867.

Yearbook of the Dallas Architectural Club and Catalogue of Its First Annual Exhibition. N.p., 1922.

Contemporary Narratives of Texas

"Austin, The Capital of Texas." *Frank Leslie's Illustrated Newspaper*, May 22, 1880, pp. 196–197.

Ballinger and Runnels County. Ballinger, Tex., 1908.

Bancroft, Hubert Howe. *History of the North Mexican States and Texas.* Vols. 15, 16: *The Works of Hubert Howe Bancroft.* San Francisco: A. L. Bancroft Co., 1884, 1889.

Bartlett, John R. *Personal Narrative of Explorations and Incidents in Texas, New Mexico, California, Sonora, and Chihuahua, Connected with the United States and Mexican Boundary Commission, During the Years 1850, '51, '52, and '53.* 2 vols. New York: Appleton, 1854.

Berlandier, Jean Louis. *The Indians of Texas in 1830.* Translated by Patricia Reading Leclercq. Washington, D.C.: Smithsonian Institution Press, 1969.

Bollaert, William. *William Bollaert's Texas.* Edited by W. Eugene Hollon and Ruth Lapham Butler. Norman: University of Oklahoma Press, 1956.

Bonilla, Antonio. "Bonilla's Brief Compendium of the History of Texas, 1772." Translated by Elizabeth Howard West. *Texas State Historical Association Quarterly* 8 (July, 1904): 3–78.

Bonnell, George W. *Topographical Description of Texas. To which is added an account of the Indian Tribes.* Austin: Clark, Wing, and Brown, 1840. Reprint. Waco: Texian Press, 1964.

The Book of Fort Worth. Fort Worth: Fort Worth Record, 1913.

Bourke, John G. "The American Congo." *Scribner's Magazine*, May, 1894, pp. 590–610.

Bracht, Viktor. *Texas in 1848.* Translated by Charles Frank Schmidt. San Antonio: Naylor Co., 1931.

Braman, E. E. *Braman's Information About Texas.* Philadelphia: J. B. Lippincott and Co., 1857.

Burke, James, Jr. *Burke's Texas Almanac and Im-migrant's Handbook.* Houston: American News Co., 1882–1883.

Castro, Lorenzo. *Immigration from Alsace-Lorraine: A Brief Sketch of Henry Castro's Colony in Western Texas.* New York: George W. Wheat and Co., 1871.

Celiz, Fray Francisco. *Diary of the Alarcon Expedition into Texas, 1718–1719.* Translated by Fritz Leo Huffman. Quivira Society Publications, vol. 5. Los Angeles: Quivira Society, 1935.

City of Dallas: Its Growth and Resources. Souvenir Edition. Dallas, 1892.

The City of Fort Worth and the State of Texas. St. Louis and Ft. Worth: George W. Engelhardt and Co., Publishers, 1890.

The City of San Antonio, Texas, the Metropolis of Texas. The Most Famous Health Resort of America. San Antonio, 1902.

Clopper, J. C. "Journal and Book of Memoranda for 1828, Province of Texas." *Quarterly of the Texas Historical Association* 13 (1909–1910): 44–80.

Corner, William. *San Antonio de Bexar, a Guide and History.* San Antonio: Bainbridge and Corner, 1890.

Crimmins, M. L., ed. "Colonel J. K. F. Mansfield's Report of the Inspection of the Department of Texas in 1856." *Southwestern Historical Quarterly* 42 (October, 1938):122–148; (January, 1939):215–257; (April, 1939): 351–387.

Cuervo, Tienda de. "Tienda de Cuervo's Ynspección de Laredo." Translated by Herbert Eugene Bolton. *Quarterly of the Texas State Historical Association* 6 (1903):187–203.

"Dallas, Texas. The Marvel of the Lone Star State." *Frank Leslie's Illustrated Newspaper*, October 6, 1888, pp. 129–131.

De Cordova, Jacob. *The Texas Immigrant and Traveller's Guide Book.* Austin: De Cordova and Frazier, 1856.

Dewees, W. B. *Letters from an Early Settler of Texas.* Louisville, Ky.: Morton and Griswald, 1852. Reprint. Waco: Texian Press, 1968.

Ewell, Thomas T. *History of Hood County Texas from its Earliest Settlement to the Present.* Granbury, Tex., 1895.

Facts About Fort Worth and Adjacent Country. Ft. Worth: Sue Greenleaf, 1893.

Falconer, Thomas. *Notes on a Journey through*

*Texas and New Mexico in the Years 1841–
1842.* London, 1842(?).

Fisher, Orceneth. *Sketches of Texas in 1840, Designed to Answer, in a Brief Way, the Numerous Enquiries Respecting the New Republic, as to Situation, Extent, Climate, Soil, Productions, Water, Government, Society, Religion, etc.* 1841. Reprint. Waco: Texian Press, 1964.

Gaillardet, Frederic. *Sketches of Early Texas and Louisiana.* Translated by James L. Shepherd III. Austin: University of Texas Press, 1966.

Galveston, The Commercial Metropolis and Principal Seaport of the Great Southwest; Its Geographical Position, Extent, Population, and Resources. Galveston: Land and Thompson, 1885.

"Galveston Harbor." *Frank Leslie's Illustrated Newspaper,* May 31, 1890, pp. 365–368.

Gillmore, Q. A. *Galveston.* New York: C. Scribner's Sons, 1879.

Hatcher, Mattie Austin, ed. and trans. "Descriptions of the Tejas or Asinai Indians." *Southwestern Historical Quarterly* 30 (January, 1927):206–218, (April, 1927):283–304; 31 (July, 1927):50–62, (October, 1927):150–180.

Historical and Descriptive Review of the Industries of San Antonio: 1885. Commerce, Trade and Manufactures, Manufacturing Advantages, Business and Transportation Facilities, Together with Sketches of the Representative Business Houses and Manufacturing Establishments in the "Alamo City." San Antonio: Land & Thompson, 1885.

Holley, Mary Austin. *Letters of an Early American Traveller, Mary Austin Holley: Her Life and Her Works, 1786–1846.* Dallas: Southwest Press, 1933.

————. *Texas, Observations, Historical, Geographical, and Descriptive, in a Series of Letters Written during a Visit to Austin's Colony, with a View of a Permanent Settlement in that Country in the Autumn of 1831.* Baltimore: Armstrong and Plaskitt, 1833.

————. *Texas.* Lexington, Ky.: J. Clarke and Co., 1836.

Hooton, Charles. *St Louis' Isle, or Texiana with Additional Observations made in the United States and Canada.* London: Simmonds and Ward, 1847.

Hunt, Richard S., and Jesse F. Randel. *Guide to the Republic of Texas: Consisting of a Brief Outline of the History of its Settlement.* New York: J. H. Colton, 1839.

Ikin, Arthur. *Texas: Its History, Topography, Agriculture, Commerce, and General Statistics to which is Added a Copy of the Treaty of Commerce Entered into by the Republic of Texas and Great Britain. Designed for Use by the British Merchant, and as a Guide to Emigrants.* 1841. Reprint. Waco: Texian Press, 1964.

The Industrial Advantages of Houston, Texas, and Environs, also Series of Comprehensive Sketches of the City's Representative Business Enterprises. Houston: Akehurst Publishing Co., 1894.

Jenkins, John Holland. *Recollections of Early Texas.* Edited by John Holmes Jenkins III. Austin: University of Texas Press, 1958.

Joseph, Donald, trans. *A Story of Champ d'Asile as Told by the Colonists.* Edited by Fannie E. Ratchford. Dallas: Book Club of Texas, 1937(?).

King, Edward, and J. Wells Champney. *Texas 1874: An Eyewitness Account of Conditions in Post-Reconstruction Texas.* Edited by Robert S. Gray. Houston: Cordovan Press, 1974.

Kinnaird, Lawrence, ed. *The Frontiers of New Spain: Nicolas de Lofora's Description, 1766–1768.* Quivira Society Publications, vol. 13. Berkeley: Quivira Society, 1958.

Lawrence, A. B. *Texas in 1840, or the Emigrants' Guide to the New Republic, by a Resident Emigrant Late from the United States.* New York: Nafis and Cornish, 1845.

"The Lone Star State." *Frank Leslie's Illustrated Newspaper,* September 27, 1890, pp. 1–16; October 4, 1890, pp. 1–20; October 18, 1890, pp. 1–16.

McClintock, William A. "Journal of a Trip Through Texas and Northern Mexico in 1846–1847." *Southwestern Historical Quarterly* 34 (October, 1930):141–158.

Martinez, Antonio. *The Letters of Antonio Martinez.* Translated and edited by Virginia H. Taylor. Austin: Texas State Library, 1957.

Moore, Francis, Jr. *Map and Description of Texas, Containing Sketches of Its History, Geology,*

Geography and Statistics; with Concise Statements, Relative to the Soil, Climate, Productions, Facilities of Transportation, Population of the Country; and Some Brief Remarks upon the Character and Customs of Its Inhabitants. Philadelphia: H. Tanner, 1840. Reprint. Waco: Texian Press, 1965.

Morfi, Fray Juan Agustín. *History of Texas, 1673–1779.* Translated by Carlos Eduardo Castañeda. Albuquerque: Quivira Society, 1935.

Morrell, Z. N. *Flowers and Fruits from the Wilderness; or Thirty-Six Years in Texas and Two Winters in Honduras.* St. Louis: Commercial Printing Co., 1882.

Morrison, Andrew. *The City of San Antonio, Texas.* St. Louis: George W. Englehardt and Co., n.d.

"Notes on Texas by a Citizen of Ohio." *Hesperian; or Western Monthly Magazine* 1 (September, 1838):350–360, (October, 1838):428–440; 2 (November, 1838):30–39, (December, 1838): 109–118, (January, 1839):189–199, (February, 1839):288–293, (March, 1839): 359–367, (April, 1839):417–426.

Olmsted, Frederick Law. *A Journey Through Texas.* New York: Dix, Edwards and Co., 1857.

Parker, A[mos] [Andrew]. *Trip to the West and Texas, Comprising a Journey of Eight Thousand Miles, Through New York, Michigan, Illinois, Missouri, Louisiana and Texas, in the Autumn and Winter of 1834–1835. Interspersed with Anecdotes, Incidents, and Observations. With a Brief Sketch of the Texian War.* Concord, N.H.: White and Fisher, 1835.

Peña, Father Juan Antonio de la. *Derrotero de la Expedición en la Provincia de los Texas, Nuevo Reyno de Philipinos, que del orden del Exmo. Señor Marques de Valero Vi-Rey de esta Nueva España ha hecho D. Joseph Azlor, Caballero Mesnadero del Reino de Aragon, Gobernador y Capitan General de dicha Provincia de Texas, Nuevas Philipinos, y de esta de Coahuila, Nuevo Reino de Estramadura, etc.* Mexico: 1722.

Pérez de Luxán, Antonio de. *Expedition into New Mexico made by Antonio de Espejo, 1582–1583, as revealed in the Journal of Diego Pérez de Luxán, a member of the party.* Edited and translated by G. P. Hammond and A. Rey. Quivira Society Publications, vol. 1. Los Angeles: Quivira Society, 1929.

Rankin, Melinda. *Texas in 1850.* Waco: Texian Press, 1966.

Roemer, Ferdinand. *Texas, with Particular Reference to German Immigration and The Physical Appearance of the Country.* Translated by Ostwald Mueller. San Antonio: Standard Printing Co., 1935. Reprint. Waco: Texian Press, 1967.

Sánchez, José María. "A Trip to Texas in 1828." Translated by Carlos Eduardo Castañeda. *Southwestern Historical Quarterly* 29 (1926): 249–288.

Sheridan, Francis C. *Galveston Island; or a Few Months off the Coast of Texas: Journal of Francis C. Sheridan 1839–1840.* Edited by Willis W. Pratt. Austin: University of Texas Press, 1954.

Smith, Edward. *Journey Through Northeastern Texas, Undertaken in 1849 for the Purposes of Emigration.* London: Hamilton, Adams, and Company, 1849.

Soulie, Maurice. *Autour de L'aigle Enchaine Le Complot du Champ D'Asile.* Paris: Marpon and Cie., 1830(?).

Steinert, W. "W. Steinert's View of Texas in 1849." Translated and edited by Gilbert J. Jordan. *Southwestern Historical Quarterly* 80 (October, 1976):177–200.

Stiff, Edward. *The Texas Emigrant; being a Narrative of the Adventures of the Author in Texas, and a Description of the Soil, Climate, Productions, Minerals, together with the Principal Incidents of Fifteen Years Revolution in Mexico: And Embracing a Condensed Statement of Interesting Events in Texas, From the First European Settlement in 1692, Down to the Year 1840.* 1840. Reprint. Waco: Texian Press, 1968.

———. *The Texas Emigrant.* Cincinnati: George Conclin, 1840.

Texas Almanac and Industrial Guide. A. H. Belo and Co., 1904.

Texas Capitol Building Commission. *Final Report of the Capitol Building Commissioners Upon the Completion of the New Capitol.* Austin: State Printing Office, 1888.

———. *Report of the Capitol Building Commis-*

sion Upon The Completion of the New Capitol. Austin: Hutchings Printing House, 1888.

———. Report of the Capitol Building Commission to the Governor of Texas. Austin: E. W. Swindells, State Printer, 1885.

———. Third Biennial Report of the Capitol Building Commission. Austin: Triplett and Hutchings, 1886.

Texas in 1837: An Anonymous, Contemporary Narrative. Edited by Andrew Forest Muir. Austin: University of Texas Press, 1958.

Texas in 1840, or the Emigrant's Guide to the New Republic being the Result of Observation, Inquiry and Travel in that Beautiful Country by an Emigrant, Late of the United States with an Introduction by the Rev. A. B. Lawrence of New Orleans. New York: William W. Allen, 1840.

Texas State Gazetteer and Business Directory 1892. Detroit, Chicago and St. Louis: R. L. Polk and Co., 1892.

Thrall, Homer S. The People's Illustrated Almanac, Texas Handbook and Immigrant's Guide, for 1880; Being an Index to Texas, Her People, Laws, State and Local Governments, Schools, Churches, Railroads, and Other Improvements and Institutions with Chronological History of the State for 1879. St. Louis: N. D. Thompson and Co., 1880.

———. A Pictorial History of Texas, From the Earliest Visits of European Adventurers, to A.D. 1879. Embracing the Periods of Missions, Colonization, the Revolution, the Republic and the State; also, a Topographical Description of the County, Together with Its Indian Tribes and Their Wars, and Biographical Sketches of Hundreds of Its Leading Historical Characters. Also, a List of the Counties, with Historical and Topical Notes, and Descriptions of the Public Institutions of the State. 5th ed., rev. St. Louis: N. D. Thompson and Co., 1879.

A Visit to Texas in 1831. Being the Journal of a Traveller Through Those Parts Most Interesting to American Settlers with Descriptions of Scenery, Habits, &c., &c. New York: Goodrich and Wiley, 1834.

Woodman, David, Jr. Guide to Texas Emigrants. Boston: M. Hawes, 1835.

History of Architecture

Alexander, Drury Blakely. Texas Homes of the 19th Century. Austin: University of Texas Press, 1966.

American Institute of Architects, Dallas Chapter. The Prairie's Yield. New York: Reinhold, 1962.

American Institute of Architects, San Antonio Chapter. Historic San Antonio 1700–1900. N.p., 1963.

Andrews, Wayne. Architecture, Ambition and Americans. New York: Harper and Brothers, 1955.

Baird, Joseph Armstrong. The Churches of Mexico, 1530–1810. Berkeley: University of California Press, 1962.

Baker, T. Lindsay. "Cleburne: A Case Study for Small City Water Systems." Southwest Water Works Journal 56 (September, 1974):34–36.

Barnstone, Howard. The Galveston That Was. New York: Macmillan Co., 1966.

———. The Architecture of John F. Staub: Houston and the South. Austin: University of Texas Press, 1979.

Baxter, Sylvester. Spanish-Colonial Architecture in Mexico. 12 vols. Boston: J. B. Millet, 1901.

Beacham, Hans. The Architecture of Mexico: Yesterday and Today. New York: Architectural Book Publishing Co., 1969.

Blumenson, John J. G. Identifying American Architecture. Nashville: American Association for State and Local History, 1977.

Bridenbaugh, Carl. Cities in the Wilderness: The First Century of Urban Life in America 1625–1742. 2nd ed. New York: Alfred A. Knopf, 1955.

Bryant, Keith L., Jr. "Railway Stations of Texas: A Disappearing Architectural Heritage." Southwestern Historical Quarterly 79 (1976):417–440.

Burchard, John, and Albert Bush-Brown. The Architecture of America: A Social and Cultural History. Boston: Little, Brown and Co., 1966.

Burke, Padraic. "To Market, To Market." Historic Preservation 29 (1977):33–38.

Bush-Brown, Albert. "College Architecture: An Expression of Educational Philosophy." Architectural Record 122 (1957):154–157.

Bywaters, Jerry. "More About Southwestern Architecture." *Southwest Review* 18 (1933):234–264.

Celoria, Miguel. "Spanish-Colonial Architecture: An Archaeological Approach." *Journal of the Society of Architectural Historians* 34 (December, 1975):295.

Conger, Roger N. *Historic Log Cabins of McLennan County, Texas.* Waco: Heritage Society of Waco, 1954.

———. "The Waco Suspension Bridge." *Texana* 1 (1963):181–224.

Connally, Ernest Allen. "Architecture at the End of the South: Central Texas." *Journal of the Society of Architectural Historians* 11 (December, 1952):8–12.

Cotton, Fred R. "Log Cabins of the Parker County Region." *West Texas Historical Association Year Book* 29 (October, 1953):96–104.

Coursey, Clark. *Courthouses of Texas.* Brownwood, Tex.: Banner Printing Co., 1962.

Darst, Maury. "Texas Lighthouses: The Early Years, 1850–1900.". *Southwestern Historical Quarterly* 74 (January, 1976):301–316.

Droege, John. *Passenger Terminals and Trains.* New York: McGraw-Hill Book Co., Inc., 1916.

Eichenroht, Marvin. "The Kaffee-Kirche at Fredericksburg, Texas, 1846." *Journal of the Society of Architectural Historians* 25 (March, 1966): 60–63.

Eisenhour, Virginia. *The Strand of Galveston.* N.p., n.d.

Fitch, James Marston. *American Building: The Historical Forces That Shaped It.* 2nd ed. Boston: Houghton Mifflin, 1966.

Fox, Stephen. "Profile: Nicholas J. Clayton, Architect." *Texas Architect* 26 (July/August, 1976): 51–52.

Gebhard, David, and Deborah Nevins. *200 Years of American Architectural Drawing.* New York: Whitney Library of Design, 1977.

George, Eugene. *Historic Architecture of Texas: The Falcón Reservoir.* Austin: Texas Historical Commission and Texas Historical Foundation, 1975.

Giedion, Sigfried. *Space, Time and Architecture.* 5th ed., rev. Cambridge: Harvard University Press, 1967.

Goeldner, Paul. *Texas Catalog: Historic American Buildings Survey.* San Antonio: Trinity University Press, 1976.

Hamlin, Talbot. *Greek Revival Architecture in America.* New York: Oxford University Press, 1944.

Harris, August Watkins. *Minor and Major Mansions in Early Austin.* Austin: privately printed, 1958.

Historic Preservation in Texas. Vol. I: *The Comprehensive Statewide Historic Preservation Plan for Texas.* Austin: Texas Historical Commission and Office of Archeology and Historic Preservation, U.S. Department of the Interior, 1973.

Hitchcock, Henry-Russell. *The Architecture of H. H. Richardson and His Times.* Cambridge: M.I.T. Press, 1966.

———. *Architecture: Nineteenth and Twentieth Centuries.* Baltimore: Penguin Books, 1958.

Jordan, Terry G. *Texas Log Buildings: A Folk Architecture.* Austin: University of Texas Press, 1978.

Jutson, Mary Carolyn Hollers. *Alfred Giles: An English Architect in Texas and Mexico.* San Antonio: Trinity University Press, 1972.

Kilham, Walter H. *Mexican Architecture of the Vice-Regal Period.* New York: Longmans, Green and Co., 1927.

Kimball, Fiske. *American Architecture.* New York: Bobbs-Merrill Co., 1928.

Kirker, Harold. *California's Architectural Frontier: Style and Tradition in the Nineteenth Century.* San Marino, Calif.: Huntington Library, 1960.

Kubler, George. *Mexican Architecture of the Sixteenth Century.* New Haven: Yale University Press, 1948.

———, and Martin Soria. *Art and Architecture in Spain and Portugal and Their American Dominions, 1500–1800.* Baltimore: Penguin Books, 1959.

Lancaster, Clay. "Builders' Guide and Plan Books and American Architecture from the Revolution to the Civil War." *Magazine of Art* 41 (January, 1948):16–22.

———. "Some Octagonal Forms in Southern Architecture." *The Art Bulletin* 28 (June, 1946): 103–111.

Lehman, Donald J. *Lucky Landmark, A Study of a Design and Its Survival: The Galveston Customhouse, Post Office, and Courthouse of 1861.* Washington, D.C.: General Services Administration, 1973.

Lehmer, Donald J. "Modern Jacales of Presido." *El Palacio* 46 (August, 1939):183–186.

Lunden, Walter A. "The Rotary Jail, or Human Squirrel Cage." *Journal of the Society of Architectural Historians* 18 (December, 1959): 149–157.

Lynes, Russell. *The Tastemakers.* New York: Grosset and Dunlap, 1954.

Meeks, C. L. V. "Form Beneath Fashion: 19th Century Depots." *Magazine of Art* 39 (December, 1946):378–380.

———. *The Railroad Station: An Architectural History.* New Haven: Yale University Press, 1956.

———. "Romanesque before Richardson in the United States." *The Art Bulletin* 35 (March, 1953):17–33.

Morrison, Hugh. *Early American Architecture from the First Colonial Settlements to the National Period.* New York: Oxford University Press, 1952.

Mumford, Lewis. *The Brown Decades: A Study of the Arts in America, 1865–1895.* New York: Harcourt, Brace and Co., 1932.

———. *Roots of Contemporary American Architecture.* New York: Reinhold Publishing Corp., 1952.

———. *Sticks and Stones.* New York: Dover Publications, 1955.

Munday, James H., and Earle G. Shettleworth, Jr. *The Flight of the Grand Eagle: Charles G. Bryant, Maine Architect and Adventurer.* Augusta, Maine: Maine Historic Preservation Commission, 1977.

Newcomb, Rexford. *Spanish Colonial Architecture in the United States.* New York: S. J. Augustin, 1937.

Newton, Ada K. "The Anglo-Irish House of the Rio Grande." *Pioneer America* 5 (January, 1973):33–38.

Nicholas Clayton. Houston: Masonry Institute of Houston-Galveston, n.d.

Perrin, Richard W. E. *Wisconsin Architecture: A Catalog of Buildings Represented in the Library of Congress, with Illustrations from Measured Drawings.* Washington, D.C.: U.S. Government Printing Office, 1965.

Peterson, Charles E. "The Houses of French St. Louis." In *The French in the Mississippi Valley,* edited by John Francis McDermott, pp. 17–40. Urbana: University of Illinois Press, 1965.

Plummer, Betty. *Historic Homes of Washington County 1821–1860.* San Marcos, Tex.: Rio Fresco Books, 1971.

Price, Edward T. "The Central Courthouse Square in the American County Seat." *Geographical Review* 58 (1968):29–60.

Quinn, Robert M. "The Architectural Origins of the Southwestern Missions." *The American West* 3 (Summer, 1966):56–66ff.

Reece, Ray. "Galveston: Historically Distinguished Architecture in Island City's East End is Too Often Overlooked by Tourists." *American Preservation* 1 (October–November, 1977): 42–55.

Reps, John W. *Cities on Stone: Nineteenth Century Lithograph Images of the Urban West.* Ft. Worth: Amon Carter Museum of Western Art, 1976.

———. *The Making of Urban America.* Princeton, N. J.: Princeton University Press, 1965.

———. *Town Planning in Frontier America.* Princeton, N. J.: Princeton University Press, 1969.

Rippe, Peter. "Harris County Heritage Society of Houston." *Antiques* (1975):490–501.

Robinson, Willard B. "Colonial Ranch Architecture in the Spanish-Mexican Tradition." *Southwestern Historical Quarterly* 83 (1979): 123–150.

———. "The Public Square as a Determinant of Courthouse Form in Texas." *Southwestern Historical Quarterly* 75 (1972):339–372.

———. "Temples of Knowledge: Historic Mains of Texas Colleges and Universities." *Southwestern Historical Quarterly* 77 (1974):445–480.

———. *Texas Public Buildings of the Nineteenth Century.* Austin: University of Texas Press, 1974.

Rogers, Mondel. *Old Ranches of the Texas Plains.* College Station: Texas A&M University Press, 1976.

Sanford, Trent Elwood. *The Architecture of the Southwest.* New York: W. W. Norton and Co., 1950.

———. *The Story of Architecture in Mexico Including The Work of the Ancient Indian Civilizations and That of the Spanish Colonial*

Empire Which Succeeded Them, Together with an Account of the Background in Spain and a Glimpse at the Modern Trend. New York: W. W. Norton and Co., 1947.

Scully, Vincent, Jr. "American Villas." *The Architectural Review* (March, 1954):168–179.

———. "Romantic Rationalism and the Expression of Structure in Wood: Downing, Wheeler, Gardner, and the 'Stick Style,' 1840–1876." *The Art Bulletin* 35 (June, 1953):121–142.

———. *The Shingle Style: Architectural Theory and Design from Richardson to the Origins of Wright.* New Haven: Yale University Press, 1955.

Shipway, Verna Cook, and Warren Shipway. *The Mexican House, Old and New.* New York: Architectural Book Publishing Company, 1960.

Short, C. W., and R. Stanley-Brown. *Public Buildings: A Survey of Architecture of Projects Constructed by Federal and Other Governmental Bodies between the Years 1933 and 1939 with the Assistance of the Public Works Administration.* Washington, D.C.: Government Printing Office, 1939.

Shurtleff, Harold R. *The Log Cabin Myth: A Study of the Early Dwellings of the English Colonists in North America.* Cambridge: Harvard University Press, 1939.

Stanislawski, Dan. "Early Spanish Town Planning in the New World." *Geographical Review* 37 (1947):94–105.

———. "The Origin and Spread of the Grid-Pattern Town." *Geographical Review* 36 (1946): 105–120.

Sturgis, Russel. *A Dictionary of Architecture and Building Biographical, Historical, and Descriptive.* 3 vols. New York: Macmillan Company, 1901.

Tallmadge, Thomas E. *The Story of Architecture in America.* New York: W. W. Norton and Co., 1936.

Taylor, Lonn. "The McGregor-Grimm House at Winedale, Texas." *Antiques* 108 (1975): 515–521.

Upjohn, Everard III. *Richard Upjohn: Architect and Churchman.* New York: Columbia University Press, 1939.

Utley, Robert M. *Fort Davis National Historic Site, Texas,* National Park Service Historic Handbook Series No. 38. Washington, D.C.: U.S. Government Printing Office, 1965.

Vocabulario Arquitectónico Ilustrado. Mexico City: Secretaría del Patrimonio Nacional, 1976.

Weisman, Winston. "Commercial Palaces of New York: 1845–1875." *Art Bulletin* 36 (1954): 285–302.

Weslager, C. A. *The Log Cabin in America: From Pioneer Days to the Present.* New Brunswick, N. J.: Rutgers University Press, 1969.

Whiffen, Marcus. *American Architecture since 1780: A Guide to the Styles.* Cambridge: M.I.T. Press, 1969.

———. "The Early County Courthouses of Virginia." *Journal of the Society of Architectural Historians* 18 (March, 1959):2–10.

White, Theo[philus] B[allou]. *Paul Philippe Cret, Architect and Teacher.* Philadelphia: Art Alliance Press, 1973.

Williamson, Roxanne Kuter. *Austin, Texas: An American Architectural History.* San Antonio: Trinity University Press, 1973.

Withey, Henry F., and Elsie Rathburn Withey. *Biographical Dictionary of American Architects (Deceased).* Los Angeles: Hennessey and Ingalls, 1970.

Wodehouse, Lawrence. "Alfred B. Mullet and His French Style Government Buildings." *Journal of the Society of Architectural Historians* 31 (March, 1972):22–37.

———. "Ammi Burnham Young, 1798–1874." *Journal of the Society of Architectural Historians* 25 (December, 1966):268–280.

———. "The Custom House, Galveston, Texas, 1857–1861, by Ammi Burnham Young." *Journal of the Society of Architectural Historians* 25 (March, 1966):64–67.

General History

Arneson, Axel. "Norwegian Settlements in Texas." *Southwestern Historical Quarterly* 45 (October, 1941):125–135.

Baker, T. Lindsay. *The Early History of Panna Maria, Texas.* Texas Tech University Graduate Studies no. 9. Lubbock: Texas Tech Press, 1975.

Barkley, Mary Starr. *History of Travis County and Austin, 1839–1899.* Waco: Texian Press, 1963.

Battle, William James. "A Concise History of the University of Texas." *Southwestern Historical Quarterly* 54 (1951):391–411.

Beasley, Ellen. "History in Towns: Galveston, Texas." *Antiques* 108 (1975): 478–489.

Biesele, Rudolph Leopold. *The History of the German Settlements in Texas, 1831–1861.* Austin: Von Boeckmann-Jones, 1930.

Blackmar, Frank W. *Spanish Colonization in the Southwest.* Johns Hopkins University Studies in History and Political Science, series 8, no. 4. Baltimore: Johns Hopkins University, 1890.

Blake, R. B. *Historic Nacogdoches.* Nacogdoches, Tex.: Nacogdoches Historic Society, 1939.

Bolton, Herbert Eugene. "The Founding of the Missions on the San Gabriel River, 1745–1749." *Southwestern Historical Quarterly* 17 (April, 1914):323–379.

———. "The Jumano Indians, 1650–1771." *Texas Historical Association Quarterly* 15 (July, 1911):66–84.

———. "The Mission as a Frontier Institution in the Spanish-American Colonies." *American Historical Review* 23 (1917):42–61.

———. "The Native Tribes about the East Texas Missions." *Quarterly of the Texas State Historical Association* (April, 1908):249–276.

———. *Spanish Exploration in the Southwest 1542–1706.* New York: Charles Scribner's Sons, 1925.

———. "The Spanish Occupation of Texas, 1519–1690." *Southwestern Historical Quarterly* 16 (July, 1912):1–26.

———. *Texas in the Middle Eighteenth Century.* Studies in Spanish Colonial History and Administration. 1915. Reprint. New York: Russell and Russell, 1962.

Branda, Eldon Stephen, ed. *The Handbook of Texas: A Supplement.* Vol. 3. Austin: Texas State Historical Association, 1976.

Brinkerhoff, Sidney B., and Odie B. Faulk. *Lancers for the King: A Study of Northern New Spain, With a Translation of the Royal Regulations of 1772.* Phoenix: Arizona Historical Foundation, 1965.

Browning, Webster E. "Joseph Lancaster, James Thomson, and the Lancasterian System of Mutual Instruction, with Special Reference to Hispanic America." *Hispanic American Historical Review* 4 (February, 1921):49–98.

Bryant, Keith L., Jr. "Arthur E. Stilwell and the Founding of Port Arthur: A Case of Entrepreneurial Error." *Southwestern Historical Quarterly* 75 (July, 1971):19–40.

Buckley, Eleanor Claire. "The Aguayo Expedition into Texas and Louisiana, 1719–1722." *Quarterly of the Texas State Historical Association* 15 (July, 1911):1–65.

Calleros, Cleofas. *El Paso, Then and Now.* El Paso: American Printing Co., 1954.

Camara, Kathleen D. *Laredo on the Rio Grande.* San Antonio: Naylor Co., 1949.

Carrol, B. H., ed. *Standard History of Houston, Texas.* Knoxville, Tenn.: H. W. Crew and Co., 1912.

Castañeda, Carlos E. *Our Catholic Heritage in Texas: 1519–1936.* 7 vols. Austin: Von Boeckmann-Jones Co., 1936–1950.

Chabot, Frederick C. *The Alamo: Mission, Fortress and Shrine.* San Antonio: Carleton Printing Co., 1936.

———. *San Antonio and Its Beginnings; comprising the four numbers of the San Antonio Series with appendix.* San Antonio: Artes Graficas, 1936.

———. *With the Makers of San Antonio: Genealogies of the Early Latin, Anglo-American, and German Families with Occasional Biographies, Each Group Being Prefaced with a Brief Historical Sketch and Illustrations.* San Antonio: privately printed, 1937.

Clark, Joseph L. *The Texas Gulf Coast: Its History and Development.* 2 vols. New York: Lewis Historical Publishing Co., 1955.

Conger, Roger N. *Highlights of Waco History.* Waco: Hill Printing and Stationery Co., 1945.

Connelley, William Elsey, ed. *Doniphan's Expedition.* Topeka: privately printed, 1907.

Connor, Seymour V. "Log Cabins in Texas." *Southwestern Historical Quarterly* 53 (October, 1949):105–116.

———. *The Peters Colony of Texas: A History and Biographical Sketches of the Early Settlers.* Austin: Texas State Historical Association, 1959.

———, James M. Day, Billy Mac Jones, Dayton Kelley, W. C. Nunn, Ben Proctor, and Dorman H. Winfrey. *Capitols of Texas.* Waco: Texian Press, 1970.

Corning, Leavitt, Jr. *Baronial Forts of the Big*

Bend: Ben Leaton, Milton Faver and Their Private Forts in Presidio County. San Antonio: Trinity University Press, 1969.

Cosby, Hugh E., ed. *History of Abilene*. Abilene, Tex.: Hugh E. Cosby, Co., 1955.

Cox, I. J. "Educational Efforts in San Fernando de Bexar." *Quarterly of the Texas State Historical Association* 6 (July, 1902):27–63.

Crocket, George L. *Two Centuries in East Texas: A History of San Augustine County and Surrounding Territory*. Facsimile reproduction. Dallas: Southwest Press, 1932.

Crouch, Carrie J. *A History of Young County*. Austin: Texas Historical Association, 1956.

Dethloff, Henry C. *A Pictorial History of Texas A&M University, 1876–1976*. College Station: Texas A&M University Press, 1975.

Didear, Hedwig Krell. *A History of Karnes County and Old Helena*. Austin: San Felipe Press, 1969.

Dunn, William Edward. "The Apache Mission on the San Saba River." *Southwestern Historical Quarterly* 17 (April, 1914):379–414.

Estill, Harry F. "The Old Town of Huntsville." *Quarterly of the Texas State Historical Association* 3 (April, 1900):265–278.

Estill, Mary S. *Vision Realized: A History of Sam Houston State University*. Huntsville, Tex.: Sam Houston Press, 1970.

Ferguson, Dan. "Austin College in Huntsville." *Southwestern Historical Quarterly* 53 (April, 1950):386–403.

Fletcher, Edward Garland. "The Beginnings of the Professional Theatre in Texas." *University of Texas Bulletin*. Austin: University of Texas, 1936.

Frontier Forts of Texas. Waco: Texian Press, 1966.

Fuermann, George M. *The Face of Houston*. Houston: privately printed, 1963.

Gerald, Rex E. *Spanish Presidios of the Late Eighteenth Century in Northern New Spain*. Santa Fe: Museum of New Mexico Press, 1968.

Gideon, Samuel. "The Quaint Old Town of Castroville." *Frontier Times* 2 (September, 1925).

Gilmore, Kathleen. *The Keeran Site: The Probable Site of LaSalle's Fort St. Louis in Texas*. Austin: Texas Historical Commission, 1973.

Gittenger, Ted, Connie Rihn, Roberta Haby, and Charlene Snavely. *St. Louis Church, Castroville; A History of the Catholic Church in Castroville, Texas*. San Antonio: Graphic Arts, 1973.

Graham, Roy Eugene. "Federal Fort Architecture in Texas During the Nineteenth Century." *Southwestern Historical Quarterly* 74 (October, 1970):165–188.

Greene, A. C. *Dallas: The Deciding Years—A Historical Portrait*. Austin: Encino Press, 1973.

Grimes, Roy, ed. *300 Years in Victoria County*. Victoria, Tex.: Victoria Advocate Publishing Co., 1968.

Grimm, Agnes. *Llanos Mestenas: Mustang Plains*. Waco: Texian Press, 1968.

Habig, Marion A. *The Alamo Chain of Missions: A History of San Antonio's Five Old Missions*. Chicago: Franciscan Herald Press, 1968.

Haley, J. Evetts. *Fort Concho and the Texas Frontier*. San Angelo, Tex.: San Angelo Standard-Times, 1952.

Hammond, William J., and Margaret W. Hammond. *La Reunion; A French Settlement in Texas*. Dallas: Royal Publishing Co., 1958.

Handy, Mary Oliva. *A History of Fort Sam Houston*. San Antonio: Naylor Co., 1951.

Hart, Katharine. *Austin and Travis County: A Pictorial History, 1839–1939*. Austin: Encino Press, 1975.

Hasskarl, Robert A., Jr. *Brenham, Texas, 1844–1958*. Brenham, Tex.: Banner-Press Publishing Co., 1958.

Heusinger, Edward W. *Early Explorations and Missions Establishments in Texas*. San Antonio: Naylor Co., 1936.

Hodge, Floy Crandall. *A History of Fannin County*. Hereford, Tex.: Pioneer Publishers, 1966.

Hogan, William Ransom. *The Texas Republic: A Social and Economic History*. Norman: University of Oklahoma Press, 1946.

Holland, G. A. *History of Parker County and the Double Log Cabin*. Weatherford, Tex.: Herald Publishing Co., 1937.

Hunter, J. Marvin. *Pioneer History of Bandera County: Seventy-Five Years of Intrepid History*. Bandera, Tex.: Hunter's Printing House, 1922.

Jackson, Marsha F. *Texana: Excavations at a 19th Century Inland Coastal Town, Jackson County, Texas*. Texas Archaeological Survey, Research Report No. 56, Palmetto Bend Reservoir Series I. Austin: University of Texas at Austin, 1977.

Johnston, Marguerite. *A Happy Worldly Abode: Christ Church Cathedral, 1839–1964.* Houston: Gulf Printing Co., 1964.

Jones, O. Garfield. "Local Government in the Spanish Colonies as Provided by the *Recopilación de Leyes de los Reynos de Las Indias.*" *Southwestern Historical Quarterly* 19 (1915–1916):65–90.

Jordan, Terry G. "Forest Folk, Prairie Folk: Rural Religious Cultures in North Texas." *Southwestern Historical Quarterly* 80 (October, 1976):135–162.

———. *German Seed in Texas Soil: Immigrant Farmers in Nineteenth-Century Texas.* Austin: University of Texas Press, 1966.

Kennedy, William. *Texas: The Rise, Progress, and Prospects of the Republic of Texas.* Ft. Worth: Molyneaux Craftsmen, 1925.

Knight, Oliver. *Fort Worth: Outpost on the Trinity.* Norman: University of Oklahoma Press, 1953.

Krieger, Alex D. *Culture Complexes and Chronology in Northern Texas with Extension of Puebloan Datings to the Mississippi Valley.* Austin: University of Texas Press, 1946.

Landolt, George L. *Search for the Summit: Austin College through Twelve Decades: 1849–1970.* Austin: Von Boeckmann-Jones Co., 1970.

Leclerc, Frédéric. *Texas and Its Revolution.* Translated by James L. Shepherd III. 1st English ed. Houston: Anson Jones Press, 1950.

Lindsley, Philip. *A History of Greater Dallas and Vicinity.* Chicago: Lewis Publishing Company, 1909.

Lott, Virgil N., and Mercurio Martinez. *The Kingdom of Zapata.* San Antonio: Naylor Co., 1953.

Lotto, F. *Fayette County: Her History and Her People.* Schulenburg, Tex.: Sticker Steam Press, 1902.

McCaleb, Walter F. *The Spanish Missions of Texas.* San Antonio: Naylor Co., 1954.

McCampbell, Coleman. *Saga of a Frontier Seaport.* Dallas: South-West Press, 1934.

McComb, David G. *Houston: The Bayou City.* Austin: University of Texas Press, 1969.

McDonald, William L. *Dallas Rediscovered: A Photographic Chronicle of Urban Expansion,* 1870–1925. Dallas: Historical Society of Dallas, 1978.

Maillard, A. *The History of the Republic of Texas.* London: Smith, Elder, and Co., 1842.

Maissin, Eugene. *The French in Mexico and Texas (1838–1839).* Edited and translated by James L. Shepherd III. Salado, Tex.: Anson Jones Press, 1961.

A Memorial and Biographical History of Dallas County, Texas, Illustrated Containing a History of This Important Section of the Great State of Texas, from the Earliest Period of its Occupancy to the Present Time, together with Glimpses of its Future Prospects; with Full Page Portraits of the Presidents of the United States, and also Full Page Portraits of Some of the Most Eminent Men of the County, and Biographical Mention of Many of its Pioneers, and also of Prominent Citizens of Today. Chicago: Lewis Publishing Co., 1892.

A Memorial and Biographical History of Ellis County, Texas. Chicago: Lewis Publishing Co., 1892.

A Memorial and Biographical History of Johnson and Hill Counties. Chicago: Lewis Publishing Co., 1893.

A Memorial and Biographical History of Navarro, Henderson, Anderson, Limestone, Freestone, and Leon Counties. Chicago: Lewis Publishing Co., 1893.

Mills, W. S. *History of Van Zandt County.* Canton, Tex.: Irby Mills, 1950.

Moorhead, Max L. *The Presidio: Bastion of the Spanish Borderlands.* Norman: University of Oklahoma Press, 1975.

Moraud, Marcel. "Le Champ d'Asile au Texas." *Rice Institute Pamphlet* 39 (April, 1952):18–24.

Morgan, Jonnie R. *The History of Wichita Falls.* Oklahoma City: Economy Co., 1931.

Morgan, William Manning. *Trinity Protestant Episcopal Church, Galveston, Texas, 1841–1953.* Houston and Galveston: Anson Jones Press, 1954.

Morphis, J. M. *History of Texas, From Its Discovery and Settlement.* New York: United States Publishing Co., 1874.

Murphy, DuBose. "Early Days of the Protestant Episcopal Church in Texas." *Southwestern Historical Quarterly* 34 (April, 1931):293–316.

Myres, Sandra L. *The Ranch in Spanish Texas, 1691–1800.* Social Science Series No. 2. El Paso: Texas Western Press, 1969.

Neumann, Ray. *A Centennial History of St. Joseph's Church and Parish, 1868–1968, San Antonio, Texas.* San Antonio: Clemens Printing Co., 1968.

Neville, A. W. *The History of Lamar County (Texas).* Paris, Tex.: North Texas Publishing Co., 1937.

"A New Bridge for Bend." *Texas Highways* 19 (January, 1972):30–31.

Newcomb, W. W., Jr. *The Indians of Texas: From Prehistoric to Modern Times.* Austin: University of Texas Press, 1961.

Newton, Lewis W., and Herbert P. Gambrell. *A Social and Political History of Texas.* Dallas: Southwest Press, 1932.

Nueces County Historical Society. *History of Nueces County.* Austin: Jenkins Publishing Company, 1972.

Nuttall, Zelia. "Royal Ordinances Concerning the Laying Out of New Towns." *Hispanic American Historical Review* 4 (November, 1921): 743–753.

O'Connor, Kathryn Stoner. *The Presidio La Bahia del Espíritu Santo de Zuniga 1721 to 1846.* Austin: Von Boeckmann-Jones Co., 1966.

Paddock. B. B., ed. *History of Texas: Fort Worth and the Texas Northwest Edition.* Chicago: Lewis Publishing Co., 1922.

Parisot, F. F., and C. J. Smith. *History of the Catholic Church in the Diocese of San Antonio, Texas.* San Antonio: Carrico and Bowen, 1897.

Polk, Stella Gipson. *Mason and Mason County: A History.* Austin: Pemberton Press, 1966.

Rather, Ethel Zivley. "De Witt's Colony." *Southwestern Historical Quarterly* 8 (October, 1904):95–192.

Rathjen, Frederick W. *The Texas Panhandle Frontier.* Austin: University of Texas Press, 1973.

Reed, St. Clair Griffin. *A History of the Texas Railroads and of Transportation Conditions under Spain and Mexico and the Republic and State.* Houston: St. Clair Publishing Co., 1941.

Richardson, Rupert Norval. *The Frontier in Northwest Texas: 1846 to 1876.* Glendale, Calif.: Arthur Clark, 1963.

———, Ernest Wallace, and Adrian N. Anderson. *Texas: The Lone Star State.* 3rd ed. Englewood Cliffs, N.J.: Prentice-Hall, 1969.

Robertson, Pauline Durrett, and R. L. Robertson. *Panhandle Pilgrimage: Illustrated Tales Tracing History in the Texas Panhandle.* Canyon, Tex.: Staked Plains Press, 1976.

Santleban, August. *A Texas Pioneer. Early Staging and Overland Freighting Days on the Frontier of Texas and Mexico.* New York: Neale Publishing Co., 1910.

Schmidt, Charles F. *History of Washington County, Texas.* San Antonio: Naylor Co., 1949.

———. "Impression of Texas in 1860." *Southwestern Historical Quarterly* 42 (April, 1939): 334–350.

Schmitz, Joseph W. *Mission Concepción.* Waco: Texian Press, 1965.

———. *Texas Culture, In the Days of the Republic, 1836–1846.* San Antonio: Naylor Co., 1960.

Scholes, France V., and H. P. Mera. *Some Aspects of the Jumano Problem.* Contributions to American Anthropology and History, No. 34, Publication 523. Washington, D.C.: Carnegie Institution of Washington, 1940.

Scott, Florence Johnson. *Historical Heritage of the Lower Rio Grande: A Historical Record of Spanish Exploration, Subjugation and Colonization of the Lower Rio Grande Valley and the Activities of José Escandón, Count of Sierra Gorda, Together with the Development of Towns and Ranches under Spanish, Mexican and Texas Sovereignties 1747–1848.* Rio Grande City, Tex.: La Retama Press, 1965.

Scott, Zelma. *A History of Coryell County, Texas.* Austin: Texas State Historical Association, 1965.

Sewell, Gerald, and Mary Beth Rogers. *The Story of Texas Public Lands: A Unique Heritage.* Austin: Texas General Land Office and J. M. West Texas Corporation, 1973.

Shanklim, Felda Davis. *Salado, Texas: Its History and Its People.* Belton, Tex.: Peter Hansbrough Bell Press, 1960.

Shelby, Charmion Clair. "St. Denis's Declaration Concerning Texas in 1717." *Southwestern Historical Quarterly* 26 (January, 1923):165–183.

Sibley, Marilyn McAdams. *Travelers in Texas, 1761–1860.* Austin: University of Texas Press, 1967.

Simonds, Frederick William. "Geographical Influence in the Development of Texas." *Journal of Geography* 10 (May, 1912):277–283.

Sinks, Julia Lee. *Chronicles of Fayette: Reminiscences of Julia Lee Sinks.* Edited by Walter P. Freytas. La Grange, Tex., 1975.

———. "Rutersville College." *Quarterly of the Texas State Historical Association* 2 (1898–1899):124–133.

Sledge, A. W. *Ballinger and Runnels County.* N.p., n.d.

Sleeper, John, and J. C. Hutchins. *Waco and McLennan County.* Waco: Examiner Steam Press, 1876.

Smythe, H. *Historical Sketch of Parker County and Weatherford, Texas.* St. Louis: Louis C. Lavat, 1877.

Stieghorst, Junann. *Bay City and Matagorda County: A History.* Austin: Pemberton Press, 1965.

Sussman, Herbert L. *Victorians and the Machine: The Literary Response to Technology.* Cambridge: Harvard University Press, 1968.

Temple, Texas, Junior Chamber of Commerce. *Bell County History. A Pictorial History of Bell County, Texas, Covering Both the Old and the New.* Ft. Worth: University Supply and Equipment Co., 1958.

The Texians and the Texans: The Czech Texans. San Antonio: Institute of Texan Cultures, 1972.

The Texians and the Texans: The French Texans. San Antonio: Institute of Texan Cultures, 1973.

The Texians and the Texans: The German Texans. San Antonio: Institute of Texan Cultures, 1970.

Thrall, Homer S. *History of Methodism in Texas.* Houston: E. H. Cushing, 1872.

———. *A History of Texas, from the Earliest Settlements to the Year 1885, with an Appendix Containing the Constitution of the State of Texas, Adopted November, 1875, and the Amendments of 1883.* New York: University Publishing Co., 1892.

Tyler, George W. *The History of Bell County.* Edited by Charles W. Ramsdell. Waco: Texian Press, 1966.

Urbanovsky, Elo J. "Mission de las Cabras, Wilson County, Texas: Feasibility Report." Mimeographed. Lubbock, Tex.: Texas Tech University Department of Parks Administration and Horticulture, 1972.

———. "Plaza de los Pastores: Feasibility Study." Lubbock, Tex.: Texas Tech University Department of Parks Administration and Horticulture, 1973.

Vigness, David M. *The Revolutionary Decades.* Austin: Steck-Vaughn Company, 1965.

Wallace, Ernest. *Texas in Turmoil: The Saga of Texas, 1849–1875.* Austin: Steck-Vaughn Company, 1965.

Walter, Ray A. *A History of Limestone County.* Austin: Von Boeckmann-Jones, 1959.

Waugh, Julia Nott. *Castroville and Henry Castro, Empresario.* San Antonio: Standard Printing Co., 1934.

Webb, Walter P., and H. B. Carroll, eds. *The Handbook of Texas.* 2 vols. Austin: Texas State Historical Association, 1952.

Weddle, Robert S. *The San Saba Mission: Spanish Pivot in Texas.* Austin: University of Texas Press, 1964.

Weyand, Leonie Rummel, and Houston Wade. *An Early History of Fayette County.* La Grange, Tex.: La Grange Journal Plant, 1936.

Wilcox, Seb. "Laredo During the Texas Republic." *Southwestern Historical Quarterly* 42 (October, 1938):83–107.

Woldert, Albert. *A History of Tyler and Smith County, Texas.* San Antonio: Naylor Co., 1948.

Works Progress Administration. *Beaumont, A Guide to the City and Its Environs.* Houston: Anson Jones Press, 1939.

———. *Houston: A History and Guide.* Houston: Anson Jones Press, 1942.

———. *Old Villita.* San Antonio: Clegg Co., 1939.

———. *Port Arthur.* Houston: Anson Jones Press, 1940.

———. *Texas: A Guide to the Lone Star State.* New York: Hastings House, 1940.

Wortham, Louis J. *History of Texas, from Wilderness to Commonwealth.* 5 vols. Ft. Worth: Wortham-Molyneaux, 1924.

Yoakum, Henderson King. *History of Texas from Its First Settlement in 1685 to Its Annexation to the United States in 1846.* 2 vols. New York: Redfield, 1855.

Young, S. O. *A Thumb-Nail History of the City of Houston, Texas, From Its Founding in 1836 to the Year 1912.* Houston: Rein and Sons Co., 1912.

Index

(Numbers in *italics* refer to illustration captions.)

Public School, Wichita Falls, 189, *190*
public square. *See* square, public

Queen Anne style, 137; houses in, 137, *138–140*
Queen City Electric Company, Dallas, 90
Quihi, 31
Quintle (Laurent) House and Store, Castroville, *30*

Rábago y Terán, Felipe, 14
railroads, 79, 82, 83, 84, *84*, 243, 246, 247; development of, 82; impact of, 83, *84*; roundhouses for, 86, 110, *112*; terminals for, 110, *112*, 247
raised cottages, 55, *57*
Ramírez, José Clemente, *20*
Ramírez (José) House, Falcón, 18, *20*
ranchers, 86
ranches, 80, *81*; sites for, 17; Spanish Colonial, 16–18, *19–22*, *21*, *22*
ranch grants, *20*, *21*
ranch headquarters, 80, *81*
ranching, 243
Rancho de las Cabras, 16–17
Ranch of the Goats, 16–17
ranchos, 16–18, *19–20*, *21*, *21*, *22*
Raymond (James H.) House, Austin, *60*, 61
Raymond (Nathaniel) House, Austin, *53*
Real County Courthouse, Leakey, 80
Reconstruction, 80; architecture during, 113–115
Red House, Washington County, 53 n
regional design, *183*, 236
rejas, *22*
Renaissance, Italian, *151*
Renaissance Revival style, 99, *119*, 144, *157*; auditorium in, *258*; commercial buildings in, 158, *160*, 161, *162*, *165*, *166*, *166*, *173*, *174*, *175*, 176, 251, *255*; fire stations in, *256*; French, *143*; government buildings in, 219, *221*, 221–222, *223*, 236, *258*; houses in, *145*, *146*, 147; library in, *251*; railroad terminal in, *247*; schools in, 189, *190*, *254*
resorts, health, 175, 178, *178*, 179, *179*
retablo, 12
Revett, Nicholas, 51
Rice, William Marsh, *176*
Rice Hotel, Houston, *176*
Richardson, Henry Hobson, 141, 169, 203, 203 n, 240
Richardson, Willard, *125*
Richardsonian Romanesque style, *170*, 189, *191*, *205*, 242; courthouses in, *235*, 235; federal buildings in, *239*; railroad terminal in, *248*
Richardson (Willard) Building, Galveston, *104*

Ringgold Barracks, 47
Rives (James) House, Mission Valley, 113, *115*
Robeline, La.: mission near, 8, *9*
Rockport: courthouse in, *227*
Roebling, August, 110
Roemer, Ferdinand, 43
Roma: architecture in, 24; church in, 73, *75*
Romanesque Revival style, 99, *102*, *118*, 137, 141, *169*; banks, *167*, *168*, *169*; churches, *203*, *206*, *207*, *257*; commercial buildings, *170*; courthouses, *226*, *227*, 227, *229*, 232, 232–235, *235*; federal buildings, 236, *239*, 239; hotels, *175*; houses, 141, *142*, 144, *146*; jails, 212–213, *216*; natatorium, *181*; terminal, *248*
Ropes, P. H.: *178*
Rose and Peterson, architects: courthouse designed by, *260*
Ross Hall, Texas A&M University, College Station, *197*
roundhouses, 86, 110, *112*
Round Top, 199; house in, 35, *35*
Ruffini, Frederick Ernst, 124 n, *125*, 224, *260*; commercial building designed by, 158, *160*; courthouses designed by, *122*, *226*; temporary capitol designed by, 240, *241*; university building designed by, *198*
Ruffini, Oscar, 132, 224; courthouse designed by, 126–127; house designed by, 132, *133*; jail designed by, 213, *215*
Runnels County Courthouse, Ballinger, *125*, 223, *223*
rural architecture, 16–18, *19–20*, *21*, *21*, 80, *81*
Rusk: iron foundry at, 105
Ruskin, John, 61, 103, 103 n
Rutersville College, 65

Sacred Heart Catholic Church, Galveston, 203, *205*
Saint Francis on the Brazos Church, Waco, 244–245
Saint John's Episcopal Church, Brownwood, 130 n
Saint Joseph's Catholic Church, Galveston, 73
Saint Louis Catholic Church, Castroville, 31
Saint Mary's Catholic Church, Bremond, 38
Saint Mary's College, Dallas, *194*, *195*, 202
Saint Mary's Institute, San Antonio, 65
Saint Matthew's Cathedral, Dallas, 202
Saint Patrick's Cathedral, Corpus Christi, 199, *200*

Saint Patrick's Catholic Church, Fort Worth, 92
Saint Paul's Sanitarium, Dallas, 99, *102*
Saint Regis Hotel, El Paso, 247, *250*
Sakowitz Department Store, Houston, *151*
saloon, 83, 86
Sam Houston State University, Huntsville, 65
San Angelo: jail in, 213, *215*
San Antonio, 11, 14, 15, 24, 86; cast-iron fronts in, 107; churches in, 24, 25; commercial buildings in, 58, 144, 158, *159*, 161, *165*, *166*, *166*; factory site in, 79; government buildings in, 27, 95, 223, 226, 236, 239; historic district in, 262; hotel in, 64; houses in, 58, 61, 62, 113, 114, 132, *134*, 137, 140, 141, 142, 144, 146; ice plant in, 91; indigenous architecture in, 19; industry in, 86; institute in, 65; lunatic asylum in, 198, *199*; missions in, 12, 13–15, 246; natatorium in, 178; opera house in, *153*; presidio in, 11, 13; public services in, 58, 89, 90, 91, 92, 95, 98; railroad terminal in, 247, *250*; ranches near, 16
San Antonio Conservation Society, 12, 262
San Antonio Daily Express, 197
San Antonio Gas Works, 89
San Antonio Hospital, 95
San Antonio National Bank, 144
San Antonio Post Office and Courthouse, 236, *239*
San Antonio State Hospital, *199*
San Augustine: university in, 65
San Bartolo Ranch, 18, *21*, *21*
Sanders, K. P., 44
Sanders-McIntyre House, Stoneham, 44
San Diego: jail in, 213
San Fernando Cathedral, San Antonio, 25
Sanger (Alexander) House, Dallas, 132, *134*
Sanger Brothers, Dallas, *134*
Sanger Brothers Buildings, Dallas, 169, *170*, *171*
Sanguinet, architect, 123; buildings designed by, 189, *189*, 234
Sanguinet and Dawson, architects: buildings designed by, *194*
Sanguinet and Messer, architects: cathedral designed by, 202
sanitarium, 99, *102*
San Marcos: chautauqua in, *151*
San Patricio mission church, 71
Santa Fe Railway Company, 223
Santiago, 4
San Xavier River missions, 14
San Ygnacio Ranch, 17